WEST SLOPE COMMUNITY LIBRARY
(503) 292-6416
MEMBER OF
WASHINGTON COUNTY COOPERATIVE
LIBRARY SERVICES

MAKING TIME FOR MAKING MUSIC

D0972759

Making Time for Making Music

HOW TO BRING MUSIC INTO YOUR BUSY LIFE

Amy Nathan

OXFORD
UNIVERSITY PRESS

Oxford University Press is a department of the University of Oxford. It furthers
the University's objective of excellence in research, scholarship, and education
by publishing worldwide. Oxford is a registered trade mark of Oxford University
Press in the UK and certain other countries.

Published in the United States of America by Oxford University Press
198 Madison Avenue, New York, NY 10016, United States of America.

© Amy Nathan 2018

All rights reserved. No part of this publication may be reproduced, stored in
a retrieval system, or transmitted, in any form or by any means, without the
prior permission in writing of Oxford University Press, or as expressly permitted
by law, by license, or under terms agreed with the appropriate reproduction
rights organization. Inquiries concerning reproduction outside the scope of the
above should be sent to the Rights Department, Oxford University Press, at the
address above.

You must not circulate this work in any other form
and you must impose this same condition on any acquirer.

Library of Congress Cataloging-in-Publication Data
Names: Nathan, Amy, author.
Title: Making time for making music : how to bring music into your busy life / Amy Nathan.
Description: New York, NY : Oxford University Press, [2018] |
Includes bibliographical references and index.
Identifiers: LCCN 2017043713 | ISBN 9780190611583 (hardcover : alk. paper) |
ISBN 9780190611590 (pbk. : alk. paper)
Subjects: LCSH: Music—Vocational guidance. | Music—Social aspects.
Classification: LCC ML3795.N15 2018 | DDC 780.23—dc23
LC record available at https://lccn.loc.gov/2017043713

9 8 7 6 5 4 3 2 1

Paperback printed by Sheridan Books, Inc., United States of America
Hardback printed by Bridgeport National Bindery, Inc., United States of America

For Carl

Contents

MAKING TIME FOR MAKING MUSIC

Dr. Morris Schoeneman (second from right) performing with the Larchmont Symphonia, the community orchestra he joined when he returned to playing violin after he retired. Both adults and high school students play in this string orchestra, which is sponsored by the Larchmont Music Academy in Larchmont, New York.

1   A Lifelong Passion

AS I STOOD in front of a photocopy machine at my neighborhood copy center, I noticed that the dapper-looking elderly gentleman at the adjacent machine was making copies of a musical score. Could he be an amateur musician? Perhaps one who might be interested in the flier I was copying? I planned to hand out the flier that weekend at an amateur musicians' Meetup group in New York City in what was to be my first effort to invite amateur musicians to fill out an online questionnaire about their musical activities. That questionnaire would form a major part of the research for this book.

Seizing on a chance for a head start, I asked my fellow copier, "Are you in a community orchestra?" That's the name for orchestras made up mainly of amateur or avocational musicians.

Indeed he was in such an orchestra. He was copying parts for a rehearsal that evening of a Bach violin concerto. I introduced myself and told him briefly about the book I was starting to work on—a book that would be for and about amateur musicians. I handed him a flier, fresh from the copier.

As he looked at the flier, he explained that he was a very new musician, although he had been an avid concertgoer all his life. He had played violin during high school but hadn't bowed a note for four decades until he retired from his medical career two years earlier. That's when he decided to pick up violin again, took some refresher lessons, and discovered to his surprise that there was a local community orchestra that was glad to welcome him as its newest and oldest member.

Then he said something that raised my spirits about the importance of the project I was beginning.

"I had no idea there was a way to make beautiful music in a community orchestra the way I'm doing now. I wish I had known about this earlier," he said wistfully. "I could have been doing this while I was working."

His comment confirmed for me an impression that I had gained from preliminary research—that many people aren't aware of the range of music-making options that are available for people who choose not to pursue music professionally but who still want to keep music-making as part of their lives. I had seen evidence of that during parent-to-parent workshops that I led at music schools in connection with two musical advice books I had written earlier. One book had been for youngsters and the other for parents. Invariably during these music school discussions, a parent would say what a shame that there would be no chance for their youngsters to keep performing as adults if they didn't become professional musicians. Not so, I would counter, noting that both of my books include vignettes about spare-time musicians who continue to make music despite having non-musical day jobs.

As the doctor rushed off to his orchestra rehearsal, he took along my flier. The next day, he emailed me, volunteering to fill out the questionnaire. That's how Dr. Morris Schoeneman, retired New York pediatric nephrologist, became one of the first people to complete the online questionnaire for this new book, *Making Time for Making Music*.

Over the course of the next several months, more than 300 other amateur musicians from around the country—and a few from overseas—joined the book's advice team by logging onto the questionnaire's webpage to describe how they fit music-making into their lives and to offer suggestions for others. Four dozen other non-pro music-makers shared their musical experiences by interview via telephone, email, or in person. I also interviewed dozens of music educators, researchers, and health-care professionals, as well as a few professional musicians.

Altogether, 441 individuals have been advisors for this book. Their stories, comments, and insights fill these pages, presenting the wide range of possibilities that are available for amateur music-making as well as offering practical advice from music lovers who know the score.

This is a different kind of advice book, not one filled with charts and lists of the top-ten steps to success or the best products to buy, but one enriched by personal accounts of challenges experienced and lessons learned. This information may help other non-pro musicians with difficulties they face, and may encourage people who are thinking about adding music-making to their busy lives to go ahead, jump in, and catch the beat.

The Questionnaire Respondents

To find avocational, non-pro musicians to complete the online questionnaire, I started with the flier I gave to Dr. Schoeneman and then handed out copies at the meeting of an amateur musician group in New York City that is part of Meetup, an online social networking organization that brings together people with similar interests. I also emailed the flier to the director of an amateur pianist Meetup group in San Diego and contacted the directors of adult education programs at twelve music schools around the United States, who let their teachers and students know about this research project. Officials at ten choirs or choruses around the country spread the word to their members. So did the leaders of four major summer programs for adult amateurs, seven community orchestras, four community bands (including one in Montréal), and an organization that maintains a worldwide database of people who like to play chamber music. Others who helped with the research are listed in the "About the Advice Panel" section toward the end of this book.

> **Every time I sing, I feel happier. It expresses things that I don't in other ways.**
> —Elizabeth Fein, singer, songwriter, psychology professor

The questionnaire consisted of fifty-one questions. A few were multiple choice, but most were open ended so that individuals could provide details on how they have been involved in making music. Ninety percent of those who started the questionnaire completed it or answered most of the questions.

The answers of the 274 individuals who completed the entire questionnaire have been tallied. Statistical information about this cohort is presented throughout the book, with a note each time that the percentages refer to the "questionnaire completers." Comments and suggestions from the forty-one others who answered most of the questions are included as part of the qualitative pool of information presented in this book, as are comments from forty-eight amateur musicians who described their musical journeys through interviews.

Those who completed the questionnaire ranged in age from 25 to 96. They make music—instrumental and vocal—in a variety of styles: classical, jazz, folk, rock, pop, early music, and world music. Many perform with community orchestras, bands, choirs, and choruses. Others get together in smaller groups—playing in chamber music ensembles or in rock, jazz, and folk bands, taking part in open mic nights, or jamming with friends. Some prefer performing solo. Others choose not to perform at all, seeing music as a personal activity that they do on their own at home. A few create their own music through composing, songwriting, and arranging, or by launching new musical ensembles and concert series.

A little less than half of the those who completed the survey are returnees to music-making. They had stopped making music but then found their way back, as Dr. Schoeneman has. Many reconnected with music long before their retirement years. Bob Gronko, a retired government employee, came back to guitar in his late 20s and has been hosting informal jam sessions at his Illinois home for years. Philip Knieper, a mechanical engineer from Baton Rouge, waited a little longer to make his return. He started playing piano again in his 40s when his young daughter began her own piano lessons.

About a third of the questionnaire completers have been making music all along—from childhood through adulthood, with no major gaps. London management consultant Hugh Rosenbaum has been playing recorder for more than fifty years and bassoon for more than forty. Retired elementary school principal Patricia Mabry has been a lifelong church choir member and pianist who now sings also in an auditioned, semi-pro chorale in Washington, DC.

Just under a third of those who completed the questionnaire were musical newcomers. Some had little musical training or experience prior to becoming adult music-makers. Before Maine educator Christine Anderson-Morehouse joined a

Colleen Schoneveld started playing violin at age 48 and then created a community orchestra for newcomers and returnees.

choir for the first time in her 50s, her earlier musical involvement consisted of two years of beginner piano lessons as a young girl and childhood campfire sing-alongs. Pennsylvania dressmaker Colleen Schoneveld started violin as an absolute beginner at age 48, but then went on to create a community orchestra for other newcomers and for returnees, too.

Others in the newcomer category had already been doing music as adults when they added a different kind of musical activity to their repertoire. Miriam Jackobs had been playing clarinet, her childhood instrument, for several years as an adult when she decided at age 70 to add violin. Then this Ohio registered dietitian switched to viola at age 76. Retired San Francisco political science professor Rufus Browning had been involved in choral singing as an adult, but took on a daunting new challenge at age 81—to become a composer. There will be more about each of these musicians in later chapters.

Statistical Snapshot: Questionnaire Completers

- **Gender profile:** Fifty-six percent of the questionnaire completers are female.
- **Age breakdown:** The average age was 59. Slightly more than half were age 60 or over when they completed the questionnaire. Nearly a quarter were over age 70. About a quarter were in their 40s and 50s. Slightly more than a tenth were in their 20s and 30s.
- **Employment status:** About two-fifths had retired. Nearly all the rest were employed in non-musical careers. None were working as professional musicians who relied on music as their main means of financial support. A few did occasional music gigs that earned them a little cash, but not enough to quit their day jobs. Four percent had been music teachers at some point. One violist earned a master's degree in music composition after retiring from a military career and is now a composer.
- **Music majors:** Fifteen percent had been music majors in college.
- **Childhood music-making:** Nearly all questionnaire completers played a musical instrument as children; more than half had played piano. About a third played string instruments as youngsters. A third played wind instruments, followed by brass and guitar. About half sang in choral groups as kids, a quarter performed in school musicals, and more than half were music-makers during college.
- **Instrumental vs. vocal music:** When they completed the questionnaire, most were instrumentalists, about a third sang in choral groups, and a quarter were doing both instrumental and vocal music.

- **Which instruments as adults:** Nearly half of the instrumentalists were playing piano as adults. Just under half were playing string instruments; followed by a third on wind instruments; a quarter on guitar, banjo, mandolin, or ukulele; 10 percent on brass; and less than that on percussion or harp. A few played other instruments, including tabla, erhu, viola da gamba, harpsichord, concertina, accordion, Celtic harp, or Finnish lap harp.

Closing the Information Gap

Dr. Schoeneman was not alone among questionnaire respondents in initially not knowing about music-making options for amateur musicians. Jamie Getz, an attorney in her mid-30s, had found herself in the same situation. "I had no idea that opportunities would exist," she says. "I assumed I would play viola through high school and that would be the end of it. If I had known, I might have asked to take more lessons as a child, when I had the time, so my viola skills would be stronger through life." She performed in her college orchestra but didn't discover post-college possibilities until her last year of law school, when she received a recruitment email from Atlanta's Lawyer's Orchestra. She quickly joined the ensemble's viola section. Later, after moving to Chicago, she searched for a similar ensemble and joined the Chicago Bar Association Symphony Orchestra. She has continued to perform with them, even after becoming a mother. (The Atlanta Lawyer's Orchestra has recently broadened its membership and changed its name to the Atlanta Musician's Orchestra.)

A surprise discovery also let Heather Rosado find ways to play flute with others. For a few years after college, she practiced on her own at home because she had a job with hours that made it impossible to register for music classes at night. New opportunities materialized when she prepared to move to New Jersey for a pharmaceutical job. As she searched online for apartments, an ad popped up on her screen for a summer band in her new hometown. She promptly joined that band, which led to her joining a year-round band and later finding a way to start playing chamber music, too. "I didn't think there would be performance opportunities if you didn't get a degree in music performance. I thought you had to go to Juilliard or Curtis to play after graduation," she said. "Now that I'm in my mid-thirties, I perform a lot and know there are options out there."

Some younger members of the advice panel actively searched out opportunities from college graduation onward. They were determined not to let music-making fade from their lives. "When college ended, I had a little panic moment of: 'How

Mandy Ray with her bassoon and her two children after a performance of Seattle's Around the Sound Community Band—two and half weeks after her son was born.

do I keep this going?'" says Amanda (Mandy) Ray, a nurse practitioner and mother of two in her mid-30s. During college, she played bassoon in her college orchestra, took lessons from a professor, and coached a youth symphony. She didn't know exactly how she could "keep this going," but she set out to forge her own path. First, she persuaded her college orchestra to let her continue to perform with them for a year after graduation. Later, however, there were times when she had to put down her bassoon "because we were moving too frequently while my husband was in the military and I was working in hospitals on the night shift. Once we settled down in Seattle and I found a job that was friendly to music-making, I found a community band and woodwind quintet."

Her husband, Brandon Ray, a singer and atmospheric research scientist in his 30s, shares his wife's sense of urgency about finding ways to keep making music. In fact, he offers a challenge to other younger adults to join the ranks of non-pro music-makers. "Some people are concerned that there are few people of my age group who sing or play instruments. By choosing not to sing or play, you add to that stereotype. If you start singing or playing, you'd be surprised by the connections you will make and the people *you* will then inspire to pursue their own passions." Throughout this book, he and his wife and other advice-team members—young and old—share ideas for how to uncover musical opportunities.

Overcoming the Confidence Gap

For some questionnaire respondents, it wasn't only a lack of information that held them back from making music as adults. They also had a lack of confidence in their musical abilities, feeling that they weren't talented enough or sufficiently skilled to keep playing or singing. Emotional baggage left over from less-than-positive childhood experiences with music burdened them. But as many questionnaire respondents discovered—and as music educators on our advice panel confirm—it is possible to reboot as an adult and overcome old issues by trying a new instrument, a new type of music, a new kind of teacher-student relationship, or by gaining a better understanding of what effective practice and performing entail.

Rebooting is how one member of our advice team managed at last to make peace with the piano, an instrument that had fascinated and frustrated her for so long. This arts administrator, who prefers to remain anonymous, had taken lessons as a child and liked the piano, but as she explains, "I grew up thinking that if I couldn't do something well right away, that meant I wasn't born to do it and there were other people who were." When she left for college, regular piano playing stopped for more than a decade. "Occasionally as an undergraduate when I was feeling brave, I would sneak into the practice rooms at the music college at my university and play one of the pianos there. Even in a closed room, I was self-conscious about being overheard by people who were more 'talented,' " she explains.

By her early 30s, she was at last in a position to buy her own piano. She signed up for piano lessons in the adult education division of a local conservatory. As an adult student, she has more control than she did as a child in defining the teacher-student relationship and in setting goals for the lessons. Fortunately she has found a teacher who knows how to help her make progress despite her insecurities. She is pleased that he doesn't mind her asking questions and encourages her to "play five notes and be an artist." She explains that by that "he means that it's better to play small segments well than to play the whole piece without artistry. It can sometimes be overwhelming to think how far I have to go, but if I allow myself to focus on one small step at a time, I can appreciate the beauty of the experience and enjoy the ride instead of postponing enjoyment for a later date. I wish I had known earlier that making music is much more about commitment to practice than it is about being 'gifted.'"

A recent book by Geoff Colvin, *Talent Is Overrated,* cites research that shows there is indeed more to successful music-making than having what some call "talent"— and that logging in many hours of effective practice plays a major role in creating top

Brown University professors Baylor Fox-Kemper (left) and Kerry Smith performing with their rock cover band as a demonstration band during a course on the history of rock music.

CLOSE UP: BAYLOR FOX-KEMPER,
PIANIST, OCEANOGRAPHY PROFESSOR

"I went to Berklee College of Music for a semester. Maybe I would have stayed in music school if I really liked it, but I decided to go into science," says Baylor Fox-Kemper. As a science major at a different school, he played in its jazz ensemble but "in grad school it was hard to continue." It wasn't only the time crunch that kept him from playing. "When I was serious about music, I was playing competitively, to be the best," he says. "For a while I thought I couldn't do it part way." After a few years, though, he realized that he could do music in a less all-consuming way. "The important thing is playing for your and the audience's enjoyment." He has joined a rock cover band with other Brown University faculty members, playing keyboard, guitar, and bass. "Now that I'm less focused on the competitive side, playing music casually that's enjoyable for me to play and to listen to feels immensely fun, fulfilling, and creative, without feeling like it's something I have to do. It's something I get to do."

performers. Other questionnaire respondents have decided to stop fretting about whether they have what it takes. "Don't worry whether you're talented enough," says Carol Katz, a retired special education teacher in Québec who started playing guitar in her 50s and percussion and bass guitar in her 70s. "With motivation, enthusiasm, and willingness to learn, you'll do well. The main thing is to enjoy your music-making."

Librarian Mary Schons, who started on banjo in her late 30s and now runs a workshop in Indiana to help other adult musicians, advises, "You won't be in Carnegie Hall unless you buy a ticket, but who cares? Jump in and forgive yourself if you make mistakes or aren't brilliant after two weeks. The point of music for me is to make the best sound you can and if you're lucky, to make that good sound with other people."

Several survey respondents had childhood teachers who actively discouraged them from making music, particularly singing. "When I was in kindergarten or first grade, during a singing session, the teacher pointed to me and said, 'You there in the back, just mouth the words,'" says Steven Duke, a retired Chicago journalist. "I never sang again until I was nearly 60. Not in front of other people, not in front of the dog, not in the shower." He played guitar on and off during his 20s and 30s, taking lessons now and then, but he never played in public or with others. "I felt I couldn't sing. So I didn't want to get into situations where I would be expected to sing in front of others," he says. It was only during his 50s when he took ensemble classes at Chicago's Old Town School of Folk Music that he broke free from that childhood curse, with the help of a supportive teacher who "created a safe and encouraging environment and pretty much forced me to sing. Now I like singing with others."

Bau Graves, the executive director of that Chicago music school, sums up the feelings of many of the educators interviewed for this book. "There's a prevalent attitude in our culture that art is only something that specially designated people can do," he says. "We don't believe that at all. We think everyone has a birth right to participate in creating whatever sort of creative life they want for themselves. We try to provide opportunities for people to do that."

No matter the reasons for their lack of confidence, nearly all our questionnaire respondents have found ways to bounce back. A common thread aiding in their musical awakening has been finding a supportive community, whether through teachers, music schools, ensembles, online options, Meetup groups, summer programs, workshops, or master classes. Throughout this book our team of advisors offer suggestions for how to create a musical support system and become more confident musicians.

> **It's not rocket science. Anyone can play an instrument!**
> —Carl Olson, guitarist, engineer

Handling Other Roadblocks

Here are other music-making roadblocks that are also tackled in this book.

- **Too old to learn:** Putting this fear to rest are research studies cited in chapter 2, along with reports in chapter 5 of older team members who have successfully started new musical adventures.
- **No time:** In chapter 6, busy team members describe how they carve out time for music, including several super-busy parents of young children.
- **Recital phobia:** Adult students don't have to do recitals, but some have actually come to like them, as they explain in chapter 7.
- **Too costly:** Music can be an expensive pursuit, but money-saving tips in chapter 7 can help.
- **Jitters:** In chapters 7, 9, and 10, team members tell how they tame performance anxiety.
- **Practice dread:** In chapter 8, team members who hated practicing as kids explain how they have come to enjoy it.
- **Aches and pains:** Pain prevention strategies abound in chapter 8.

Demographic Drumbeat

Now is a particularly good time to be an avocational musician because of the increasing number of opportunities for adults that are becoming available as a result of demographic changes. As the baby boomer generation has begun reaching retirement age, there has been a substantial increase in the number of people age 65 and older who have time on their hands, an interest in remaining active, and a longing to return to activities they enjoyed in their youthful years—exactly the position Dr. Schoeneman found himself in when he retired.

In the decade from 2004 to 2014, the 65-and-older segment of the US population increased by 28 percent, a faster rate of increase than for those under age 65, according to US Census reports. With life expectancy increasing as well, projections are that by 2030, one out of every five people in the United States will be 65 or older. By 2060, that segment of the population will be more than double what it was in 2014.

Music schools have taken notice not only of demographic projections but also of surveys showing adult interest in music. A National Endowment for the Arts (NEA) survey found that about 28 million adult Americans (12 percent) played instruments in 2012. In a separate 2014 survey of older adults, the NEA reports that 19 percent of those age 55 and over sang or played instruments. A Chorus America survey found that 18 percent of US households reported in 2009 that one or more adults sang in a chorus, an increase of two percentage points from 2003. In addition, a 2009 Gallup Poll revealed that 85 percent of US adults who don't play musical instruments wish they had learned to play one.

The pool of new music-making enthusiasts may increase even more as a result of reports in the popular media about neuroscience research that suggests that adults who are actively engaged in music-making may benefit from a delay in the onset of some of the cognitive declines of aging. This enticing idea is discussed in the next chapter.

As a result of the rising interest in music among the older demographic, music schools have begun offering more programs for older adults—and for younger adults, too, in order to bring them onboard before they reach retirement age. These programs benefit music schools by allowing them to make better use of their facilities, which often stand idle during the morning and early afternoon because programs for youngsters generally occur in the late afternoon or evening. Daytime programs for retirees can help a school's classrooms and studios generate revenue day in and day out. The director of Peabody Conservatory's Preparatory Division in Baltimore reports that adult students make up about 25 percent of its enrollment. A community music school in New York City estimates that in ten years their adult students may outnumber the children. The National Guild for Community

Arts Education reports that students age 25 and over in its member schools rose from 10 percent in 2009 to 15 percent in 2013, with the number of students age 65 and up more than doubling in that four-year span.

In addition, organizations have sprung up that offer musical ensembles specially for older adults, such as the New Horizons International Music Association, a consortium of more than two hundred community bands, orchestras, and choruses in the United States, Canada, and other countries. New Horizons ensembles are geared primarily to adults age 50 and over (although some also welcome younger adults). They are safe havens for those who have never been involved in music or who put music on hold for many years. The New Horizons motto—"Your best is good enough"—is a comfort for late bloomers.

For help in locating arts and music programs for older adults, the National Center for Creative Aging (NCCA) has a searchable online database of programs nationwide and serves as a catalyst for launching new arts programs. Lifetime Arts also encourages organizations to offer creative aging arts and music programs, including in public libraries. In addition, retirement communities and senior centers may sponsor music-making opportunities. AARP is another informational resource, as is Next Avenue, a new media service and online newsletter for older adults operated by Minnesota's PBS affiliate. In 2016, Next Avenue released a report entitled *Artful Aging* about what it calls the Artful Aging Movement. Aroha Philanthropies helped fund this report and also offers grants for arts projects. As Heidi Raschke, editor of the report, states: "In the 1960s, boomers changed the world by transforming youth culture. Now they're set to do it again by transforming the culture of aging." Websites for these organizations can be found in the resources section.

Most of the retirees on our research team became music-makers before retiring, but about a fifth waited until after retirement. Some retirees joined New Horizons ensembles, while others joined multi-age ensembles, as Dr. Schoeneman did. Younger adults can benefit from the new burst of programs for older music-makers because, as just noted, many such offerings welcome adults of all ages. In addition, there are also new ensembles created specifically for younger adults, including two New York groups that younger members of the advice panel participate in: the Young New Yorkers' Chorus and the Camerata Notturna chamber orchestra. Both are geared to those in their 20s and 30s.

About the Amateur Label

Until the early twentieth century, amateur musicians played a major role in the world of music, regularly getting together with friends to play music in living rooms and parlors or to join local singing societies and glee clubs. These spare-time music-makers included such luminaries as Thomas Jefferson and Albert Einstein. Home-based get-togethers provided the main way for ordinary people to hear great masterworks as well as popular tunes—by performing the music themselves. With the invention of the radio and the phonograph, however, people could hear great music at home without having to perform it. The tradition of informal music-making began to decline and the gulf between amateur and pro widened, especially as the recording industry developed ways to edit recordings to remove the inevitable errors that professionals make while performing. Near-flawless recorded performances set a standard of musical perfection that amateurs (and pros) have a hard time matching in live performances. This transformation is described in books by Robert Philip, Mark Katz, and Alan Rusbridger that are listed in the bibliography.

Accompanying these societal changes has come a shift in the emotional overtones carried by the word "amateur." In recent years, less resonance seems to come from the word's Latin root—*amare*, to love—which implies that an amateur does something for the love of it. A bit more heaviness seems to arise from the word's second definition in the Oxford English Dictionary, that an amateur is someone who is "inept at a particular activity."

However, a new shift in definitional overtones may occur in the future because of the increasing influence of a new breed of amateurs—the amateur journalists and videographers who have made history in recent years with their frontline reporting via cell phone and social media (as noted in an article by Anna Lee listed in the bibliography). The new "artful aging movement" may also prompt a rehabilitation of the amateur label, as artfully aging amateurs increase in number.

Several amateur musicians who have written memoirs about their musical activities have struggled to come to terms with the "A" word. The late Wayne Booth, a cello enthusiast and eminent English professor, wound up embracing both meanings of the word, as he explained in his memoir *For the Love of It*. He acknowledged that he and the amateurs with whom he played chamber music fit both definitions: "We play for the love of the playing, yet we often reveal signs that we lack professional skill or ease." A major amateur musician organization of which he was a member recently changed its name from Amateur Chamber Music Players to Associated Chamber Music Players (ACMP), perhaps to avoid the naming issue or to welcome professional musicians who want to make use of ACMP's worldwide database of people who like getting together with others for the kind of living room chamber music that used to be so popular. Other organizations have retained amateur in their names, including one of the most prestigious, the Cliburn International Amateur Piano Competition.

Hoping to solve the terminology dispute, a few years ago I started using a new term in my two earlier books on music and also on the fliers that invited people to fill out the questionnaire for this book: spare-time musician. But that term implied a casualness that irritated one questionnaire completer, Dr. Marc Wager, a suburban New York French-horn–playing pediatrician who is out many evenings a week rehearsing or performing. There is nothing casual about his devotion to music. "It's one of the most important things in my life," he says. He prefers the word amateur because of its French translation: "one who loves."

Other advice-team members bristle at the amateur label. Charmarie Blaisdell, a retired professor who sings in a Maine community chorus, suggests "non-professional singer" as an alternative. Rey Forrest, a technical writer in Washington, DC, who sings in a church choir and in an auditioned chorale, explains, "I consider myself a professional singer. It depends on your dedication, your attitude toward what you do. It's not determined by whether you get paid or not. There are amateurs who sound like professionals, who work at it day in and day out."

Another alternative—Recreational Music Making—has been used by programs that offer group piano lessons for adult beginners, but this term also has a whiff of casualness. Avocational is a possibility, but it sounds rather clinical. "Passionate adult musicians" is an amateur substitute that has appeared in online publicity for summer music programs, apparently to indicate that amateurs are welcome without using the "A" word. But this term is problematic as well. Surely professional musicians are just as passionate about music as those for whom music isn't their primary career.

Silas Meredith suggests doing away with the whole amateur versus pro debate. "There's an idea out there, often passed on implicitly to music students, that the only true way to make the most of your musical gift is to become a professional musician. This idea does a lot of harm. You don't have to be a professional runner to get the full benefit of running. There's a lot of value in having a society of people who make their own art in their off hours," says this data analyst who plays piano, guitar, and bass with friends at small social gatherings, often in his New York City apartment. "I've derived more pleasure being an amateur musician than I think I ever would have as a professional. I get to focus only on the music that I like. I can take a break and recharge anytime I need. I can take risks, do things that I'm bad at just to push my boundaries. If I had to focus all my waking hours on the aspects of music most likely to pay my bills, I'd enjoy it a lot less."

Judge Blanche M. Manning performing with the Chicago Bar Association's Barristers Big Band.

The issue of economic stability played a role in the life decisions of some advice-team members who had aimed initially at becoming professionals but then realized that the kinds of music jobs they were likely to land would not provide a secure financial future. They turned to less financially risky careers. When they later found a route back to music as non-professionals, they often discovered a creative silver lining in what had been a painful career decision. "Having been raised as a competitive musician, I really appreciate playing with adults now who have a sustained joy in music removed from ego and competition," explains retired librarian Sandy Steinberg. She had been a flute major with a degree in flute performance, but now plays with an upstate New York community orchestra and chamber groups.

Sofia Axelrod came to singing only during graduate school, loved it, and then wished that she had started sooner so she might have become a pro. "I had this regret for a while," she explains, "but then I realized that for me it's better to be a scientist who sings, than a struggling singer who has a PhD in neuroscience." She performs often in the lobby of a New York hospital near the university where she works as a researcher. "I love that I can sing the repertoire that suits me, wherever, whenever," she says. "I don't have to go to auditions and hear that I am not good enough."

Dr. Elizabeth Nevrkla, a retired British physician and lifelong chamber musician, recalls, "As a young doctor working long hours, I used to feel frustrated that there was so little time for playing the cello. Looking back from the perspective of a seventy-year-old, I realize that I have played far more of the chamber music repertoire that I love than many of my professional musician friends, without the competitiveness of the professional world. I was told this when I was young but was too frustrated at the time to value the advice. Now, from the perspective of retirement, I would give the same advice to young players struggling to fit it all together."

The use of the word amateur will be kept to a minimum in this book. The non-pros on the advice team will be identified mainly by their musical interest: bassoonist, cellist, composer, guitarist, pianist, soprano, and so on. A few members of the advice panel feel a little embarrassed to be called "guitarist" or "violinist," feeling that their skill level doesn't merit such a lofty title. In this book, all music-makers are regarded as "musicians." Each one fits somewhere along the lengthy musical continuum that extends from the 70-year-old violin newcomer and brand new choir member at one end, up through those who are semi-pro, and then continuing on to polished professional musicians at the other end. As a struggling non-pro musician with less-than-terrific piano and singing capabilities, I land toward the early part of that continuum. But no matter how far along we are, we're all musicians having fun making music.

> **CLOSE UP: BLANCHE M. MANNING, SAXOPHONIST, CLARINETIST, RETIRED FEDERAL JUDGE**
>
> "I have played tenor saxophone since high school," says retired federal judge Blanche M. Manning, who majored in music for her first two years of college. "I would have tried to be a musician," she notes, "but my dad said, 'No way.' I became a school teacher and later decided to go into law." Through all her career changes, including as the first African American female judge of the Illinois Appellate Court and nearly twenty years as a federal judge in Chicago, she kept playing, including for several years in her own band, Diversity. She even hosted rehearsals of the Chicago Bar Association's Barristers Big Band in her federal courtroom. "Other judges would come up and listen. It was great. Nobody objected," she says. She has kept playing well into her 80s and gets together with a professional musician friend each week "to work on things, keep up to date. The jobs I held, there was a lot of pressure involved in being a federal judge, appellate court judge, and a teacher. Music helped make me happier. It was relaxing. It was a nice outlet for me and it still is."

Enthusiastic Music-Makers

The non-pros on our team of advisors—both the questionnaire respondents and the interviewees—are an impressive and inspiring group who are passionately devoted to music. Nearly all are enthusiastic about the role music plays in their lives. "It's wonderful to participate with others in something much larger than yourself. There's a kind of magic when it happens," says Stephen Whitner, a choir member and retired marketing manager in Seattle. Dr. Lili Barouch, a Baltimore cardiologist and violinist, agrees, "It brings me happiness and peace."

Such positive responses might be expected, given how advice-team members were recruited, by soliciting volunteers who are involved in taking music lessons

Stephen Whitner singing with Seattle Pro Musica.

or participating in ensembles or workshops. But not all went well for every team member during their musical journeys. Accounts of difficulties encountered and how individuals dealt with them are included in this book. The next chapter, however, focuses on the positive, presenting comments from advice-team members and others about the many benefits of making music.

THE BOOK'S "PROGRAM NOTES"

Just as pre-concert program notes can help listeners hear more in a piece of music, the following overview of this book's structure can help readers gain more from what it has to offer.

- **Chapter topics:** Each of the next ten chapters focuses on an area of concern for avocational musicians.
- **Introductory anecdotes:** The sharing of experiences from advice-team members begins at the opening of each chapter, with anecdotes that serve as an introduction to each chapter's topic.
- **Unfolding stories:** The stories of some advice-team members unfold gradually over the course of the book, as they comment on aspects of their musical involvement in different chapters.
- **Repetition:** There is some repetition because suggestions may relate to more than one area. Also, some readers may not read cover-to-cover, but will dip in here and there, depending on their interests.
- **Musician ID's:** When non-pro musicians on the advice panel are introduced for the first time, their employment status and location are noted, along with the instruments they play or whether they are singers. In subsequent chapters, they are identified mainly by their musical activities. Professional musicians are clearly identified as such. Most advice-team members agree to be quoted by name, but a few prefer to remain anonymous when discussing sensitive issues.
- **Bibliography and resources:** The bibliography lists books, articles, and videos mentioned in the text, plus others of interest. The resources section lists websites of interest.

Soprano Sarah Muffly (second from left) performing with the Young New Yorkers' Chorus, an auditioned choir geared to singers in their 20s and 30s.

2   The Benefits of Keeping On with Music

"PLAYING FLUTE IS totally absorbing so that day-to-day worries are completely blocked from my mind. I love the way music fills the space in your head," says Mary Linard, a retired medical lab technician in Montréal and long-time singer who started playing flute in her 60s, with lessons at a community center. Then in her 70s, she began playing percussion in a New Horizons ensemble. Her description of the all-involving nature of music-making is one of the many benefits discussed in this chapter.

The sensation that Ms. Linard has when she plays flute is similar to how Sarah Muffly feels while singing. "Singing is one of the only things I do where I'm fully present. I'm not thinking about anything else. I don't want to check my cell phone. It's refreshing to engage in an activity with that level of concentration," says this New York educational data specialist. Seattle retiree Stephen Whitner agrees: "When I'm singing, whether it's going well or badly, there's no space left for anything else. It's a very present-time, captivating activity."

Of course, it is possible to let your mind wander while singing or playing an instrument, go on automatic pilot, and let muscle memory take over, especially if you're doing a familiar piece or an étude you'd rather not be practicing. But if you're truly focused, it can be all-consuming. "You cannot think about anything else—your problems at work or at home or in the world. You can think only about the music, singing your melody, connecting with the other people in the group," says Carol Davidson, a Massachusetts school administrator who plays viola in a community orchestra and in chamber music groups.

"You get a feeling of 'flow' when you do chamber music. That's why we do chamber music. We like that feeling," says Paula Washington, a violist, New York high school music teacher, and chamber music regular. She is commenting on the "flow" state of immersion in an activity described in Mihaly Csikszentmihalyi's book, *Flow: The Psychology of Optimal Experience.* Jonathan Pease experiences something similar while practicing piano alone at home. "When practice is going well, I can feel very 'in the moment,' deeply connected with the music," says this New York office worker. So does human resources director Theodore Sapp, describing his involvement with the songs he sings in a Virginia church choir and in musical theater productions: "The music I choose to perform resonates at a deeper level. I connect and become one with the song so I can convey the sentiments of the words and melody."

The all-encompassing sensation that these musicians experience reflects the multitasking nature of music-making that has intrigued scientists for many years. When musicians play an instrument or sing, they need to do a great many different kinds of tasks simultaneously: *reading* symbols (if using a score); *planning* how to proceed; *remembering* the skills that will be needed; *moving* fingers, hands, arms, or mouth; *listening* carefully to self-monitor; *communicating* and *coordinating* with others (if in an ensemble); while at the same time *expressing emotion*.

Neuroscientists and educational researchers have been focusing on music's multitasking as a route to learn more about the human brain and the nature of learning. Although much remains to be understood about how musician's brains do what they do, researchers have concluded, much as our advice-team members have, that making music seems to be very good for adults. The next section presents an overview of some of the major research findings that have led to that conclusion.

Music and the Brain

Researchers have seen visual representations of music-making's multitasking in scans of musicians' brains while musicians are at rest, while they listen to or think about music, and while they make music. The scans show that being involved with music seems to activate more regions of the brain than appear to be involved with many other kinds of tasks. Making music "is one of the most complex and demanding cognitive challenges that the human mind can undertake," says McGill University neuroscientist Robert J. Zatorre.

Although he is not willing to say that music is the *most* complex task a person can undertake, he notes that "it is certainly the case that music contains this interesting complexity. That is part of the reason we study it. We are exploring how these systems work and how they change with learning and expertise. We want to understand the rules by which the brain operates and the rules by which the brain changes its characteristics with learning. If we can figure out those rules, we will be in a better position to develop rehabilitation strategies that would improve functioning of someone with dementia, or a stroke, or a degenerative disease like Parkinson's. To do that we need to understand the basic mechanism of how the brain works." His research team has been designing modified instruments that can be played safely in MRI machines so researchers can use brain scan technology to explore how brains function while people are learning to play an instrument, as well as how brain activity differs when someone matches pitch vocally compared to matching pitch while playing a modified cello.

These experiments are among the many in recent years that follow up on a surprising discovery made more than twenty years ago when Harvard neuroscientist Gottfried Schlaug found that MRI scans show that the brains of professional musicians differ from those of non-musicians by having a larger corpus callosum. That is the part of the brain that serves as a bridge between its left and right hemispheres. Before then, scientists thought that only one side of the brain was involved in music. A larger corpus callosum suggests that greater-than-normal communication is going on among different regions of a musician's brain, perhaps through newly created neural pathways. Ever since this game-changing discovery, scientists have been trying to learn more about the cross-brain communication that goes on in musicians' brains.

Researchers still don't understand exactly how a musician's brain pulls off its astonishing coordinating act. They also can't prove that music-making is what causes the differences in musicians' brains. There could be something that predisposes a person to want to make music and this predisposition causes the brain differences. Some studies, however, suggest that it is the making of music itself that is the cause. In a study by Dr. Schlaug's group, MRI scans of young children's brains began to show the structural changes typical of musicians' brains after the youngsters had fifteen months of keyboard lessons.

Leaving aside the chicken-versus-egg debate, researchers feel that they have learned enough to conclude that musicians' brains give them an advantage in other aspects of life and may possibly lessen some of the cognitive decline of aging. Below is a brief rundown of key findings. The bibliography lists articles that fill in the details.

- **Brain plasticity:** Dr. Schlaug's research group has also found that musicians have a larger amount of gray matter than non-musicians in the areas of the brain that work together in music-making. Amateur musicians have less of this gray matter than professional musicians, but more than non-musicians, suggesting that music-making may cause the changes (assuming that pros practice more than amateurs). This finding implies also that the more one makes music, the more there is of this gray matter. Increased gray matter may mean that new neural pathways have been created to let music-related cross-brain communication occur more easily. The brain's ability to modify itself and create new pathways is called "brain plasticity."

- **Plasticity persists:** Music-related brain changes seem to persist even if music-making stops. Northwestern University neuroscientist Nina Kraus found that adults who had instrumental music lessons as youngsters but hadn't been music-makers for forty years still had faster brainstem responses to sounds than adults who never had music lessons.

- **Crossover skills:** Musicians' brains also seem to help with non-musical tasks, particularly "executive function" tasks—those that involve coordination, planning, and problem-solving. University of Maryland neuropsychologist Brenda Hanna-Pladdy gave seventy adults, age 59 to 80, a battery of executive function cognitive tests. The amateur instrumental musicians in the group outperformed non-musicians on the executive function tests. In another of her studies, amateurs who had stopped playing their instruments still outscored non-musicians, another indication that a musician's better-connected brain may last a lifetime. Even musical newcomers perform better on cognitive tests than non-musicians, according to two studies of adults age 60 and over who had no previous music training. Those who were given several months of piano lessons as part of these studies performed better on cognitive tests than those who had no piano lessons. In one study, those who took piano lessons reported increased feelings of well-being than the others. "You're never too old to begin to play a musical instrument," concludes the University of South Florida's Jennifer Bugos, author of one of the piano studies. You're never too old, apparently, to tune up your brain either.

- **Cognitive reserve theory:** Strong ability on cognitive function tasks may give musicians "cognitive reserve." The extra neural pathways in musicians' brains could be called upon to lessen some of the mental decline of aging. Because executive function skills are among the first to go when dementia strikes, being good at those tasks may mean that a person has "strong neural connections and flexibility in the brain so that when the lesions of dementia appear, the brain will automatically be more able to cope and find new ways to do tasks," explains Canadian neuroscientist Aline Moussard. This cognitive reserve theory gains support from a Swedish study of twins—25 percent of whom were identical twins—that found that "twins who played a musical instrument" in older adulthood were less likely to develop dementia . . . compared to their co-twins" who hadn't been playing instruments. Cognitive reserve is cited with another group thought to have good brain plasticity—bilingual adults, who, according to some studies, develop dementia four years later than monolinguists, on average. In addition, a 2014 NEA study of older adults, age 55 and up, found that those who created art, including singing and playing instruments, and who also attended arts events reported having higher levels of cognitive functioning and lower rates of hypertension than those not involved in the arts.

- **Research impact:** The cognitive reserve theory is speculative, but it has caught the attention of our questionnaire respondents from reports that have appeared in popular news media. "I am hopeful that music will stave off mental decline ahead," says choral singer and viola da gamba player Kathy Fleming. This Baltimore arts administrator is partly joking, but also wishing it's true. Carol Eisenbise, a retired special education teacher in Pennsylvania, is similarly hopeful. Having started playing string bass in her 60s, she exclaims, "They say learning a new instrument will help prevent dementia. I believe it! Taking string bass lessons at 62—talk about making new brain synapses!" However, fending off cognitive decline isn't the main reason our team members pursue music, even for Ms. Eisenbise, who notes, "I had wanted to play string bass for decades and decided I better do it now or forget it."

CLOSE UP: RUFUS BROWNING, COMPOSER, SINGER, PIANIST, RETIRED POLITICAL SCIENCE PROFESSOR

"I knew when I fully retired in 2005 I would take up something musical. I settled on voice, then added a little piano at age 79. Playing piano is hard for me to learn, but it's worth the effort," says Rufus Browning. "Frequently I'm in a state of bliss because I'm inside the most beautiful and artfully constructed music—the ecstatic chord progressions of a simple Bach chorale! Then I started composing at age 81. It is intellectually fascinating and incredibly satisfying to create one's own music. I became involved in composition because I dreamt I was composing and it felt blissful. That very morning I saw a flier for a summer workshop on composition. I signed up and wrote the melody for a song based on a poem I had recently encountered which reminded me of my mother, who was a composer. I have an excellent teacher who opens doors for me and helps me out of the boxes I find myself in. A melody flows out of my head—that's inspiration—but then it's real work to develop it. That's the challenge!"

Rufus Browning at a concert where he sang a few songs, including one he composed.

"Stress Melts Away"

"Some people jog, do yoga, or meditate. I play music. For the two hours a week when I'm at rehearsal for community band, I get a break from the challenges of being an adult—work, children, bills, housing. For that two hours, the stress melts away and I feel refreshed," says Mandy Ray. "True, there are the occasional rehearsals after which I feel frustrated and dejected, but they are rare. I love playing bassoon, haven't stopped since I was 13, and feel gratified rehearsing, learning, and perfecting a piece as an individual and part of a group."

Music-making as a calming stress-reliever is the most commonly mentioned benefit noted by our questionnaire completers. "I can get through my week so long as I play music with my folk music group on Sunday night," says Debra Koran, a Chicago school counselor who sings and also plays guitar and mandolin. Dr. Deborah Edge, a retired Washington physician and double bassist, observes, "Once you start playing, a calmness comes over you." Chicago software designer Joseph Arden agrees, "Guitar practice is my relaxation. The guitar is like a best friend that is always there for you."

Researchers suggest that neurochemicals may explain the calmness that our advisors experience. Listening to music activates areas of the brain that are involved in releasing dopamine, a neurotransmitter associated with "positive mood and affect," according to Canadian neuroscientist Daniel Levitin, who discusses this in his book, *This Is Your Brain on Music*. Because listening to music plays a major role in making music, musicians no doubt experience this neurotransmitter-associated, mood-elevating benefit while practicing and performing. Studies by British psychologist Robin Dunbar suggest that performing music—not just listening to it—may release other mood-enhancing neurochemicals: endorphins, substances known for producing "runner's high." However, the endorphin release in these studies was measured indirectly by gauging musicians' increased tolerance for pain while performing, suggesting an involvement, while not actually proving it. Other studies have shown an increase in positive affect for those doing choral singing, compared with when the same people simply listen to music.

A member of our advice team did a mini experiment of her own to assess the calming influence of playing tabla, Indian hand drums. "I noticed in my first year

Dr. Wen Dombrowski playing tabla, a South Asian instrument that consists of a pair of drums.

of learning tabla that, unlike the experiences I've had with other drums, playing tabla felt like a mindfulness exercise that required my total focus, attention, and inner calm. If I practiced for fifteen minutes, I would feel refreshed, as if I had taken a nap," notes Dr. Wen Dombrowski, a New York and California-based physician who specializes in health-care innovation and technology. She had a Muse EEG headband that measures brainwaves that she was evaluating for work. She slipped it on to see if her brainwaves differed while checking emails compared with playing tabla. "When I play tabla, there is an immediate flip in the brainwave pattern," she says. "The brainwaves associated with stress go down and ones associated with the subconscious go way up." But after she advanced to more complex songs, she sometimes found it harder to get into a meditative mode when practicing tabla. "Keeping track of all the notes can be mentally tiring, like doing math problems," she says.

Music's calming magic doesn't always kick in during practice time for choral singer Liz Langeland either. "The physical act of singing has a calming effect when I'm singing complete pieces or singing with others to produce an amazing, rich, collective sound, but not necessarily when I'm at home woodshedding," she says. But this Seattle nurse adds that another kind of singing definitely relieves stress: "Singing with the car radio on can release lots of pent-up emotion!"

Releasing stress through music has helped Lydia Zieglar deal with the challenges of being a working mother. An automobile accident in her 20s caused a cervical disc problem that ended her violin-playing, but she came back to music years later through her son, by helping him practice cello and eventually joining a cello class that one of his teachers started for adult beginners. "Cello is better for my spine than violin and I love cello's deep tone. My doctor told me it's important to have something for yourself, that if I don't take care of myself, then I can't be at my best in taking care of those who are depending on me. Music is my 'something,'" says this Maryland mathematician, who adds, "My family prefers that I work out my stress on my instrument rather than on them."

I am one 'chilled out' adult when I play viola.
—Miriam Jackobs, violist, clarinetist,
registered dietitian

"New Friendships"

Steven Duke keeps on with music in part because "it gives me the opportunity to meet new people, form new friendships. I like the companionship of making music with others. It makes me feel less alone in the world." Gerri Hall, a Maryland professional gardener and choral singer, adds, "Joining a choir means you become like 'family' with a group of people."

Making friends is the second most frequently mentioned benefit of staying involved in music, as noted by our questionnaire completers. "You end up with a real cool set of musical friends," says Stephen Taylor, a French horn–playing engineer in New Hampshire. In fact, music offers one of the best ways to meet people when moving to a new community, according to Brandon Ray, who moved around a lot after college while on active duty in the military. "When I was stationary in one location and was not deployable, I made it a priority to get involved with music groups, singing in a church choir and doing musical theater. That has given me the chance to meet people outside of work."

Bringing his cello with him in 1939 when Fritz Lustig fled from Nazi Germany was "his passport to finding lifelong friends in England," says his violinist/violist son, Stephen Lustig. "Within two months of arriving in Cambridge as a refugee, his hosts introduced him to musicians and he was playing in a chamber music concert at Cambridge University. He had just turned 20." Both father and son are members of our advice team. The elder Mr. Lustig, a retired accountant, has continued playing quartets once a month well into his late 90s, partnering with his son and "a couple of young ladies who are only 91," his son reports.

For Roland Wilk, "music is a wonderful way to make friends all over the world," not just in Ontario, where this retired software developer lives and plays clarinet, French horn, and bassoon. He has expanded his circle of friends by attending summer music camps for adults in Canada and the United States, and by using the worldwide database of musicians maintained by ACMP (Associated Chamber Music Players) to find chamber music partners while traveling. Music has helped Sarah Muffly maintain contact with friends, whether musical or not, by inviting them to performances of her chorus. "I think some friends like coming to the concerts because it's an inexpensive way to go to a live performance of good music in New York City," she notes. "My involvement in the choir has encouraged others to join it, too."

Musical friends helped violist Louise Lerner during her legal career and beyond. "Music-making kept me sane through college, law school, and many years in a high pressure job in Washington. Most of my closest friends I met through music. Since retiring, I rely on music to get me out of the house—playing viola in an orchestra and in chamber music pick-up groups." As retired school psychologist Mike Alberts notes, "Without music, retirement would be much more boring." This guitarist organizes regular jam sessions at which he and fellow Chicago musicians perform. "It is an essential part of my everyday life."

Fritz Lustig in 1939 at age 20 (in top photo) when he played his first chamber music concert in Britain, shortly after fleeing Nazi Germany with his cello. The lower photo shows him more recently.

For some team members, musical friends have truly been a lifeline. "My whole department was outsourced and I got laid off," recounts Cassandra Pettway. "When you don't work and lack money, you stay home. I wasn't socializing. I lost contact with people. I was out of shape." Then she ran into a former co-worker who told her about the New Horizons program at Michigan State University's Community Music School in Detroit. She had played clarinet as a child and had kept the instrument but hadn't played it since eighth grade. "I grabbed that clarinet and joined the band. It became a new life for me," she says. She started taking lessons and also learned to play saxophone in the New Horizon jazz band. "My brain started ticking and I got a band family. Now I'm trying to develop a swinging, soulful

Cassandra Pettway playing with the New Horizons Jazz Band of Michigan State University's Community Music School in Detroit.

style." This same band program was also a lifesaver for Nancy Harris while she was going through a difficult divorce. "It was a way to have a break, an escape," says this Michigan food inspector. She had been playing flute on her own since college but never knew there were bands for adults until she saw a notice at the school where she signed up her son for band camp. "If I had known there were bands for adults, I would have joined sooner."

Family Ties

In some cases, a new musical friend has wound up as more than a friend, becoming also a husband or wife. Ken Williams, a technical writer and cello enthusiast in Seattle, reports, "I met my wife at a chamber music session." They still play chamber music together. So do Leslie and Leon Vieland, pianist and cellist respectively. They also make music with a grown son (a clarinetist), a daughter (a flutist and violist), and with Mr. Vieland's pianist sister during family get-togethers at their New Jersey home. "Any family visit includes music-making," says Mr. Vieland, a retired scientist. "How lucky we are!"

"Playing guitar has brought me closer to my children. I feel that I set an example for them about practicing and having patience," says Joseph Arden, who helps his kids with their music lessons. Norma Foege has seen the impact that her involvement with music has had on her children, now grown. "Both of my children studied instruments and now their children play instruments," says this retired New York schoolteacher and visual artist. She continued to play piano while they were growing up and also reports, "I always sang to my children and now sing to my grandchildren." Dr. Marc Wager feels that his devotion to French horn has imparted another lesson. "There were times when my kids resented that I was out so much at rehearsals," he acknowledges. "But I think I set a good example for them that music is important and that they need to make time for their own creative passions when they become adults."

Kids aren't the only family members who have been inspired by a relative's music-making. When Miriam Jackobs started violin at age 70 and viola at 76, that prompted her brother to pull out his old violin and start playing again, too. Arthur Carvajal's father began clarinet lessons after retirement, motivated by the many concerts he attended in which his lawyer son played trumpet in Chicago Bar Association ensembles. Spouses of several advice-team members have joined in the music-making music. Mohamed Magdi Hassan's whole extended Sudanese-American family has been inspired by his keyboard playing of traditional Sudanese music at weddings and other family gatherings. His playing helps root those events in the family's rich cultural heritage. "I feel on top of the world when I play," says this Texas geospatial analyst. "It means a lot to family and friends to have me playing at these special occasions."

Neela Wickremesinghe notes another way music has brought her family together. This architectural conservator started on clarinet as a kid, sometimes practicing with her father, an avocational clarinetist. By college, she had moved on to saxophone and searched for a group to play with in New York during graduate school and beyond. She joined the Lesbian and Gay Big Apple Corps, a symphonic band, in which she plays baritone sax. "I love being able to continue to participate in a hobby that I have done for over twenty years. I also love that it is a way for me to connect with my parents, who instilled a love of music in me. As an out lesbian with a good, but still strange relationship to my dad, it is a way for me to celebrate my identity through a nonthreatening community band that my dad loves to watch."

Making Beautiful Music

"There is nothing more satisfying, in my opinion, than blending with a group singing in perfect harmony," says Bob Weaver, a singer and retired Massachusetts mathematics professor. The joy of making beautiful music is a key motivator for our team members. "It gives you a positive appreciation of art created by geniuses and an opportunity to share in it," observes Eric Godfrey, a violinist and retired sociology professor in Wisconsin. For pianist Dale Backus, spending time with composers like Beethoven is time well spent. "His music is so deep and rich. Every note matters. You get to work out the puzzle, work through his brain and his expression, to what's going on," says this Colorado engineer, who has played in several amateur piano competitions.

Steve DeMont, a technical writer in Seattle and a newcomer to saxophone, loves using what he has learned in a jazz theory classes "to analyze and work through a tune when practicing. I'm constantly listening to music, sometimes the same tune over and over. It drives my wife nuts. But it's my way of studying a tune and a musician's technique and tone. There's so much to discover. It seems never-ending."

Joyce Richardson, a retired New York social worker, feels that she has become a better audience member from playing in a recorder quintet, as well as tooting away on her euphonium (a small tuba) in a New Horizons concert band. She has noticed that "when I go to concerts or hear music on the radio, I have begun to 'hear' more."

"Part of My Healing"

"My husband was diagnosed with Alzheimer's several years ago and music is my lifeline. As long as I can play music, I feel like I can cope. The friends I have made through music are an important part of my support system with an invalid husband," says Joan Herbers. Several times a week this retired biology professor gets together with friends in Ohio to play chamber music as a violinist, violist, and sometimes as a pianist, too.

Music has served as a therapeutic life preserver for several other members of the advice panel when disease, death, divorce, and job loss created challenges. Deanna Zoe Smith observes, "Since being widowed, singing gives me an outlet for my grief, a structure to my life, and the joy of song." She used to work as the sternman on her late husband's lobster boat but now fills her days with music, singing in two Maine choruses. For Adine Usher, "playing the piano is something I simply have to do." This New York educational consultant notes, "I find it emotionally satisfying. It got me through breast cancer. It got me through my husband's death."

> **Music creeps into every empty space to fill your soul.**
> —Mary Linard, singer, flutist, percussionist,
> retired medical lab technician

Music rescued Mr. Whitner, too. "I started to sing again a few months after the death of my wife of thirty-two years. It was an important part of my healing," he says. He had stopped singing for over a decade, partly for his job but then later because of "the illness and death of my wife. I went back to singing because I missed doing music and discovered a wonderful community. It was a way of rediscovering myself, and provides a level of emotional richness and satisfaction that nothing else does for me."

Music therapists are well aware of the help in times of crisis that music can provide. Both making music and listening to it can "encourage healing and promote a general sense of well-being" as well as "reduce pain and feelings of isolation," according to Karen Popkin, music therapist at New York's Memorial Sloan Kettering Cancer Center. When she visits patients at the bedside, she brings a cart of instruments— guitar, small drums, bells, and other handheld percussion. Some patients are too weak to play, but those who join in "often find that they increase their sense of energy and have an opportunity to release pent-up worry and stress," she says. Her hospital and several others sponsor choruses for cancer survivors that seem to lift the singers' spirits, as do choirs that other groups offer for Alzheimer patients, who often remember songs from long ago while other memories have faded, as can be seen in the documentary, *Alive Inside.*

In addition to providing stress release, music therapists have found that music-making can provide positive physical therapeutic benefits, such as alleviating symptoms for those with Parkinson's disease. Singing has also been shown to help stroke survivors recover the ability to communicate. People with breathing difficulties have made gains by playing simple wind instruments in music therapy sessions—recorder, slide whistle, harmonica, or melodica. "It's a workout that pushes open the airway a little," explains Wen Chang-Lit, music therapist at New York's Louis Armstrong Center for Music and Medicine. "It lets them be creative and it's fun"—more fun than blowing into a breathing tube, making it more likely that they will keep tooting and "expanding their lung capacity."

Music therapist Rebecca Vaudreuil uses songwriting with veterans and service members diagnosed with post-traumatic stress disorder (PTSD) and traumatic brain injury as a way, she says, to help with "acknowledgment, processing, and communication of their feelings into a musical product that they are able to listen to, share with others, and talk about." Therapeutic songwriting activities have been part of the work she has done at Naval Medical Center San Diego, Walter Reed Military Medical Center, and Camp Pendleton's Concussion Care Clinic.

CLOSE UP: CORPORAL DEMI BULLOCK, GUITARIST, RECREATIONAL PROGRAM DIRECTOR

Music therapy helped former Marine Corps Corporal Demi Bullock return to music-making. A longtime guitar player who developed PTSD after serving two tours in Afghanistan, it took a while for her to feel ready to connect with music therapy. She first experienced music therapy at Naval Medical Center San Diego, through the Semper Sound program run by Resounding Joy, Inc. What finally clicked for her was developing a relationship with a music therapist whom she had gradually grown to trust and who encouraged her play with other veterans in a rock band. "I was extremely anxious," she wrote on her blog. "It turned out I had a blast with the band . . . and rediscovered my passion for music." Playing with the band enabled her to manage symptoms in a different way. She then became a military intern with Resounding Joy. Together she and music therapist Rebecca Vaudreuil pioneered and developed the east coast Semper Sound program at the Soldiers' Home in Chelsea, Massachusetts. "I play guitar, ukulele, and piano for fun," says Corporal Bullock. She aims to continue using music to work with military populations.

Help with the Day Job

Several advice-team members report that making music doesn't just relieve workplace stress but actually helps their day jobs, as they describe in the following examples.

- **Presentation confidence:** "When I perform as a singer, I change my whole demeanor. I walk more confidently. I speak more confidently," says Elaine Lee Paoliello, a Seattle medical writer who sings in an auditioned chorus. She taps into the confidence learned through music performance when giving presentations at work, allowing her to "come across as more professional" and not as nervous as she really may be.
- **A habit for learning:** "The awareness that one never stops learning, which I've gained from music, along with openness to suggestions and guidance from others, underlies my professional life," says Arabella Lang. She plays violin in chamber music groups, when not writing position papers on legal issues for Britain's House of Commons. Patricia Mabry feels that "studying and performing a wide range of music of different styles, languages, and cultures" as part of the Heritage Signature Chorale, a high-level Washington chorus, helped her during her years as a school principal, "making me more equipped to deal with different personalities, cultures, and levels of strengths and weaknesses in the work place."

Elaine Lee Paoliello singing with Seattle Pro Musica.

- **Teamwork skills:** Dr. Alvin Crawford, a clarinetist, saxophonist, and University of Cincinnati orthopedic surgeon, notes how similar the give-and-take he has honed in jazz bands is to the teamwork needed in an operating room. "All team members—nurses, anesthesia, neuro-monitoring, X-ray, and house staff—must play in harmony, same key, same beats to the bar to achieve the best surgical result," he says. Teamwork skills also helped singer Theodore Sapp. Insights gained from performing in musicals helped him deal with a problem he was having as a human resources director. "For a short while, I was letting some things fall through the cracks at work, not getting things resolved in a timely manner. I realized that much like you can't carry a show yourself, I couldn't do it all myself at work and had to do a better job leveraging resources available to me."

- **Improvising:** Dr. Brad Reddick sees a connection between his work with kids and the improvising he does playing lead guitar in blues and rock bands, which he describes as "catching a wave and staying afloat." This North Carolina child psychiatrist explains, "With kids, I create an improvisational space, with all kinds of toys they can interact with as we create play together. Play is how kids process and requires improvisational skills on the part of the clinician in facilitating it therapeutically. If they feel comfortable creating this play on equal footing with me, they're not so intimidated by the 'scary child psychiatrist.'"

- **A link to kids:** Dr. Jeff Bostic, a Washington child psychiatrist who plays drums in several rock and folk bands, feels that his ease in talking about all kinds of music gives him an "in" with kids. Talking with them about their music "is a way to communicate where they don't feel like you're trying to preach to them. They'll talk about what really matters to them," he explains. Ms. Koran has noticed something similar in her work as a middle school and high school counselor. "I can connect more closely with students when we are discussing music and the power it has in our lives," she says. In addition, when she joined a community chorus—something that was new for her—that helped her feel "more empathetic with students. I was learning new things each week in the chorus, working in a team, as my students do every day."

- **Professional contacts:** Mr. Carvajal reports that music has helped him "establish rapport with legal adversaries who are disarmed when they learn I am a lawyer musician." Dr. Wager has gained new patients for his pediatrics practice from parents who hear him play French horn. Sarah Wright, a Minneapolis pharmacist and violinist, says her musical hobby "has come up in job interviews. Employers are curious about people they are hiring, if they have achievements in other areas." However, Alex Jones notes that he didn't talk much about playing clarinet when he started as a professor of electrical and computer engineering because it might not be "viewed particularly positively in my field, since we're supposed to spend time competing for research grants. When I got tenure, I became a little less cautious." His wind quintet played recently at his Pennsylvania university's graduation.

- **Immediate gratification:** "Many of the things I do at work provide delayed gratification," says Ann Rogers, a professor of nursing in Atlanta who plays flute and bassoon. "There are years between the generation of an idea for research, submitting a grant proposal, doing the research, and finding the answer." But music, she says, "provides immediate gratification."

"My Truest, Deepest Self"

"I feel music is my truest, deepest self," says Catherine Kasmer, who put her guitar aside for seventeen years while raising her kids and starting her teaching career in Chicago. "During a particularly difficult time, I felt music calling to me again and I was shocked to find that it was right there on my fingertips. I began again with renewed vigor and have vowed to keep music alive and vital in my life from now on. I dream in music. I think in music. I am glad I can have music in my life in a pure way, just for fun, friendship, beauty, and art, and not have to worry about making money with it." Others on our advice panel also comment on how making music helps them feel more complete.

- "It's as though I've reconnected with a part of my soul that had been missing for all these years," says New York arts consultant Polly Kahn, describing her return to cello.
- "Returning to music broke me out of my work/home routine and reminded me that despite my highly analytical work life, I still have a creative side," says Kathy Dockins, a pre-employment background investigator in Seattle who started flute again in her 40s.
- "For most of my life, I have been a 'technique nerd' in everything I do. But I always knew I had a musical heart. At age 38, I had the means and opportunity to get into music. It has changed me. I have developed a better sense of empathy and communicate better," says Jay Choi, a new violist and owner of a California fencing academy.

- "I feel renewed and uplifted by singing. God has given me a gift that I must share," says Lucia Elder, a nurse who has sung in church choirs all her life and is part of a Maine community chorus.
- "It keeps me feeling younger than my age," says John Murray, a retired chemical engineer in Houston who returned to clarinet in his 80s.

Laurel Kuxhaus playing oboe. Mark Dalrymple with his trombone.

3 Making Music All Along

"COMMUNITY BANDS HAVE been on my radar since high school because the one in my town rehearsed in our high school band room each week. As students, we thought of them as the people who mess up the band room," says Laurel Kuxhaus, explaining how she always knew that there would be a way to keep playing oboe as an adult, even though she would choose to pursue a career in biomechanics after earning degrees in both engineering and music at college. Now an engineering professor in northern New York, she has been making music all her adult years, with no major gaps. So have about one-third of our advice-team members who completed the questionnaire on their musical activities. This chapter tells their stories.

Professor Kuxhaus had her first taste of performing with adult avocational musicians one summer during college when she played in two community bands. Each of those bands had only one rehearsal for their weekly performances. "That's when I really learned how to sight-read," she says, mastering the skill that has helped many a musician wing it in performances for which they didn't have enough time to rehearse. During graduate school, she played in university ensembles and also in local community orchestras. "I realized that while there can be varying levels of musicianship between (and sometimes within) ensembles, there are good players everywhere, some of whom have careers in widely different fields." When she landed a teaching job in a new community, she tracked down musical opportunities and found a slew of them. During one recent year, she performed in a community band, two orchestras, a wind ensemble, a regular quartet, and frequent pick-up chamber music get-togethers, as well as in the pit for three high school musicals. She also attended a chamber music camp that summer. Such a full schedule "motivates me," she says. "I'm an oboe player. I'm always needed."

Not all of our lifelong music-makers participate in so many different groups, although many find more than one way to keep on with music. Pennsylvania-based software developer Mark Dalrymple comes close to Professor Kuxhaus's tally. A trombonist and bassoonist who occasionally plays recorder and handbells, he managed over the course of one recent year to play in more than eight instrumental ensembles, in addition to singing in a church choir. North Carolina financial consultant Robin Henning is also busy, singing in a choir plus playing saxophone in several jazz bands.

Other long-term music-makers focus on just one type of musical activity. Barbara Napholtz, a New Jersey software developer, concentrates on daily piano practice to prepare duets and other pieces to perform at a summer piano camp or to play in recitals organized by a music Meetup group. Elaine Lee Paoliello's main music activity involves singing with a Seattle chorus. Boston scientist Liman Zhang's music-making doesn't involve any public performances. She prefers playing the erhu, a Chinese stringed instrument, on her own at home "as a personal relaxing activity."

Ms. Paoliello and Professor Kuxhaus, both in their 30s, have a way to go to catch up with the oldest member of the lifelong contingent of our advisors: Fritz Lustig, the retired London accountant described in chapter 2. He filled out his questionnaire for this book at age 96 and has played cello in chamber music groups all his adult life, as well as, he says, in the "occasional orchestra." In addition, he has attended the same summer music camp for more than sixty years.

Some long-term music-makers acknowledge that there were moments when other commitments took priority and their music-making slowed down. "I have never quit playing but have played at varying levels of intensity, depending on work demands," says New York lawyer and cellist Irene Ten Cate. New York publisher Marion Berghahn adds, "Giving birth and recovering from it took me away from piano, but only briefly. I always went back to my playing whenever I had thirty minutes available. I can't imagine life without it." In the following pages, she and others who have managed to make music all along describe how they keep going.

Seeing a Way Forward

Quite a few members of our lifelong music-makers knew early on, as Professor Kuxhaus did, that they would somehow always find a way to make music. Mike Tietz began playing chamber music with adult amateurs during high school. Not only did that let him know about the vibrant world of avocational music-making, but he also became aware of the networking that lets musicians find playing opportunities. "I knew it would just be a matter of making the right contacts after completing my education and moving back to New York City after law school. That turned out to be the case," says this retired lawyer. He plays several other instruments in addition to cello, loves doing chamber music, and also conducts a community orchestra that he founded. He began networking even before entering high school, when, at age 12, he joined a youth orchestra and met a fellow middle-schooler, violist Paula Washington, another of our team members. "She and I still play chamber music together. She plays in my orchestra. We're only a few months apart in age and refer to ourselves as brother and sister because we're the only ones in our current immediate families who knew each other's parents. If you're lucky enough to play instrumental music, it's for life."

Flutist Linda Rapp had a role model to inspire her—a physics professor at her university who was also a professional organist at a local church. "I never talked with him about it, but because of him, I knew that it was possible to do this," she says. His dual life made her feel more comfortable when she switched from a music major to engineering. "I knew I would find ways to make music. I was sad that I might not play with high-level players." Luckily, this materials engineer has always found excellent

Cellist Mike Tietz (right) with violist Paula Washington after a performance of the Broadway Bach Ensemble, which he founded and conducts.

musicians to play chamber music with who live near her in upstate New York, as well as others she meets at a summer chamber music program.

Mr. Dalrymple, the multi-instrumentalist mentioned earlier, had parents who were avocational musicians and played in the Arkansas Symphony. Their experiences made him aware of non-pro options and also let him realize the financial perils of trying to become a professional musician. "I made the decision in high school that it would be easier to have a music habit on a computer salary than the other way around," he reports. For his first job in Virginia after college, "a friend of my folks got me hooked up with a pretty good community band and from there I made more contacts." He has been making contacts ever since.

Those who sang as children and teens in a church or synagogue choir had firsthand experience with one of the most popular ways that adults keep on with music. For them, joining a choir after college seemed perfectly natural. In addition to being a deeply meaningful and spiritual experience, choir singing can often be fairly easy to fit into a busy week. Choirs are generally low time-commitment ensembles. In some choirs, their one rehearsal a week occurs an hour or two before the ensemble is to sing in a service.

Choir membership also provides a way to improve musical know-how gradually so that later when time and opportunity permits, some choir members were ready to pursue other musical challenges. Church choirs helped Patricia Mabry stay connected with music while raising two daughters and earning a doctorate in education during her many years as an elementary school principal. "Singing in church and college choirs for more than forty years prepared me to stretch my musical gifts to the next level and audition for a semi-professional chorus," she reports. For John Murray, singing in church choirs for sixty-four years kept music in his life until an opportunity arose during his 80s to return to clarinet—which he hadn't played since elementary school—when his Houston church started a clarinet choir and later a New Horizons band. "I always had time for church choir," says this retired chemical engineer. "Now that I'm retired, I have time for choir and band. It's a good feeling of contributing to the group, of feeling needed."

As an adult, Joe Meisel initially pursued the aspects of music-making that he enjoyed the most during high school: writing songs and playing guitar. He had been in a rock band as a teenager that played original material that he wrote. When he no longer had enough time to join a band—in graduate school, during his first jobs, and while starting a family—he kept writing songs as he had in high school, whenever inspiration struck. "I would go to coffee house open mic nights, where people with guitars can go in and play two or three songs," he explains. He kept up his guitar skills, too, so that he was ready to join a rock cover band when the opportunity arose just after moving to Brown University in Rhode Island to become deputy provost. Drumming enthusiast Janet Blume, a senior associate dean there, mentioned that she had a faculty band that

Guitarist and singer songwriter Joe Meisel.

was breaking up and wanted to form a new band. He became a member of the new band and began collaborating again with other musicians, "something I missed from my high school days and was delighted to start doing again," he says.

> **Other than work and family commitments, piano comes first—before groceries, before housework, before cooking!**
> —Barbara Napholtz, pianist, software developer

Crafting a Musical Support System

A number of other lifelong team members also spent a few years working on music on their own until they found a way to connect with fellow musicians again. Virginia environmental scientist Julie Fitzpatrick went the solo-practice route during two years of graduate school. "I played occasionally for personal enjoyment, but I did not participate in an orchestra as a graduate student," she recalls. She had played cello in a community orchestra as an undergraduate but didn't feel she had time for that as a grad student. Joshua Dadeboe was a solo practicer during college because "my college didn't have an orchestra. I took my violin with me and would pull it out once in a while to play." Now an accountant in Pennsylvania, he had fallen in love with violin at age nine and was determined not to let his skills slip during college.

Tinkering away solo has its drawbacks, however, as Svetlana Gladycheva, a Maryland physics lecturer, observes. "For most of my adulthood I played piano, varying from occasional pieces that I remembered by muscle memory to attempts to resume learning scales, études, and new pieces. But learning on my own would always die out after a month or two because of lack of formal stimulus." That changed when she created a music support system that made it easier for her to stay involved with music. So did Ms. Fitzpatrick, Mr. Dadeboe, and others of our lifelong music-makers.

For most of our advice-team members, having a support system is an important element underpinning their connection to music whether they have been making music all along, returned to music after a long gap, or are musical newcomers. The basics of creating such a support system are presented in this chapter, using examples from the experiences of those who have been making music all along. However, returnees and newcomers have used many of the same strategies to craft support systems. Each of the elements of the basic supportive network that are described here receive more detailed discussion in subsequent chapters.

- **Joining ensembles:** This is one of the pillars of our team members' musical support systems. Three-fourths of those who completed the questionnaires for this book make music as part of an ensemble—singing in choirs and choruses, performing in musical theater productions, playing in community orchestras and bands, performing with smaller groups such as chamber music ensembles or small bands, or taking part in informal jam sessions and open mics. This is the route Ms. Fitzpatrick and Mr. Dadeboe took. They each got back into practicing more regularly when they had time to join community or church ensembles after they finished their education. More recently, Ms. Fitzpatrick's encouragement to keep practicing comes from the many chamber music groups in which she plays. Some chamber groups can be as small as the piano duets that Ms. Berghahn and a friend put on every New Year's Eve. "It's fun to play with others rather than just for yourself, and good to have an aim. It is a great motivator to play toward a deadline," she says. That's also why Patrick Holland has joined choruses, large and small, wherever he has moved during his career as a chemistry professor, including singing now with two choruses in New Haven. "Then I have an obligation to others and don't want to let them down. I have to find ways to schedule it and not let it slide," he explains. There is more about the many ways of making music with others in chapters 9 to 11.

- **Finding instruction:** "Coming back to taking lessons at age 37 was a watershed in really developing a personal music life," says Deborah Wythe, recently retired from a New York museum. For many years she had been trying to find time to play piano on her own at home. Once she started taking lessons again in her 30s, making time to practice has been easier. "My teacher's method of focusing on three things to work on at a time has helped—gives me specific goals to reach before the next lesson. It makes me carve out practice time. Keeps me accountable." Ms. Berghahn has found that piano lessons not only keep her focused but also introduce her to potential chamber music partners. "I have always found a teacher wherever we moved," she says. "My current teacher organizes workshops at least once a year for his more mature students." Taking lessons is part of the support system for about half of our questionnaire completers. Chapter 7 offers ways to connect with instruction.

- **Music school community:** In addition to offering private and group lessons, music schools can provide a supportive community of fellow musicians and an abundance of other kinds of learning and performing opportunities. Many have instrumental and vocal ensembles, chamber music workshops, performance workshops, master classes, and informal jam sessions. These options are discussed in chapters 7, 9, and 10.

Flutist Linda Rapp (left) next to fellow advice-team member, clarinetist Karen Greif, as they rehearse a wind quintet by György Ligeti at the Bennington Chamber Music Conference summer program in Bennington, Vermont.

- **Summer camps:** "I don't do a good job of making time for practicing, but what motivates me to take out the cello is when my week at Bennington is coming up soon," says lawyer Susan Lauscher, referring to the chamber music program held each summer in Bennington, Vermont. During the rest of the year she plays now and then with a string quartet at home in Colorado. "I wish I could do it [the quartet] more regularly but I have a busy job, travel for work, home obligations, and the limited number of people in this area who are on the same playing level as I am makes it difficult." A summer music program is an important element of her support system as it is also for Eloise Bensberg who has been singing in the ensembles of the Berkshire Choral Festival for more a dozen summers. That motivates her to keep up with voice lessons back home in Baltimore, where she sings in a high-level chorus. Chapter 9 has more on summer programs.

- **Morale-boosting groups:** Some lifelong music-makers gain strength from joining musical support groups where they meet like-minded musicians and perform in low-stress situations. Often these support groups are part of Meetup, an online social networking organization that links people with similar interests. Ms. Berghahn participates in an informal piano group that isn't part of Meetup. She and other pianists get together every few months in a friend's apartment, where a teacher gives a master class. Ms. Lauscher has made use of a support group that doesn't hold meetings but puts her in

Angela Bowman, fiddler and lead singer in a Cajun band.

touch with chamber music partners through its online database—ACMP (Associated Chamber Music Performers). Its website also has helpful articles, a listing of summer programs and workshops, and other useful information. For more on support groups, see chapter 9 and the resources section.

- **New genres:** Several long-time music-makers reinvigorated their musical lives and enlarged their support system by learning a new instrument or musical genre. After Lynn Malnekoff had been playing viola for more than thirty years in a community orchestra, she decided to learn country fiddling, taking lessons at Chicago's Old Town School and joining in its jam sessions and ensembles. She still plays in an orchestra, but also performs in Celtic, folk rock, and klezmer groups. "I'm having a ball," says this retired social worker. Ms. Gladycheva escaped the frustrating cycle of on-again-off-again piano practicing by adding a new instrument in her 30s—flute. Now she takes flute lessons and plays flute in several ensembles, which has surprisingly revived her enthusiasm for piano, leading her to find a friend for playing four-hand piano pieces. Team members' new musical ventures are discussed in chapters 5, 7, 9, 10, and 11.

Putting Networking to Use

"Opportunities are out there," says retired architect and trumpeter Bruce Burgess. "All one has to do is search them out." He and other lifelong music-makers have used various networking methods to uncover musical options. Once they begin making connections, the web of contacts

---

CLOSE UP: ANGELA BOWMAN, SINGER, FIDDLER, TEXTBOOK EDITOR

"For me, it's about community," says Angela Bowman, a developer of textbooks and educational software. She has been making music all her adult years, just not the same kind of music, having evolved from classical singing in college to leading a Cajun band on voice and fiddle. Her transition started in her late 20s, when she developed an interest in traditional *sean-nós* Irish singing. She began taking fiddle classes at Chicago's Old Town School of Folk Music and attended its jam sessions "so that I could participate in the social aspects of Irish music instead of the lonely art of unaccompanied song," she explains. Soon she formed an old-time string band that played at neighborhood bars "or wherever anybody asked us." When some band members moved away, "I was looking for new music to play and went to a Cajun concert. I loved Cajun music—its plaintive intensity." She began going to Cajun jam sessions and teamed up with an accordion player, guitarist, and fiddler to form a Cajun band. She creates bands "so I have a reason to practice and improve. It's easier to make time for music if it involves other people."

expands in a snowball effect. The amateur music world is collegial, as noted earlier in the success that Mr. Dalrymple had when he moved to Virginia after college and joined a community band recommended by his parents' friend. From that band's musicians, he learned about a community orchestra that he also joined. That orchestra's conductor was also the music director for another local orchestra, which Mr. Dalrymple joined as well and through which, he says, "I met my wife." This word-of-mouth networking strategy proved successful once again when he moved to Pennsylvania. He wrote about this strategy on his blog, listed in the bibliography.

Mr. Burgess tapped into a different kind of support system to get his networking ball rolling when he moved to Virginia for his first architectural job. "I thought that joining the musician's union would open doors for playing in Richmond, and it did," says this trumpeter. He subbed in commercial bands and later landed a fairly steady gig as the only non-African-American musician in a jazz band that played backup for such visiting stars as Stevie Wonder and The Temptations. But when he moved to Vermont in his 30s, he realized the dance band strategy wouldn't work there. He adapted to the local scene, where one of the mainstays of local music-making are summertime town bands. He joined one that he has played with for more than thirty years, and later joined another one, too. Keeping his networking antennae well-tuned led to learning of other possibilities that require travel, which he has been pursuing more fully after retirement, including participating in play-along programs offered by professional orchestras in Baltimore, Richmond, and Buffalo, which are described in chapter 9.

Other networking strategies include Internet searches, contacting music schools, music stores, and local colleges, and not being shy about speaking up. The latter was management consultant and bassoonist Hugh Rosenbaum's approach. "When I first arrived in London," he says, "I called a horn player whose name had been given to me and said, 'I understand you are the best amateur horn player around and I would like to come play with you.' Well, he had never been told *that* before, and immediately organized some players to play wind quintets with me. I have been playing with him and some of those first ones ever since."

> **I've been playing music longer than anything else I've done in my life.**
> —Dr. Sherman Jia, violinist, violist, neurologist

Creating Musical Opportunities

When faced with a lack of opportunity to make music, several lifelong music-makers started their own ensembles. Laurel Kuxhaus did that when she found there was no community band in Potsdam, New York, after arriving there to start a teaching job. "A few friends and I rekindled the Potsdam Community Band and it's still going with over sixty members."

"It is time consuming to go this route, but it can be rewarding," says clarinetist Alex Jones, who co-founded a wind quintet when he was disappointed with the performance level of a community orchestra he joined early in his academic career. He had done something similar during college. As a freshman, he auditioned unsuccessfully for the college orchestra, being informed that slots were filled by seniority. "So I grabbed the principal string players from the orchestra, formed a quintet, and we worked up the Weber Clarinet Quintet. The string players helped us get it on the fall concert and it was a hit. It wasn't long until I was in that orchestra."

Others of our lifelong music-makers have created performance possibilities for themselves. Soprano Karen Meyn put on a recital of classical and theater songs at a church in the coastal Maine town where she and her husband moved after she retired from teaching preschool. Dr. Mary Lane Cobb produced a cabaret series at her church because "I love theater music and cabaret style. It was emotionally stimulating to plan each program and receive feedback from the audience. The ability to take a beautiful piece of music, learn as much as I can about it, perform it to the extent of my ability, make it my own, is a tremendous life-affirming experience," says this soprano and retired New York public health physician. Subsequent chapters provide more on organizing new ensembles (chapter 9) and on putting on solo performances (chapters 10 and 11).

CLOSE UP: DR. SHERMAN JIA, VIOLIST, VIOLINIST, NEUROLOGIST

Dr. Sherman Jia had a taste of making music with high-level non-pro musicians during medical school, a time when many students put music aside for four years. Luckily his medical school encouraged musically minded students to join the Longwood Symphony, whose members are medical students and health-care professionals in Boston's medical centers. He became its concertmaster and gained a firsthand glimpse of busy professionals fitting music into their lives. Several medical schools have such ensembles, but when he moved to San Francisco for a neurology residency, he found that the UCSF Medical Center didn't have an instrumental music program for its students, faculty, and staff. So he started a chamber music program and an orchestra, too—the Strings Collaborative—to go along with the medical center's existing choral music program. "Connecting with other care providers who are musicians is a way to break down hierarchical barriers in medicine," he explains. "It's incredibly rewarding to foster a community of musicians and find ways to combine music and medicine in the art of healing. It's also really fun."

Flexibility

Adjusting as life circumstances change is another key to staying afloat in music. When workplace demands make it hard to get to ensemble rehearsals, "I do everything in my power to make it happen. Sometimes that means going back to the office after a rehearsal," explains Ms. Ten Cate. Registered nurse Liz Langeland adjusted her work schedule so she could fit in the twice-a-week evening choral rehearsals of Seattle Pro Musica. "For many years I worked the overnight shift so I could keep evenings free for rehearsal," she explains.

For one violinist on our advice team, being flexible was emotionally complicated because it involved adjusting her career expectations. She had considered becoming a professional musician. After earning a master's degree in violin performance, she tried the pro route by playing in a regional orchestra for a year but didn't find the experience satisfying. So she activated "Plan B" and went to law school, while also taking violin lessons and playing chamber music. When she joined a law firm, she found, through word of mouth, a community orchestra that was musically fulfilling and that connected her to others in the same situation: young people passionate about music but with careers in other professions. "It's a young, fleet group of musicians, playing challenging repertoire at a high level, while having fun," she says.

Dr. Jeff Bostic also dreamed of a professional career—as a rock drummer. He played gigs for a while after majoring in music at college, but then shifted to his Plan B: medical school. "I got to a certain level on the pyramid and was around guys who were so much better than I was. I saw I was only going to be a mediocre player. If you're honest with yourself and don't blame the world, saying 'They don't understand my music,' you can see that you need to develop another strength," says this Washington, DC, child psychiatrist. He has continued to sit in with bands, some that land paying gigs, and one called Pink Freud and the Transitional Object, whose members are child psychiatrists. This band performs each year at the annual meeting of the American Academy of Child and Adolescent Psychiatry.

Elizabeth Fein lost her musical network when she moved to Pittsburgh for a new position as an assistant professor of psychology. At first, her demanding new job didn't leave time for finding new bands to sing with and write songs for as she had been doing since college. She adapted by occasionally singing at karaoke nights while also doing something else that she could fit into spare moments—write song lyrics. "I've done this my whole life. It feels good to put experiences into words in this way," she says. By her second year of teaching, she managed to find time to start a new band with musicians she met through an online forum. "The band is inspired by melodic melancholic bands from the 1980s, like New Order," she reports.

Another Pittsburgh musician, Catherine Getchell, made adjustments to keep making music during graduate school, while working on a degree in counseling. In addition to a heavy academic load, she had a part-time counseling job, leaving little time for weekly orchestra rehearsals. Even so, she fit in some trumpet practicing each day. "My chops go down if I don't," she says. When she heard about a community orchestra that needed an extra trumpet for a concert now and then, "that was something I had time to do—a couple of rehearsals and a concert, a couple of times a year." Now with a more fixed schedule as director of a university's disability resources, she can make rehearsals for an orchestra that calls on her as a sub and also for the community band she plays in with her trombonist husband. "It's a fun thing for us to do together. We motivate each other."

Mr. Dadeboe also had to be flexible to continue in music. Before he became a father, he played violin in a community orchestra in Maryland that was a long drive from his Virginia home. But with a new baby in the house "that became too much and I had to let the orchestra go," he says. He switched to an instrumental ensemble at his church, which was nearer to home. The church orchestra rehearsed on the same night each week as a church dinner, so the whole family could go and do other things while he rehearsed. He was also in an ensemble at another nearby church that didn't play every week and whose rehearsals he sometimes skipped because he is a good sight-reader. He still carved out time to practice. "I love violin," he says. "That's why I make time for it. I've been known to wake up at 3:00 in the morning to

Joshua Dadeboe on violin.

practice." After moving to Pennsylvania, he found another church ensemble to play with whose schedule meshed well with his. Although he is no longer playing the big orchestral repertoire he loves, he feels playing in these ensembles is important. "I am the only regular violinist at my home church. As an African American, I feel like a role model for young boys in the congregation."

The issues faced by the lifelong musicians introduced in this chapter—creating a support system, using networking, being flexible—are also central to the experiences of those who come to music later as adults, either as newcomers or as returnees. However, there are other issues that are particular to returnees and newcomers which are explored in the next two chapters.

Dr. Sherman Jia (center last row, holding up a viola) with the Strings Collaborative at UCSF.

Dr. Mark Wager playing French
horn. Dr. Darlene Ifill-Taylor with
her piano.

4 Returning to Music-Making

"IN MEDICAL SCHOOL, I had very little time to practice. So I gave up French horn for a year," says Dr. Marc Wager, a New York pediatrician. "I was miserable! When my medical school, Albert Einstein, started its own orchestra and when I was asked to join the Doctor's Orchestra in Manhattan, I was much happier." He determined never to put music aside again, and now fills his evenings playing in community orchestras, in the pit for musicals, and with chamber music groups. "My mother says it's my therapy. I need it to stay sane."

His year without French horn is one of the shortest music-making gaps among the amateur musicians on our research team. A little less than half of those who completed the questionnaire for this book are returnees. They put music-making on hold for a while but then reconnected with a way they had enjoyed making music in their childhood, teen, or college years. This chapter describes the reasons for their musical gaps as well as how they re-engaged with music, the difficulties they encountered, and the strategies that made their returns successful.

Dr. Darlene Ifill-Taylor's pause was nearly as brief as Dr. Wager's. She stopped singing for her first two years of medical school. "That was devastating," she says. "I felt like I lost my left arm. In my third year, I saw an ad for auditions for a choir. I auditioned and got in. I remember going to rehearsals with my scrubs on and my pager. Somehow it just worked out. I thought, 'I'm never again going to go without being involved in something musical.'" This North Carolina psychiatrist has continued singing and has begun writing her own songs. For her and Dr. Wager, their brief gaps served a useful purpose—turning them into dedicated music-makers going forward.

Most of the returnees on our advice panel took longer to fit music back into their lives. Peg Beyer's gap came while she pursued an MBA and launched a career in commercial risk management. "The cello sat in the corner for ten years," she says. From time to time she would pick it up, but "it was frustrating how much skill I had lost." She was still living in Buffalo, where she had gone to college and had played in community orchestras as an undergraduate. Her dry spell ended when she decided to check out one of those community orchestras again. "I attended a rehearsal where they played the Rachmaninoff Second Piano concerto, my favorite. The hunger returned. I was at the very next rehearsal and never turned back." Balancing work and rehearsals has been tricky. Reviving her cello skills wasn't easy either, as she describes later in the chapter. But the struggle has been worth it. "Music has been something I do for myself," she says.

"I put my violin down for close to two decades, but resumed playing in my late thirties after being invited to a master class taught by Pinchas Zukerman that revived my interest," reports Maryland lawyer John Warshawsky, who now plays viola in a community orchestra. "As a trial attorney and parent, it can be challenging to find the time but I feel more complete and consider myself to be, among other things, a musician." Dr. Susan Reeder's gap was even longer. She didn't make her return until she had retired, having put piano and guitar on hold for forty years, due to the demands of child-rearing, graduate and medical schools, and an active medical practice. She has been having so much fun for the past few years taking weekly group guitar classes at a Chicago music school that she decided to move to the Chicago area instead of driving there from Michigan each week. "I wish I had known how much fun it is," she says, "although when I was working, I really didn't have the time."

Knowing whether and when to connect again with music depends on so many personal variables. Some false starts may occur, as the late John Holt points out in his memoir, *Never Too Late*, which several of our team members found inspiring. He explains why his early efforts as an adult on flute didn't go as well as his later pursuit of cello: "I was still not psychologically or emotionally ready to play a musical instrument . . . . I was not yet ready to be at the center of my own learning."

For nearly all the returnees on our advice panel, coming back to music has turned out well. That is to be expected given how the panel was assembled, by soliciting participants currently involved in music-making. However, their journeys back haven't been easy, often involving many months—and in some cases years—of hard work at regaining skills, as well as devising creative time-management strategies. For some returnees, reconnecting has been complicated by emotional issues and self-doubt left over from earlier musical experiences, as they explain later in this chapter.

Why They Stopped

The two most common reasons that our advice-team members cite for taking a break from music are becoming new parents and enrolling in post-college educational programs—graduate school, medical school, law school, veterinary school, nursing school, and so on. Nearly as commonly mentioned is the stress of starting a new career. Other reasons include military service, caring for an ill spouse, having an injury or illness, a natural disaster, not having access to a piano, or not knowing of ways for non-professionals to keep on with music. For those whose youthful experiences with music had given them a sense that they weren't quite good enough, it took time to have the perspective and courage to try again. For others who had considered becoming professional musicians, it took a while to feel that there was still a place for them in the world of music. The next four sections of this chapter focus on reasons why our returnees decided to re-engage with music, followed by a look at their struggles to revive musical skills, and the attitude adjustments some have made to enjoy music again.

"I Missed It Terribly"

"I stopped playing flute during law school and for several years after because I had no time and no outlet for playing with others. I missed it terribly and was thrilled to find other players who wanted to form a flute trio," says Illinois attorney Judith Grubner. A longing to sing again propelled Sophia Jimenez to join a chorus even though she had planned to devote all her time and energy during her first year after college to finding a publishing job in New York City. "Eventually I broke down. Even though I hadn't found a full-time job yet, I acquired an almost-free used keyboard and joined a chorus. Not singing makes me feel dead inside and made being mostly unemployed even harder. I found out about this chorus during a job interview, when I mentioned that I hadn't found a choral group yet and the interviewer recommended the chorus she was in." Ms. Jimenez soon landed a job as an editorial assistant, perhaps in part from the boost of confidence singing again gave her. Missing the joy of making music is ultimately the central reason why all our returnees came back to music no matter what prompted them to realize this, whether it was a change in schedule or opportunities that were too good to ignore.

Schedules Loosen Up

For a few who stopped music during graduate school, slipping back into music was relatively easy once they earned their degrees. During most of graduate school, Joan Herbers not only had no time for playing violin in an orchestra, but also didn't have access to a piano, which she had enjoyed playing as a child. "When I finished graduate school and got my first job, I bought a piano and found an orchestra to play with," she says. Eric Godfrey's eight-year break from music—while earning a PhD in sociology—left him with shaky violin skills. "After I resumed playing, it was six months before I could open the bedroom door while practicing and let my wife hear me," says this Wisconsin professor, now retired. He managed to regain both his confidence and technique and has enjoyed playing violin ever since.

Dr. Alvin Crawford encountered several gap periods as he launched his career as an orthopedic surgeon, but then came to a point where he felt he had time to play clarinet and saxophone in Cincinnati community orchestras and jazz bands. "In addition to being pure pleasure, it has been a respite from the nuances of health-care reform," he observes.

Given the limits that child-rearing can put on available free time, some parents waited until their kids were grown and gone before returning to music. "When my last two children—twins—went off to college, I looked for something to fill the void and returned to singing," says Eileen Shea. Now retired from college teaching, she has been singing in two suburban New York community choruses for more than fifteen years. Peggy Radin also waited until her nest had emptied because, as she explains, "While raising two children on my own, one problem I couldn't solve was practicing flute. My son would overturn my music stand while I played. I got the message and took a hiatus until they both left home for college." Her return to flute "was rough for about three months but luckily I met the right teacher," she says. This law professor soon became busy playing in community orchestras and chamber music groups, which she continues to do as a retiree in Toronto.

Other parents made a musical return earlier. Riva Edelman started playing violin again when her youngest child was three years old and had begun attending nursery school. "I could practice during the three hours he was at school. I had stopped violin and orchestra my freshman year in college, so my gap was about sixteen years. When I went back to violin, I began by taking lessons with a very good teacher," she says. Now in her 80s, this retired New York schoolteacher is an avid chamber music player. Maryland statistician Liz Sogge returned to violin when her youngest child entered kindergarten. It wasn't just the whiff of a bit of free time that sparked her return, it was also because her children "didn't enjoy their own music lessons and objected to practicing," she explains. "So I decided to take violin lessons to model practicing." The lessons benefitted her too, "extending and improving what I had learned as a child." Before long she won a position in an auditioned community orchestra. Parents who made music while their children were young explain in chapter 6 how they handled the complex schedule juggling that was often required.

> **Keep practicing. There are good days and not so good days. Don't get discouraged.**
>
> —Peggy Radin, flutist, retired law professor

Inspired by Kids

In several instances, it was their children's involvement in music that inspired parents to rekindle their own musical interests. "I came back to music after my daughter asked me to play the flute part of a wind quintet she was learning in middle school. Playing with her reminded me how much I enjoyed flute," says Ann Rogers, a professor of nursing who hadn't played since college. "I sounded terrible but was shocked by how little I'd forgotten. My fingers remembered all but the very highest fingerings." She now takes weekly lessons at the university where she teaches, has participated in the Baltimore Symphony's summer program, and plays in an Atlanta flute choir. For Colorado physician Dr. Karlotta Davis, the invitation went the other way. "When my daughter was readying herself for a high school senior piano recital, which was likely to be her last, I asked if I could play with her," says Dr. Davis, who hadn't played flute for thirty years. "I went to a band store, bought a flute, began lessons, and performed on her recital. I have not stopped." She plays in local orchestras, a wind ensemble, and a flute choir "As long as I am not on call, I will perform for gallery openings, fundraisers, and parties."

Mike Alberts ended a twenty-five year guitar gap so he could jam with his teenaged son, an accomplished guitarist. "We still play together every time we get together," he says. Dr. Henry Wang's return to music came as a result of his son, too, although a much younger one. When his son started Suzuki lessons, this Alabama physician realized how much he had missed playing violin for the past twenty-five years and began taking lessons himself.

Mary Edwards joined in the fun her kids were having in community musical theater productions by singing in some of the shows when the director invited her. Now this retired New York IT specialist sings in a community chorus. A touch of envy for the fun her kids were having in a Washington, DC, youth orchestra led Erika Singer back to piano. This lawyer, who at the time was a stay-at-home mom, also joined a choir, which she says "is the closest I'll ever get to my kids' orchestra

CLOSE UP: DALE BACKUS, PIANIST, SAFETY ENGINEER

"I was on the path to becoming a professional pianist, but I burned out after my master's degree. I thought, 'I need time away from this,'" says Dale Backus. "I also thought, 'You're going to be a starving musician.' So I got interested in piano technology and took two years on that. Then I left piano for five years to get an engineering degree and start a family. We have two children. I played a little but not seriously. I got back into music when my wife organized a recital for me at the music center in Colorado Springs. That was a great motivation. As soon as she scheduled the hall and we had a date and time, I thought, 'I better get ready.' The passion is still there, not because I have to do it, but because I want to do it, that I get to do it. I'm so lucky to have the balance that I do." Since then, he has entered several competitions for amateur pianists, winning one in Colorado in 2006. "It's important to have a supportive family and support their passions, too. My wife has a different passion that I support—horses. It needs to go both ways."

experience—the excitement of working in a group with a conductor to pull a piece together for a successful performance."

Opportunity Knocks

Enticing opportunities that were hard to refuse caught the attention of some returnees, such as the lunchtime suggestion that ended Texan Robert Tung's thirteen year hiatus from trombone. "I had lunch with some co-workers who asked me to sit in with their brass quintet," says this computer product manager. Playing with them "reminded me how much I love music." That led him to join their quintet, as well as a jazz band and a community orchestra, too.

Here are a few other unexpected opportunities that motivated returnees.

- **Gift certificate:** Science writer Amanda Healan's return happened in part because her husband gave her a gift certificate for lessons, after her double bass "sat in its case for a few years during grad school and about three years after moving to Chicago," she says. The lessons and music school jam sessions injected a sense of excitement that keeps her going, as she learns folk and rock styles of playing, so different from the classical music she did earlier.
- **Birthday surprise:** Alecia Watson began violin in fifth grade and loved it, but stopped in ninth grade "because of a band teacher who was forced to teach orchestra, was not pleasant, and made it unbearable for me," explains this program analyst. She had used a school violin because her family couldn't afford to buy one. This meant she couldn't keep on with violin on her own after quitting the school orchestra. When she was in her 30s, family members

remembered how much she missed violin and bought her one as a birthday surprise. "It's not like riding a bike. I couldn't even play 'Mary Had a Little Lamb.' I had to learn it all over again, take private lessons and everything." But within a year she was playing in the orchestra at her Virginia church. "I've gained new friends and have been exposed to more opportunities that I didn't know existed."

- **Reunion concert:** Dr. Teddy Tong's opportunity arrived in an email from college classmates inviting him to play violin in a reunion concert, a challenge he accepted, even though he hadn't played for more than thirty years. "I grabbed the opportunity and picked up my violin, working pretty diligently," he reports. Several months of refresher lessons let this Los Angeles ophthalmologist play in that concert, motivating him to look for chamber music groups so he could keep playing.

- **Chance remark:** Sofia Axelrod's musical return came in her mid-20s because of a chance remark from a singing teacher with whom her father had started taking lessons "After hearing me sing me a few scales, the teacher urged me to take lessons. I had always secretly wished to be a singer, so I gladly obliged," she recalls. She had done choral singing as a child but was regarded by her family as a pianist and violinist, instruments she stopped playing in her teens when "new friends, parties, and the opposite sex were more interesting." Thanks to this teacher's observation, she has found what she feels is her true musical calling, one that "allows me to truly express myself" when she performs in recitals and, as noted earlier, in mini-concerts in a hospital lobby.

- **School project:** "The middle school music teacher in town invited parents and others who played an instrument and had given it up to play with students in what she called the Second Chance Band," says former illustrator Philip Anderson. He had been a drummer during high school but hadn't played in decades. He started drumming again for this middle school project, and then kept on drumming, joining with others to perform at county fairs and nursing homes. When he developed a problem with his hands and had to stop drumming, he took up choral singing, something he didn't think he could do until he joined a church choir at age 58, started voice lessons, and then joined a nurturing community chorus. He is now the lead singer with a band that performs at the Maine mental health facility where he works as a residential technician. (More on this in chapter 11.)

- **Friends' example:** Arabella Lang has a law degree but took time out to do a post-graduate course in violin performance before starting her career as a legal analyst. "I didn't play much after music college as I thought it would be a letdown," she notes. She had played with some amateur orchestras that she found "unsatisfying" and thought that must be what all amateurs are like. "It was only after I moved to London and got back into it through playing quartets with friends that I realized there's a huge range of non-professional musicians, which means that many are of a really high standard with whom it's a privilege to play."

- **New ensemble:** Katherine Erwin didn't play flute during the first few years of practicing law, but that dry spell ended when a group of fellow attorneys formed an orchestra sponsored by the Chicago Bar Association. She became a founding member. "It was a joy to come back to flute, although I had to sneak out of my law firm early to attend rehearsals," she admits.

- **Recovery from loss:** As noted in chapter 2, music has been a solace for those coping with the death of a spouse. Karen Mitchell sought to regain her sense of self after the death of her husband of forty years. She had been without a piano for several years. So she bought a digital piano and joined a group piano class that she heard about from the piano store, thus finding herself with an instant support group. "Playing piano is a way for me to express myself," says this retired workers' compensation assistant. "I am always happy when I play."

Polishing Rusty Skills

A few of the returnees managed to re-connect with music fairly easily, picking up where they had left off before the gap. The two physicians whose stories open this chapter hadn't been away from music for long and didn't feel the need to turn to a teacher for help, although both used teachers later to bring their musicianship to a higher level.

Even some who had been away from music for longer periods didn't feel the need for a teacher right away either. "Coming back was very natural," says Ms. Grubner, who as noted earlier came back to flute when she joined a flute trio. "I don't recall any challenges to playing again after the gap, other than recovering my embouchure [mouth position], which didn't take long." Gene Lege taught himself to play trombone again even though his gap had lasted thirty years. "I remembered the positions and basics, but had to retrain my embouchure and how to do lip slurs and tonguing techniques. I pretty much had to relearn how to play," he explains. This software developer now plays in several symphonic and jazz bands in Houston, including two New Horizons ones.

For other returnees on our advice panel, coming back was more of a challenge. "There were little things, like as you play you can't remember the key you're in and have to keep looking towards the left on the score to be sure to hit all the flats and sharps. Things didn't come quickly when I returned. It wasn't easy. I had to work at it, and there was also a breakdown in confidence because it no longer came naturally," says Ms. Beyer, who, as described earlier, plunged into community orchestra rehearsals after a ten-year gap from cello. "For the first few years, I was still heavily into my career with little time to practice so I would push on and do what I could, sitting in the back of the section, sometimes 'air-bowing'[pretending to bow] when there were passages I couldn't do. But being an over-achiever, that didn't satisfy me for long." Eventually she turned to teachers for help and went to summer music programs where she learned from the coaching there.

Lorne Wald performing with the Montréal New Horizons Band.

CLOSE UP: LORNE WALD, TRUMPETER,
RETIRED DATA SECURITY SPECIALIST

"On the verge of retirement, I heard about the Montréal New Horizons Band from a friend. It seemed like a good idea: I had fun playing in the high school band. I was open to new activities to fill the days, there was no musical ability expected or required, and there was an opportunity to be with four friends who were retiring at the same time," says Lorne Wald, who hadn't played trumpet since high school. "At times, it was frustrating to struggle to do things I'd found easy forty years before. On the other hand, having done them before, I was confident I would be able to do them again. The fact that we were all pretty much rank beginners relieved any particular performance anxiety. Nevertheless, there is still some internalized pressure to do well, so there's some good stress happening. Every so often I congratulate myself on my improvement (which often occurs just before I berate myself). The band motto— 'Your best is good enough'—can be a stress reliever, provided you don't use it as a cop-out. There is a special sense of wonder when an ensemble begins to mesh and perform as one."

Finally she gained the courage to call the local professional orchestra and began lessons with its principal cellist.

Laura Rice also tried to tough it out when she returned to violin after a gap of several years, "sitting in the back of the second violin section in a community orchestra. It was shocking to see how much I had lost. I could hardly read 16th notes, much less play them. But I kept at it. Things came back," says this New York high school teacher, now retired. Later, she began taking lessons again and went to chamber music workshops and summer music camps.

Many other returnees sought out teachers as soon as they decided to return to music, as Dr. Tong did. Refresher lessons not only resuscitated dormant skills but also improved them. Dr. Tong feels the lessons he has taken after his long gap help him play violin better than in college. "I was relying on the nimbleness of my fingers as a young person and played a lot of pieces by ear, but this new teacher emphasizes the fundamentals, working on études, so that my skills are better grounded," he says. "As a consequence, everything, including my tone, has really improved. It has helped me enormously in a very short time."

Returning to playing cello after an eight year gap helped my playing. I am much less concerned about missing a note, and much more focused on making music.

—Sally Long, cellist, paralegal

Joining an ensemble or choral group can also be instructional by providing opportunities to learn by doing. "It's the best way to get your intonation, rhythm, and full sound back," says Paul Seeley, a university fundraiser who came back to French horn after thirteen years off while he was preoccupied with raising kids. His return was "incredibly frustrating and slow," but he pulled it off with help from a teacher and by playing with ensembles in Chicago. The secret of his success: "good instruction and hard, consistent work." Laura Rice also credits joining a community orchestra as a key element in her successful return. "Orchestra was good, because it met weekly, and concert music needed to be mastered. Without that, I probably would not have stuck with it," she says. "Play with others as early in the process as possible. Be patient with not much progress. Love it for this moment, not some future dream." There is more on instructional options and ensembles in chapters 7 and 9.

How Long Before You Sound Good Again?

The answer to that question depends in part on how long the gap has been and what pre-gap music-making was like. If the gap was fairly short, sounding good again may not take long, as was true for the two doctors described at the start of this chapter. Laurel Bishow had a quick comeback, too, even though she hadn't played flute for thirty-five years. She connected with a teacher who helped her remember the basics. "After a month of relearning, I was ready to join a local band," says this teacher's aide from Pennsylvania.

Others took longer to sound good again. Chicago physician Dr. Larry Lindeman started playing guitar during medical school, stopped for about twenty-five years, and then started again in his late 50s. "My guitar strings were literally rusted, but nine months later I could play competently," he recalls. "It wasn't as hard as I thought, kind of like riding a bicycle,"

Returning to violin was no ride in the park for Ms. Watson, as she noted earlier. Nor was it for Dr. Lili Barouch, who picked up violin again in her mid-30s, after a fourteen year gap. "I started after I was diagnosed with rheumatoid arthritis. I didn't know how long I would be able to play, so I figured I should begin as soon as possible. My daughter (then age 5) had started playing piano. So it was a perfect time to begin. I sounded awful for a year," she explains. "I sounded like I did when I was nine years old, based on the level of music I was able to play when I started again. I really had to force myself to play. It took a year of hard work before I sounded decent."

For Lauren Hill, the hardest part of coming back to bassoon from a two-year gap after college was "I had completely lost my endurance. Eventually the endurance came back, I started auditioning when opportunities came up, and two years later I joined the orchestra I'm in now. It has worked out well, but it took quite a bit of time and practice," says this New York marketing manager. She had once considered becoming a professional bassoonist. "I promised myself that I would never leave the bassoon behind completely. Even though it's not my full-time job, it's a huge part of my life and identity."

Mr. Seeley recommends taking the long view on the rate of progress in reconnecting with music. "Potential returnees should not feel daunted by the length of time or difficulty of playing again, or feel nostalgia for the good old days. The rewards of playing and improving with practice far outweigh the temporary pain of the initial return, which will be quickly forgotten once good tone returns." It can be reassuring to remember the neuroscience research cited in chapter 2—that childhood music-making has prepped the brain in ways that last a lifetime, which may help in reviving long-idle musical skills.

Attitude Adjustment

For some returnees, reconnecting with music required finding a way to handle emotional baggage left over from earlier experiences with music. Several returnees had been on the educational treadmill that could lead to a professional career in music when, for various reasons, they decided not to continue. It took a while for them to connect with music again, as was true for some lifelong musicians described in chapter 3. "My gap happened during and right after college when I felt there was no point in my playing piano because I was not good enough compared to my peers," explains New York psychology teacher Hamadi Henderson. He had started as a double major in psychology and music and then switched full-time to psychology. "I broke out of that mindset when I accepted that I didn't have the ability to become a virtuoso, but I could still learn some lovely music. The challenge was internalizing this mentality."

Shedding the need to be perfect helped Rebecca Berg, a Colorado creative writing teacher, return from a gap of nearly twenty years. She stopped playing cello during college when she changed from a cello performance major to an English major. Her gap was complicated by the high expectations she had sensed from her professional musician parents. After dropping cello, "it was painful for a while to listen to classical music. But I gradually realized that without music in my life something that was alive for me was missing," she explains. At age 39, she made a gradual return, spending six months playing on her own before taking part in a chamber music "round robin" session in Denver, during which people are assigned to groups to play with for an hour and then regroup in new combinations. "My group was playing a Haydn quartet and from the first moment when all the instruments started to play, I got a chill up my spine," she says. She found a teacher who helped her discover a new way to think about playing cello by using a problem-solving approach. The

Rebecca Berg and her cello.

teacher calmly encouraged Ms. Berg to figure out how to fix any glitches rather than berate herself for making a mistake. "If you play in order not to do something wrong, you're not playing as musically as you might," says Ms. Berg. She is now an avid chamber musician. She also shares the problem-solving approach with students she works with as a part-time teacher for cello beginners, both children and adults.

Even those who never ventured down the pro-music educational path have had to come to terms with childhood feelings of not being good enough. Ellen Tenenbaum tried to keep up with piano as a young working mother but was plagued by self-doubt left over from dreary childhood lessons. "I felt I sounded bad at the piano, nothing came out the way I wanted it to, so I closed up the piano. It was painful," says this former director of implementation studies at a Washington, DC, research company. But music kept calling to her. In her early 50s, she found a piano teacher "who believed in me, encouraged me, pushed me to improve. I had to undo so many bad habits and negative, unproductive thoughts. You have to chip away and then one day improvement happens." She gained confidence by joining a music support group where people perform for each other in stress-free situations. She also took a performance class at a music school and now performs regularly in solo recitals at senior centers, churches, and community centers. "It feels so right. It's what I was meant to do," she says. There's more about her solo performing in chapter 10.

Daniel Savin's not-good-enough feelings stem from being turned down for his college orchestra when he tried out during his freshman year. "I shipped my double bass home and did not play it again for eighteen years until I was home for vacation

Daniel Savin strumming his double bass in a New York City park.

one weekend and my mother insisted that I get my bass out of her house, as she needed the space. I brought my bass back to New York City, found a teacher, and then followed my curiosity and found opportunities to play," says this astrophysicist. He joined a music support group, took chamber music classes, became a confident chamber musician, and started an ensemble at his synagogue.

Nancy Williams won a victory over the self-doubt that kept her away from piano for twenty years when she signed up for lessons at the same time that her young son started piano lessons. Finding her way back and learning to play piano at a high level, despite a hearing loss, has motivated her to start a blog and website—Grand Piano Passion—that features essays about her own musical journey, as well those of other amateur musicians. The website features helpful articles, including on making music with hearing loss.

"Be patient and not afraid to make mistakes," Ms. Singer advises. That's good advice for newcomers, too, whose concerns are featured in the next chapter.

Ted Dawson (far right) on guitar, performing with a jug band he played with for several years.

5   Trying Something New

"DURING MY ENTIRE adult life, I have been enchanted by the rich, mellow sound of the cello," says Dr. Helen Heeren, a Pennsylvania psychotherapist. She has also been a regular audience member at symphony orchestra concerts all her adult life. In her mid-60s, those two passions came together when she says she decided "to become a maker of music, in addition to enjoying it as an audience member. I thought, 'If not now, when?'" She had done no music-making during her earlier adult years, and hadn't done much as a child either—just two years of piano lessons, plus church choir and school musicals. Undaunted, she bought a cello, found a strings teacher who liked working with adults, began taking lessons, and after a few years became skilled enough to play in a community orchestra. She has since joined another local orchestra and an informal cello chamber music group, too. "It is a glorious experience to be part of a larger whole and hear us playing music that I have enjoyed listening to others play. A dream come true. Music-making touches my deepest soul."

She is one of the nearly one-third of questionnaire completers on our advice team who are musical newcomers—people who are engaging with music in a different way as adults than they had before. This chapter features their stories.

Ted Dawson, like Dr. Heeren, had also been listening to and loving music all his life—in his case, rock, blues, and pop—without having a chance to make that kind of music himself until his mid-30s, when he signed up for guitar lessons at a music school. This Arizona resource room teacher had played cornet in his high school marching band but found that unsatisfying. "I never got the sense that we were 'making music.' It was just stomp along, play my part, rest for four measures, play again—very mechanical. I never got into enjoying music back then the way I do now. As kids, we were listening to metal bands and hair bands, but in high school we were playing marches and old ditties. Now I play what I like to listen to. Big difference," he says. He even had his own jug band for several years that played gigs at farmers' markets and bars.

Suzanne Ziemba was in her mid-60s when she became a maker of the music she loved. She had stopped by a music store's booth at a fair, filled out a form to win free piano lessons—and won! "I have always wanted to play piano. I didn't have the opportunity to play any instruments when I was young. I was someone who thought she was tone deaf and couldn't carry a tune," says this Florida health insurance supervisor. She was in a school chorus as a child but not in any instrumental groups. After six months of group lessons on digital pianos at the music store, she bought her own digital piano. "I am like a child now, learning to make beautiful music. I didn't know I would go this far from those free lessons."

Mastering a new musical skill as a busy adult isn't easy, as these three happy music-makers have discovered. It takes time, effort, and a willingness to be a beginner again, which can be an uncomfortable adjustment for some. In the following pages, advice-panel members share their experiences starting anew.

Newcomer Success Is Possible

It is definitely possible for adults—even older adults—to learn to play a new instrument they had never tried before or to sing for the first time in a chorus. Dr. Heeren, Ms. Ziemba, Mr. Dawson, and the more than seventy-five other newcomers on our advice panel provide heartening examples that successful new musical experiences are within reach for anyone willing to put in the time and effort. Research studies cited in chapter 2 support this conclusion. So does the track record of hundreds of New Horizons ensembles. For more than twenty-five years, New Horizons has been turning thousands of older adults into instrumentalists and choral singers.

Most of the newcomers among our questionnaire completers were in their 40s and 50s when they began something new, but nearly 30 percent were age 60 and over. Our oldest newcomer is Texan John Murray. He had been in choirs all his life but returned to clarinet in his 80s, and then at age 84 started on a new instrument, bass clarinet, partly, he says, because there are "fewer notes on the page than for a little clarinet." A bass clarinet offers another advantage for an older newcomer. The instrument's long body can rest on a peg on the ground, making it less tiring to play than holding up a regular clarinet.

Leading the list of instruments that our newcomers decided to master for the first time as adults are cello, guitar, and piano. Next in popularity are violin, viola, percussion, recorder, and saxophone, followed by other traditional band and orchestra instruments—bass clarinet, bassoon, double bass, euphonium, flute, oboe, and trumpet. A wide array of other instruments intrigued at least one or two newcomers, including accordion, bagpipes, bodhrán, celtic harp, concertina, djembe, dulcimer, harpsichord, lute, mandolin, tabla, ukulele, viola da gamba, and instruments used in Indonesian gamelan ensembles.

CLOSE UP: MIRIAM JACKOBS, VIOLIST, CLARINETIST, REGISTERED DIETITIAN

"My latest musical activity is due to a fall I had at age 70 that necessitated surgery for two subdural hematomas pressing on either side of my brain. I awoke from the surgery with a *strong* desire to play violin," says Miriam Jackobs, who had been playing clarinet. This urge to play violin reminded her of the man in Oliver Sacks's book *Musicophilia* who, after being struck by lightning, had a desire to play piano. She took private violin lessons for about a year, but then life got complicated and so she put violin aside for a while until a New Horizons string orchestra started at the University of Cincinnati. She joined their group violin lessons at age 75 and began playing in their ensemble. About a year later she switched to viola. "Playing with other folks motivates me to play as well as I can, to study, and practice," she says. "I had a goal: to play viola in an orchestra that is doing Handel's *Messiah*." She achieved her goal after only two years in New Horizons, when she joined a community orchestra that played parts of the *Messiah* at a holiday concert. "What an experience! The urge is still there."

A few efforts at trying something new didn't succeed, often because individuals found that they didn't like the new instrument after playing it for a while. Others decided the learning curve was too steep for the amount of time they had available. In a few cases, physical issues posed problems. Vince Motto tried to start on alto saxophone in his late 70s, but stiff, arthritic fingers made it hard to press the keys correctly. "I understood what I was supposed to do, but cannot get my fingers to follow my brain," says this retired New York insurance executive. He switched to drums and has done well in the percussion section of a New Horizons band. London publishing consultant Stephen Lustig had better luck mastering saxophone. He started lessons at age 64, after many years of playing violin and viola. "I wanted a new musical challenge and I like the sound of the sax—not easy getting muscle memory to work on all those fingerings, but great fun," he reports.

The complexity of the newly chosen instrument proved overwhelming initially for some team members. "When I started bassoon at the age of 50, it was one of the most challenging endeavors of my life. It was like I was on a different planet, learning a new language. The instrument is heavy and requires stamina," says Linda Rand, a Canadian editor who had been playing flute for years. But she mastered bassoon and in a few years was playing it in a Montréal community orchestra and with chamber music groups.

Most of the newcomers on our research team have done well in their new musical adventures. Some have become serial newcomers. Michael McFadden started cello at age 65 as a retirement project, after a career in computers. "A 'bucket list' item that I wanted to learn because I love the sound," he says. Earlier this Arizona retiree had learned to play piano in his 30s, guitar in his 50s, and was also a lifelong church choir member. Roland Wilk, another serial newcomer, taught himself to play recorder in his mid-20s, which led to him learning to play clarinet and then French horn "because I became bored with clarinet," he says. In his 40s, he added bassoon. This retired Canadian software engineer, who had played only accordion as a child, plays all these instruments, although not at the same time, in orchestras and chamber music groups, noting, "I love them all—totally different characters."

Why Something New

For many of our newcomers, the new aspect of music that they chose to explore as adults was something they had been wanting to try for a long time. For Joyce Richardson, it was a way to rebound from an unsatisfying childhood musical experience—the piano lessons that never captured her interest. "Playing piano was lonely. I avoided practicing and then felt guilty because I was unworwthy of having a teacher who had gone to Juilliard," says this retired New York social worker. She wishes she had played an instrument as a child that would have allowed her to play in a band or orchestra. As an adult, she has found a way to do this by starting recorder lessons in her late 30s and joining a recorder quintet to play Renaissance music, which she had learned to love in a madrigal choir in high school. She still plays with that quintet but added another group in her late 60s after she retired. She learned to play euphonium (a mini tuba) in a New Horizons band so she could play other music she loves—jazz and show tunes. "It's fun to sit in the low brass section, play low notes, and be really loud. I want to practice now so I don't let the team down."

Piano as a "lonely" instrument doesn't bother John Hollwitz. This New York college professor started piano lessons at age 50 after reading the book *Piano Lessons* in which NPR host Noah Adams describes turning 50, buying a Steinway, and

Joyce Richardson playing euphonium with the New Horizons Band of the Third Street Music School in New York City.

learning to play it. "I couldn't afford a Steinway, but his example spurred me to start taking lessons and acquire a good upright Yamaha," he explains. He has continued lessons for more than a decade and doesn't mind the solo nature of much of his current involvement with piano—private lessons and recitals a few times a year with his teacher's other students. He is not interested in playing in more formal public concerts, due in part to performance anxiety. "What I like as an adult is learning the sophistication of technique and playing an instrument that I've always liked, instead of one I was forced to study as a kid—accordion—which I grew to detest."

Some of our advisors had a practical reason for adding on a new instrument—to open up more performance opportunities. Several violinists added viola, because there are generally fewer amateur violists than violinists. A musician who can play both can find a spot in a quartet more easily. Cello returnee Peg Beyer added viola in her 50s because there were too many cellos at the string camp she attends each summer. Dr. Karlotta Davis, a flute returnee, added piccolo and alto flute to her repertoire because "there seem to be twenty-seven million flutists vying for the same opening in ensembles." Being proficient on other flutes could help in winning a spot in an ensemble. Katherine Erwin, another flute returnee, added bassoon partly because her orchestra needed one and also because she had always liked it. Playing bassoon has given her opportunities to solo with the orchestra.

Kids provided the inspiration for some parents trying something new. Ann Rogers added on bassoon because, as she explains, "I learned from my daughter, who majored in bassoon, that she had more opportunities to play than I did as a flutist." Violinist Joan Herbers reports that she began playing viola at age 55 "because my daughter refused to take her viola to college and it haunted me sitting unplayed."

Peg Beyer at a SCOR! Strings Camp for Adults that she attends in Rochester, New York.

Janet Blume came to drums in her late 40s when her younger son wanted to play drums. "I decided to take lessons, too. We were learning at the same time. I would practice more, but he could drum circles around me at all times," recalls this senior associate university dean who had tried unsuccessfully to play violin as a child. After several years of drum lessons and a stint playing drums in her older sons' bagpipe competition bands, she started a rock cover band, first with fellow engineering professors and later by recruiting professors from other departments. "I never thought I'd be in a rock band. It is totally fun."

Theodore Sapp started piano lessons in his 30s to make it easier to learn the pieces he sings in choir and in musical theater productions. "Playing the accompaniment on piano rather than banging out the notes for a song would be beneficial," he explains. Pianist Jonathan Pease did the opposite. He took singing lessons, partly to prepare for joining a choir with his wife after she retires, but those voice lessons wound up helping his piano playing by "focusing my attention on dynamics and phrasing at the piano."

Health issues caused some to start anew. Lydia Zieglar switched from violin to cello when neck problems from a car accident made playing violin impossible, as described in chapter 2. Amy Dennison, a professional oboist and the program manager of the Preparatory Division of the University of Cincinnati's College-Conservatory of Music, recently became an amateur cellist in her institution's New Horizons string orchestra. She chose cello in case her Parkinson's disease progresses

Janet Blume and her drum set.

to the point of interfering with the note-perfect expectations of a professional oboist. As a cellist in an ensemble where joyful music-making outranks perfectionism, she figures she would still have a way to keep making music.

Hand injuries that Suzanne Epstein developed in her 50s while playing cello made it impossible to continue with the instrument she had enjoyed since childhood. Not wanting to lose music from her life, she has become an accomplished singer who gives art song recitals and sings with chamber music groups. "It was difficult taking on this new role, both because I had no idea if I could become any good and because the identity felt so different," says this Maryland research scientist. Although she knew a lot about music, "as a singer, I was a beginner. It was quite an adjustment," she says. Adjusting to beginner status can be a challenge for all newcomers, both instrumentalists and singers.

Beating Those Beginner's Blues

"I would get so frustrated that I wasn't picking it up as fast as I wanted. I kept thinking, 'I should know how to do this,'" says Michelle Billingsley, a Chicago executive assistant who decided to learn to play guitar in her early 30s. She is a lifelong pianist and accomplished singer. She thought that adding on a new instrument would be quick and easy. She learned that "it takes time for your muscles to adapt and your brain to start making connections."

"Adults are used to feeling competent," observes Kathy Fleming. "The hardest thing to overcome as an adult playing a new instrument is getting over how bad you sound at first. That fear of sounding subpar makes it hard to even start. We all just have to get over that." Her experience with beginner status started right before the Baltimore blizzard of 2010 when a friend she sang madrigals with lent her an alto recorder and encouraged her to try it. Being snowed in gave her time to experiment. She sounded terrible at first but soon was doing better. "I fell in love with early music," she says. The goal of wanting to play that music helped her deal with her beginner's discomfort. She has gone on to master the whole family of recorders—soprano, alto, tenor, and bass—and bass viola da gamba, too. She plays them in an early music ensemble that performs at retirement communities.

Here are suggestions for new instrumentalists, followed by a section on picking an instrument. Tips for singing newcomers appear later in the chapter.

- **Encouragement required:** "Five-year-olds usually come to a first lesson with no sense of what a violin sounds like. So when it sounds pretty horrible, they're not that bothered," explains Louise Hildreth-Grasso, who teaches violin to kids and adults at Peabody Preparatory in Baltimore. "But adults come for lessons because they really like how a violin sounds and are upset when it doesn't sound like Itzhak Perlman. 'Well, he has a few years on you,' I tell them. Adult students require way more encouragement than my younger students. Adults need to realize that it takes time, that it's not quick, but if they keep working at it, it will get better. Those who really want to learn violin, do learn violin."

- **No negative self-talk:** "Many adults have misconceptions when they start. They have seen musicians and think it looks so easy. Then they try and find it's not so easy. They think maybe it's not the right instrument for them, or maybe they're not meant to do music. Sometimes it's related to childhood issues, from a teacher who told them, 'Don't play because you don't have it.' Getting rid of these preconceived ideas takes time," says Audrey-Kristel Barbeau, director of a New Horizons ensemble in Montréal. Will Baily has seen the same negative self-talk in beginning adult students at his Nebraska piano studio. "They really want to do it, they're very courageous, but there's something inside them that's saying, 'No, you can't.'"

- **Do-it-yourself:** Some newcomers tried to learn a new instrument on their own, using methods books or watching instructional videos on YouTube. This strategy worked for experienced strings players who added on viola, but other do-it-your-selfers eventually found a teacher. "I just strummed chords from a John Denver song book or got chords from the internet," says Mr. Dawson, describing his first efforts on guitar. "I didn't learn much." So he started taking group classes and private lessons, and attended jam sessions, too. "I find ways to play with others whenever I can. I listen, which I think is very important, learning from better players in person." David Inverso reached the same conclusion after trying to teach himself to play tenor saxophone. "I had lousy timing and tone and had no idea how to fix it," says this Seattle software developer. "I tried sitting in on a jazz ensemble and a woman sitting next to me bolted from her chair and moved across the room. Humbled and frustrated, I took lessons for quite a few years and played in a sax quartet while taking lessons."

- **Group support:** Many newcomers have taken private lessons. Others prefer group lessons. "Group lessons are a low-stress, friendly way to learn. We joke that it's cheaper than therapy," says Ms. Zieglar, who is learning in a group class with other cello beginners. Brenda Dillon, who teaches group beginner piano classes in Dallas, adds, "What I've learned from teaching group piano classes for adults is that they're incredibly supportive of each other. They really bond. In one class several years ago, a student had it in her mind that she wasn't proceeding as well as the others and was going to drop out. Other students called her up, took her out to lunch, and did a 'piano intervention.'" That student changed her mind and kept on with piano. Chapter 7 has more on group lessons.

Allow yourself to sound bad at first. All that hard work turns into something truly beautiful.

—David Inverso, saxophonist, software developer

- **Ease into it:** Some newcomers ease into lessons gradually, not making a commitment until they're sure this is something they are ready to tackle. "I started small, signing up for a summer Piano Boot Camp," says Dr. Rena Johnson, a choral singer who inherited a piano and decided to learn how to play it, "to keep the brain healthy." When the summer lessons went well, she signed up for the fall semester with the same teacher and has kept going. "I realized there were some things I could learn online, but I wanted to learn proper piano technique," explains this Washington, DC, physician. Dr. Wen Dombrowski also used the lesson-sampling approach, signing up for short-term workshops to explore different kinds of drumming. "In New York, you can pay by the class or sign up for weekend intensives," she explains. An Indian tabla workshop she took a few years ago introduced her to an instrument that she found so fulfilling that she has continued taking weekly tabla lessons for more than three years.
- **Beginner-friendly ensembles:** Instruction is built into some ensembles, including the New Horizons ones. But even ensembles that don't offer coaching can help newcomers, if the conductor is willing to make allowances. Physician Dr. Esthela Urriquia found such a conductor in the Cincinnati community orchestra she joined two years after starting violin at age 69. "The conductor told us newbies that we can play every third or fourth note in hard passages, just stay with the rhythm," she notes. A lifelong pianist, she added on violin when she enrolled her grandson in Suzuki violin lessons and decided to start violin, too. Beth Chapple, who had played French horn during high school, found an accommodating conductor in the Seattle community band she joined three months after renting a trumpet and starting lessons. "They were welcoming and it was the perfect level for a starter group," she explains. This

freelance editor continued with that starter band for nearly a dozen years, while also moving up to a higher level orchestra. One of the orchestras that Dr. Heeren plays with is very beginner-friendly—the Really Terrible Orchestra (RTO)—inspired by the original RTO in Scotland. Her RTO was started by another newcomer on our research team, Colleen Schoneveld, who tells how she did it in chapter 9.

Instrument Choices

Are some instruments easier than others for an adult newcomer to learn? "Almost any instrument is easy to make some music on," says Bau Graves, director of Chicago's Old Town School of Folk Music. "But while it's easy to learn a little, you can spend the rest of your life learning the rest and never hit bottom."

CLOSE UP: KEDAR GANGOPADHYAY, TABLA PLAYER, INVESTMENT BANKER

"I grew up listening to Indian classical music and liked its tonal and rhythmic beauty," says Kedar Gangopadhyay. As a youngster, he played violin at school in New Jersey. "There was never a choice to play Indian music. In school, I was exposed to Western music. None of my relatives play Indian instruments, but my mom was a classical Indian vocalist. I got pretty advanced in violin, but my father made me quit to focus more on academics. Between high school and my late 30s, I didn't play an instrument. After college, I started listening to Indian music more. Why not get into it? Not that it would bring me closer to my roots. I had already grown up very Indian. It's that tabla is a beautiful instrument with so many possibilities." He began taking group tabla lessons at the Chhandayan Center for Indian Music in New York. Tabla consists of two drums similar in size to bongos—one is played with fingertips, the other with the heel of a hand. His violin years help—not musically—but in knowing the value of practice. "I get frustrated, but I know to keep going. I've been enjoying this, especially when your hard work pays off."

"There's not one that stands out as easier. Each instrument has its own little quirks," says Brandon Tesh, director of New Horizons bands at Third Street Music School in New York City. "Flute, clarinet, alto sax, trumpet, trombone, or percussion are good starting band instruments. Two or three times a year we hold a 'petting zoo.' We'll have the instruments out so people can come in and hold the instruments, hear them, maybe make some sounds. If there are issues having to do with physical capabilities, we steer them in a different direction. Such as, are they able to hold up a trombone, do they have dental issues that might interfere with some woodwind or brass instruments."

Music schools often hold instrument demonstrations, as do New Horizons programs, including the one sponsored by the University of Cincinnati's conservatory. Its director, BettyAnne Gottlieb, explains, "We hold recruitment demonstrations at retirement facilities and during intermission at Cincinnati Symphony Orchestra concerts." She feels that an instrument's sound should be the deciding factor. Studies show that people differ in the kind of sound that appeals to them. Students are more likely to practice instruments whose sound they like.

Other factors to consider are an instrument's size and weight. Those who play guitar, flute, and clarinet like their instruments' portability. "Some people say there's arm fatigue playing violin and viola," notes Ms. Gottlieb. That's because these instruments are held up in the air, unlike cello and double bass whose endpins rest on the ground. Also worth noting, she says, is that "violas are a little larger and heavier than violins. We use smaller violas so they won't be as heavy." The large double bass can be a challenge to transport, but one member of her orchestra "has created a contraption to roll his bass around on wheels to get it from his car to rehearsal."

Also worth keeping in mind: Not all instruments are included in all kinds of ensembles. They often have different roles within an ensemble, with some usually getting the melody (violin, flute, clarinet, trumpet, guitar, banjo) while others have a more supportive role (trombone, viola, bass, percussion). Another key issue is cost, with big price differences among various types of instruments. Some newcomers who started by renting a student-level instrument recommend finding a store that offers rent-to-buy agreements. That way the amount paid on the rental can be applied later to purchasing an instrument. If a newcomer progresses to wanting a professional-level model, prices rise considerably, with professional-level string instruments costing many times more than woodwind or brass. A few of our team members found good deals on used instruments at a music store or online from Ebay and Craigslist. As with any major purchase, it's wise to shop around and also seek advice from a teacher or experienced musician.

Switching instruments is possible. So is moving into a new instrument category gradually, to make sure you like it before making too much of an investment, as retired corporate accountant Barbara Try did. She started playing bells at age 66 when she met a community orchestra conductor who needed someone to play bells. She had so much fun with the bells that she joined this Arizona orchestra's percussion section. She has since added chimes, drums, timpani, and "all sorts of noise makers" to her percussion repertoire. Joining the orchestra inspired her to start practicing piano more. By age 78, she was not only in the percussion section, but was performing with this ensemble on piano and keyboard, too.

Barbara Try with instruments she plays in the East Valley Pops Orchestra (formerly Silveridge) of Mesa, Arizona.

The "Can't Sing" Myth

"I was totally unable to sing when I was younger. I didn't even know I could sing until I was in a guitar class and was paired up with another person to sing small snippets of a song. Now I love to sing," says Dr. Larry Lindeman. He made his singing breakthrough in his late 50s, a few years after returning to guitar lessons. Fellow Chicagoan Steven Duke discovered that he could sing at about the same age, when the same encouraging guitar teacher helped free him from the curse that an elementary school teacher had placed on him, when she told him to "just mouth the words" while the rest of the class sang, as described in chapter 1.

Others on our research team also spent many of their adult years thinking they couldn't sing. Philip Anderson recalls that a 5th grade music teacher, after hearing him sing, wouldn't let him in the chorus. "That does a number on you," he says. He sang rock songs in a band that he played drums with during high school but thought choral music wasn't for him until his late 50s when he joined a church choir for the first time and then moved on to a supportive community chorus in Maine. "I found that I can actually do this, that it isn't terrifying," he says.

"The default thinking in this country is that most people are bad singers and a few lucky people are very good. This is an unfortunate hoax," says Mr. Dawson. He never thought of himself as a singer until he started going to folk music jam sessions when he began guitar lessons. He had fun singing along and realized that he too could be a singer.

Singing experts agree that it's a shame that so many people have the mistaken idea that they can't sing. "Children who have been told they can't sing well are even less likely to engage with music in the future," says Steven Demorest, music education professor at Northwestern University. "Being called 'tone deaf' can have devastating effects on a child's self-image." He notes that only a tiny subset of the population is truly tone deaf, with a condition called *amusia* that prevents them from hearing changes in pitches.

"Virtually everyone can learn to sing," says Dr. Robert T. Sataloff, chair of the Department of Otolaryngology at Drexel University College of Medicine. If people can use their voices to speak and "can distinguish between two pitches as the same or different, they can be trained to sing." There's no guarantee that they'll sing as well as Pavarotti. "But they will get better than when they started," he says. "Deaf people can learn to sing if they have some hearing restored, even if by cochlear implant. If they are completely deaf, they can learn to sing somewhat, with training by feel, sometimes facilitated with visual feedback."

Recent research by Professor Demorest has shown, however, that if adults used to sing but haven't been singing much for several years, their ability to sing in tune is less on target than for children who sing regularly in music classes at school. This might suggest that "adults who may have performed better as children lost the ability when they stopped singing." Singing seems to be a "use it or lose it" skill—one that can be revived or taught anew to adults so that they can learn the basics of relaxing their throats and using their breath to produce the sound. This transformation can happen by taking some voice lessons, or by first getting a taste of singing in a setting where they won't be judged, such as sitting in on a rehearsal of a choir or of a non-auditioned chorus that is welcoming to newcomers.

Science educator Christine Anderson-Morehouse used both strategies when she decided at age 55 to become involved in singing. She received an email about a new group called Women Who Can't Sing and decided to join. "It's a group of four women meeting weekly year-round in someone's living room with a choral instructor," she explains. The group has a new name, Songbirds, because now they can all sing. Soon after starting with this group, she joined a Maine community chorus, "even though I could barely sing on key. It was great—an opportunity to be with real singers and improve more quickly. I'm learning ways for using my breath and vocal chords appropriately. It's all about supported breathing both for creating a good sound and protecting your vocal cords. I like the feeling of wellness that I come away with each time I sing with others. I feel confident now singing for fun at parties. Heck, I even enjoy the carpool to chorus each week!"

Her response is typical of what researchers have found when they study choral singers—that singing in a group makes people feel good. Her choral success has inspired her husband to take lessons with her vocal coach. He too had been told as a child to just to mouth the words. "Now he's singing," she says.

Turn off those singing shows on TV that make fun of 'bad singers' and go find a song to sing.

—Ted Dawson, guitarist, singer, resource room teacher

New Singer Options

The chorus that Ms. Anderson-Morehouse joined—Midcoast Community Chorus of Rockport, Maine—is an example of one that's newcomer friendly. "A brand new singer is partnered with a mentor, somebody who sits next to the new person to help," says Mimi Bornstein, who founded this chorus and was its first director. "We do warm-ups and there is practice on vocal technique that is worked into all rehearsals." The chorus offers classes for those who can't read music and provides online recordings of practice tracks for every song. Chorus members can listen to the recordings at home, so they can hear the part they are to sing and how it fits into the whole piece. Listening to practice tracks helps all the group's singers, not just those who can't read music. Ms. Bornstein has found that the very act of singing together with others helps newcomers improve. "The energy that you get swept up in when you sing with others has a lot to do with how well you sing and how much you can open up. The average age in the group is 55. It's amazing the sound they make." Plus she points out that in a non-auditioned chorus as large as this—with about 140 members—if one singer has trouble matching pitch, "that one voice really isn't going to stick out that much."

Similarly supportive strategies are used in other beginner-friendly choruses. "I build in a fair amount of teaching during our rehearsals," says Juli Elliot, director of a New Horizons chorus in Rochester, New York. So does Martha Rodríguez-Salazar, who leads several community choruses offered by the San Francisco Community Music Center. Some of her choral groups were initially part of the Community of Voices study done in coordination with researchers at the University of California San Francisco to see what impact choral singing would have on cognitive functioning and emotional well-being of new singers. The study's choruses were made up of adults from diverse ethnic backgrounds, age 60 and over, often with no previous musical training. Although official study results weren't available by the time this book went to press, many choir members voted with their feet, giving a hint of what the results might be. Many had so much fun learning to be choral singers that they have continued singing in the choirs long after the research study ended. Choral ensembles for newcomers have been springing up elsewhere as well. There are Tuneless Choirs in Britain and Wales for those who think they can't sing. In Milan, Italy, there's a chorus for "*stonati*" (Italian for "out of tune") sponsored by La Verdi, an arts organization.

The Harmony Project chorus of Columbus, Ohio, is also beginner-friendly. "We don't use any sheet music," says David Brown, the director of this 250-member, multi-age, non-auditioned chorus. He teaches all the songs by ear. He gives the chorus members pages with the lyrics but no musical score. He makes his own arrangements for each song, being careful not to have any notes that are too high or too low. Chorus members listen at home to recordings of him singing each part separately. "We ask people to sing along to the recordings at home, then come into rehearsal once a week where I refine things, tweak it, and pull it together," he explains. Some in the choir cannot always match pitch and others may waffle back

Members of San Francisco Community Music Center's choirs for older adults.

and forth between soprano and alto lines, but there are enough who consistently sing true to their parts that "what you get is a blend of harmony across the choir. What we're going for is harmony. However we get there is okay." His goal is for the chorus to "breathe together and phrase things together in a way that tells a story rather than aiming for a more choral music approach." This chorus also has a public service component, which is described in chapter 11.

Choirs in houses of worship are often supportive choices for beginners. "I kind of ease them in," says Joyce Garrett, choir director at Alfred Street Baptist Church in Alexandria, Virginia. "I don't recommend that they immediately start taking lessons, but I'll say, 'Just come and sit in a rehearsal and see if it's something you would like to do.' I put them between two seasoned singers in the middle of the ensemble so they get used to hearing the pitches of the notes around them. I don't require that they read music. I teach phrase by phrase. People can record their part on their phones or I send them links to the songs on YouTube to listen to at home."

Even high-level choral societies build in a certain amount of voice training, according to Stanley J. Thurston, who leads auditioned choral groups in Washington, DC, including the Heritage Signature Chorale with which several of our advice-team members sing. He also leads choral groups made up of less-experienced singers. For all the groups, he tries to include work on vocal technique and vocal health.

Voices do get better, but Mr. Thurston warns, "It takes a while for it to become second nature, especially for people who have not been singing for a while." Voice lessons can help. Suzanne Epstein, the former cellist who switched to singing, started by joining a chorus and then found a voice teacher to help her prepare to audition for more advanced choruses. Peter Beck also used this two-step process to start singing: joining a chorus first and later signing up for lessons. "After a painful situation where I overdid things, I took some lessons to know how to take care of my voice," says this Chicago writer who plays banjo and other folk instruments.

"It doesn't require decades of voice lessons to sing in a choir or in community musicals," observes Dr. Sataloff. He feels that "at least a short course of singing lessons" can help people not only improve their voices, but also "recognize if they are being asked to do things in a choral rehearsal that would be harmful to their voices." Many choral directors are careful not to ask singers to do more than is safe, but some may not. It's wise to be alert. For more on instruction for singers and tips for healthy singing, see chapters 7 and 8.

New Artistic Pursuits

Several of our advice-team members found other ways to explore something new musically: by learning to play different styles of music; by doing some arranging, composing, and conducting; or by creating their own ensembles and concert series. Attorney John Vishneski did all of these new activities when he helped start the Barristers Big Band as an offshoot of the Chicago Bar Association Symphony Orchestra in which he plays clarinet. "I was trained as a classical clarinet player," says Mr. Vishneski. "Starting the Barristers Big Band was a whole new world of music for me. I had never played jazz or improvised. I handle the challenge by finding ways to learn about jazz through reading, playing with recordings, and playing with the band. I pay close attention to what superior players do. Classical and jazz music are both areas where I will be learning new things all my life."

Later chapters describe some of our team members' musical offshoots in more detail, as well as offer suggestions for handling the basics of a musical life: instruction, practice, performing, and injury prevention. But first, a chapter on time—a major roadblock that keeps many adults from becoming music-makers.

Phyllis Kaiden (front row center) at a weekend workshop to raise money for Chamber Music Madness, a Seattle nonprofit that encourages young people to play chamber music. "I play music regularly with these women," says Ms. Kaiden. "We met because of our love of chamber music and benefit now from an informal but powerful sisterhood."

6 Making Time

" 'I DON'T HAVE TIME,' is what I hear myself and others say. But we all have twenty-four hours in a day and we each choose how to spend that time. I decided music-making is a priority and I balance it with other activities," says Phyllis Kaiden, who started viola at age 52. She acknowledges that it has become easier to make time for music after she retired. But for ten years while she was still working as a librarian and software developer in the Seattle area, she managed to fit in time for viola lessons, orchestra rehearsals, and chamber music, too.

Time is a main reason why some adults shy away from getting into music, feeling there is no way to include it in their jam-packed schedules. In this chapter, our advice-team members, including several parents with young children, describe how they manage to make time for music.

The amount of time that needs to be carved out may not be as large as some fear. It depends on the nature of the musical involvement. As noted in earlier chapters, some music lovers participate in several ensembles and attend multiple rehearsals a week. Others are much less musically active and enjoy making music without putting in huge blocks of time.

In terms of practicing, there is quite a range in the amount of time spent on music at home. Five percent of our questionnaire completers said they usually don't practice at all. Just over a quarter practice only one or two days a week. Of those who do practice, nearly 15 percent put in thirty minutes or less each time. Judging from the experiences of these advice-team members, it seems that it is possible to do music as an adult while spending a fairly minimal amount of time on practice.

Most of the questionnaire completers, however, put in substantially more practice time. A little more than a quarter practice every day. Just under half practice three to five days a week. Of those who practice each week, more than three-fourths spend a half hour or more each time; about half of them spend at least an hour on practice each time, and sometimes longer.

Those who practice more often and for longer periods may make more progress than the others, but as Liz Sogge observes, "Avoid the feeling of running a race. There is nothing wrong with never playing at the level of a world-class violinist." As a working mom with little spare time, she may not practice as much as would be ideal, but she still manages to participate in the second violin section of an auditioned community orchestra, occasionally serving as section leader.

Some of our team members say they would like to practice more, but they have adjusted their expectations to fit the reality of their competing time commitments. The keys to conquering the time issue involve setting reasonable goals and also doing serious schedule planning. Theodore Sapp, the human resources manager who sings in a choir and often in community musicals, plans carefully each week so that rehearsals don't interfere with any meetings or deadlines. "Finding the time will never come," he says. "I had to make the time in order to get this accomplished."

A Master Schedule

Many of our advice-team members create a master schedule each week, as Mr. Sapp does. Eloise Bensberg, a Baltimore accountant who sings in two choirs explains, "I put everything on the calendar as soon as I know about it. The choir schedules are known well in advance. I plan the rest of my life around music." Some team members keep digital calendars on computers or smart phones, often with the possibility of having audio or email reminders to prod the forgetful. Roy Hitchings uses a computer to plan his days, as he did before he retired. "I schedule rehearsals and practice on my computer just like I would for a meeting," notes this retired hospital CEO who sings in a church choir and a community chorus in Maine. Yes, even retirees find it helpful to make a schedule. Dr. Morris Schoeneman notes, "Rehearsing and practicing take up a lot of time, so it becomes hard to schedule my other retirement activities: tutoring, attending French conversation groups, playing tennis, keeping fit, volunteering at my synagogue, doing errands."

Ms. Bensberg recommends thinking carefully about an ensemble's time commitment before joining. "Consider whether you can meet the rehearsal and performance requirements. Find something you can fit into your life," she notes. That's why baritone saxophonist Neela Wickremesinghe says, "I commit to a season at a time. I am the kind of person who does things once they are written down in my planner. Carve out the time and stick to it!"

Being in an ensemble with regular rehearsals makes scheduling easier. That applies also to groups that musicians organize among themselves, which is why Angela Bowman has arranged for her Cajun band to play one night a month at a Chicago bar. It's not a formal concert, just a recurring opportunity for her band to play together, with a side benefit of sometimes collecting tips in a jar. "We practice mostly at this monthly residency," she says. "We sit in the corner of the bar and work out new material. We set that up knowing that it's hard for us to schedule one-off rehearsals, especially since our accordion player has three kids. It's easier for him to have something regular."

Music lessons are another item to add to the schedule, although only about half of our questionnaire completers study with a teacher. Others may have taken lessons in the past but weren't doing so when they filled out the questionnaire for this book. Either they didn't have time for lessons, couldn't afford them, were receiving pointers from the conductor in their ensembles, or felt their skill level was adequate for their musical activities. Doing without formal instruction for a while can add some air to a packed schedule. So can spreading out when lessons occur. Only about half of those receiving instruction have weekly lessons. About a quarter meet with an instructor twice a month. The rest receive instruction less often, from once a month to a few times a year.

Theodore Sapp singing in a production of *Sister Act* at the Annapolis Summer Garden Theatre in Maryland.

For those who have lessons, some choose week nights. For others, weekends are better. Philip Knieper tried both when he returned to piano after his young daughter started piano lessons. "Originally, we both started with Saturday lessons, but those were often difficult to work around for non-typical weekends," says this Louisiana mechanical engineer. "So, I made a commitment at work to leave on time (versus the typical late) one day a week, and we've been able to make most Monday evenings work for us. When things at work are unmanageable, I've had to miss the occasional lesson here and there, but I made the decision in advance that I would accept those localized losses as part of the greater gain."

Making adjustments at work can also help. Chicago violist Adrienne Kitchen made arrangements with co-workers and the judge she was clerking for so she could leave early on the day each week that her orchestra had rehearsals. Dr. Marc Wager bargained on his work hours when he first joined his pediatric practice. "Initially I had very little control over my schedule. The senior partners wanted me to stay late, so I asked for a longer lunch hour to go home to practice," he says. "Without that, I wouldn't have had the time to practice, and I find that I can't play French horn and sound good without practicing regularly. If I don't sound good, I don't enjoy it."

Peg Beyer made a more drastic work adjustment when she cut down on her hours, after thirty years in risk management. "I gave up the corner office and went down to thirty hours a week so I would have more time to practice and play. I no longer brought work home. I didn't work Fridays so I would have a solid three days where I could get in several hours." Dr. Helen Heeren has rearranged her work setup and her social life, too. "I adjusted my office schedule so that I could make rehearsals and lessons," says this cello newcomer. "Sometimes I have had to choose not to participate in all of the social activities I would like to. I have very understanding friends."

CLOSE UP: PHILIP KNIEPER, PIANIST, MECHANICAL ENGINEER

"When I played piano as a teen, I was playing at a high level of difficulty. I enjoyed playing publicly and had many wins at performance competitions. But after a twenty-five year hiatus, I am significantly less capable," says Philip Knieper. "Even though my teacher has me playing pieces far beyond a beginner, I'm very aware of every mistake. I love being able to create music. I play hoping to recover at least a shadow of the confidence I once had. In many ways, I like how the music I make now is essentially for myself. As a husband, father, and engineer, much of what I do is to support my wife and family, raise my children, or support the company. Since I am not confident enough to play for others, the music is for me alone. It really feels like a fresh start, a wonderful stress reliever after work or at the end of a long week. Every victory feels fantastic—even the smallest ones."

Fitting in Practice

As hard as it can be to make time for rehearsals and lessons, setting aside time for practice can be trickier, because it is so open-ended, with nobody counting on you to show up at a certain place and time. One solution is to make it a habit by doing it at the same time every day or the same day every week. Weekends work best for some. For those who try to fit in some practice on weekdays, early morning offers the advantage of knowing you've done at least some practicing in case the rest of the day becomes hectic. Michelle Billingsley has become a fan of the early-morning approach, although at first she tried an after-work routine. "When I first started playing guitar, I used to put off practicing until after I got home from work," she says. "Then it seemed like every time, something would happen and I'd be too tired or crabby to do anything but zone out on the couch. Now I get up and play before work. It's nice to wake up and tinker around." Early morning works well for Kedar Gangopadhyay and his tabla practicing. "My focus is better," he says, "I'm also not looking at my cell phone."

Others have had better luck with an evening routine. "I make it a rule to practice at least one hour after dinner," says Maryvonne Mavroukakis, a Washington librarian who took up cello in her 40s. Mary Schons prefers evening, too. "When I've had a horrible day at work and after I've had a beer and have fed the cats, I like to wind down with practice," says this guitarist and banjo player. She adds, however, that "sometimes I'll play something quickity-quick in the morning before work to make the day go better." Dr. Heeren practices way after dinner time, "usually 10:00 p.m. to midnight. I am lucky that I do not need a lot of sleep," she says.

Here are other strategies for fitting practice into a busy schedule.

- **Break it up:** "Because I work at home, I can practice intermittently throughout the day, say in three ten-minute sessions," says Beth Chapple, a freelance editor and trumpet newcomer. Dale Backus divides up his piano practice, especially when preparing for a recital or competition. "I want to do half an hour in the morning and an hour at night," he says. Splitting up practice makes it easier to find chunks of spare time, while also improving the quality of the work. Practicing too long at a stretch can cause minds to wander and muscles to strain, as noted in chapter 8.
- **Five-minute plan:** "The best advice I got from my piano teacher: 'When you have five or ten minutes—practice. Don't wait for the hour that never materializes,'" says Joe Guttentag, a retired tax lawyer who returned to piano in his 40s. Several team members have received that same advice and found that it works. Lydia Zieglar's cello teacher added a no-guilt clause. "She told

me, 'Try to put your hands on your cello every day for five minutes. Often that five minutes will lead to more, but if it doesn't, put it away with no judgement,'" recalls Ms. Zieglar.

- **Down time:** "I use 'waste' time for studying the music—on public transport, sitting in doctors' waiting rooms," says Mary Linard, who has a lot of music to study for the chorus she sings with and the ensembles in which she plays flute and percussion. Dr. Valerie Clemons goes over songs while driving her car, taking care not to be a distracted driver. "I rehearse on long or short drives. Once the music is in my ear and in my head, it just comes out all the time. I'm singing the songs throughout the day, either out loud or in my head," says this Maine physician who sings in a community chorus. Experts say that mental practice—going through a piece in your mind without singing or playing the instrument—counts as practice.

- **The roast-in-the-oven plan:** Ms. Chapple reports that she might start "one of my approximately ten-minute practice sessions when I am done with work but starting housework and dinner preparation. I put a roast in the oven and then practice." So does Ms. Sogge, who notes, "I don't expect to find whole hours, so I seize the opportunity to practice fifteen or twenty minutes whenever there is time. I prefer preparing food that roasts for an hour or so. During this time, I practice."

- **Always ready:** "My uke sits on my piano so it is very visible. I can pick it up anytime and play," says Janet Howard, a retired Kentucky schoolteacher who started ukulele in her 60s. Ms. Schons also leaves her instruments out, explaining that "everything is all set up and ready to go. I bought a secondhand music stand and guitar stands for my instruments so I can grab them whenever the moment strikes. My chord books are all on the shelf next to my practice chair."

- **Workplace possibilities:** Several team members get in some practicing at work. "The residents and fellows know when I'm in each morning," says Dr. Alvin Crawford, emeritus professor of orthopedic surgery who brings his clarinet into the office for an hour of practicing from 6:30 to 7:30 a.m. "On occasion, it's the most stress-free hour of the day," he notes. John Hollwitz, the professor who started piano at age 50, put an electronic piano in his office for lunchtime practice. Katherine Erwin sometimes uses conference rooms at her law office to practice flute or bassoon. Stewart Olsen plays trumpet in several Energy City New Horizons ensembles in Houston, but when starting his career as an engineer decades earlier, he would keep a trumpet under his desk at work. Back then, computers didn't work as fast as they do now. While waiting for a computer program to compile or print, he would pull out his trumpet and practice. "The stairwell echo effect was fun late at night," he says. "The security guards got plenty of midnight trumpet music."

- **Travel accommodations:** Peggy Radin practices flute even when traveling. "People in hotels tolerate loud TV but will pound the wall about music. I figured out, though, that almost no one is in a hotel after check-out time and before check-in time." That's when this retired law professor practices in her hotel room. She has also practiced in hotel conference rooms. "Sometimes when invited to an academic venue, I said I would accept if they would reserve a practice room for me in their music building," she notes. Mr. Backus, who travels a lot as an engineer, reports, "I find practice pianos in the oddest places. I found one in the officers' lounge on Diego Garcia in the middle of the Indian Ocean. I tuned the piano and practiced at night. I always bring my tuning equipment with me." A music major in college, when he shifted to engineering, he took piano technology courses and learned to tune and fix a piano. Some pianos in hotels are digital, but he doesn't mind, even though the feel of pressing the keys differs from his acoustic piano. "I get to move my fingers, work on muscle memory, and keep my chops up."

- **Fewer time-eaters:** "The alternatives to practicing or playing—watching TV, surfing the Web—just aren't as appealing," says Peter Beck, a Chicago writer who plays a variety of folk instruments and was a music major in college. "It was tremendously beneficial to have established good practice habits when I was young. Being disciplined about the need to practice and keep up my chops is key. Plus, I dislike sounding unprepared in public, so I practice even for jamming."

- **Goals:** Violist Paula Washington recalls that her cousin, Ann Hobson Pilot, former principal harpist of the Boston Symphony, once told her, "No one practices out of virtue but only if there is something on the horizon—a lesson, a recording date, a recital. So don't beat yourself up; put something on the horizon." Practice time may miraculously materialize when there is a goal to prepare for, including the sudden urge to do at least some practicing the day before a lesson. As Mr. Knieper observes, "Having a commitment to a lesson and a teacher, I have a constant deadline to work towards. With such a busy work and life schedule, it is far too easy to procrastinate practicing." For Mr. Guttentag, age 86 when he filled out the questionnaire for this book, his goal has been to prepare pieces for the recital he plans to hold for his 90th birthday.

You have to make the time, or it slips away and you never do it.
—Dr. Helen Heeren, cellist, psychotherapist

About the Neighbors

Living in an apartment or condo adds complications to carving out practice time. "I try to practice at a time when a lot of the neighbors are out. I kind of know their schedules, so I work around that. They do complain about the noise, but what can I do?" says Heather Rosado, who plays flute in two bands and in a chamber music class. "Normally, it's weekend afternoons, although sometimes I practice on a weeknight if I get home at a normal time." In addition to not bothering the neighbors, others are shy about practicing in an apartment because they don't want others to hear their mistakes. Even those not in an apartment may worry about bothering others— sleeping spouses, kids, or roommates. One team member, a soprano, had a difficult challenge because her husband couldn't stand the vibration he experienced when she hit the higher pitches in her range.

Our team members have found ways to practice so it doesn't bother others, often by doing what Ms. Rosado has done, work around people's schedules. Additional options include practicing away from home, as the soprano did who has the husband with sensitive ears. She found a nearby church that let her practice there. Finding a way to practice at work has helped several team members, as noted earlier. Another possibility involves practicing at a music school where either the musician or his or her kids are taking lessons. That can give parents something to do instead of just hanging out waiting for their youngsters. Glenn Kramer, a pianist and art director who was looking for a better piano to practice on when he was preparing to enter a piano competition, discovered that it is possible to make arrangements with a hotel to practice on grand pianos in empty banquet halls.

Ms. Howard and a group of fellow ukulele players often practice together in a public area in a retirement community. She isn't a resident there. Nor are her ukulele friends, but their adult-education ukulele classes were held there. The center's staff is fine with them stopping by to practice. "We sit in the back and sometimes residents come by and sing along or dance," she says. During the summer, they practice in a public park.

For many musicians, using a practice mute can quiet the sound of an instrument so that late-night or early-morning practice isn't as audible. There are mutes of different types that work for string and brass instruments. Although, as Ms. Schons notes, "Even with the practice mute on my banjo, it must drive my neighbor crazy." A drum pad is a low-noise option for percussionists. Playing an electric guitar without turning on the amplifier is a possibility. There are also technological advances can that help with the noisy practice problem, as noted in the next section.

I promise there is nothing good on TV. Facebook is a waste of time. If you learn a new song, you carry that with you everywhere you go.
—Ted Dawson, guitarist, singer, resource room teacher

Technological Assistance

When John Hollwitz started taking piano lessons at age 50, he bought an upright Yamaha acoustic piano. Because he lives in an apartment condo, he later installed a digital system in the piano. "When the digital system is switched on, the piano becomes silent and requires headphones to hear it," he explains. "This means I can practice later in the day or early in the morning before work without bothering anyone. That has helped open up a lot of useful practice time."

Other team members have "hybrid pianos." These are acoustic pianos that have digital capability already built in which can be switched on or off as needed. Mr. Knieper, who owns a hybrid piano, explains, "During normal hours I play it in acoustic mode and during the night (once the kids are in bed), I flip it to silent mode and play using headphones." There are differences of opinion on digital versus acoustic pianos, which will be discussed in the next chapter.

Adine Usher, who lives in a condo townhouse, has an acoustic grand piano in her living room that she uses for most of her practicing, as well as an electronic keyboard in an upstairs guest room that can be played silently when she plugs in headphones. If she practices late at night, she uses the keyboard so as not to disturb her neighbors. She takes the keyboard with her when she stays for a week or so at her sons' homes. This lets her serve as a role-model for her grandkids on the importance of keeping on with music no matter what.

Here are no-noise options for other instruments.

- **Strings:** Electronic string instruments don't have a resonating chamber as a regular string instrument does, and so they don't make a sound when you bow the strings unless you plug in an amplifier or listen through a headset. Electronic string instruments don't have the same feel or tone as an acoustic instrument, but they are useful for quiet practicing. They are sometimes used by musicians playing non-classical gigs. Yamaha makes silent models for all string instruments. Cecilio and Stagg make them for several string instruments.

- **Guitar:** No-noise guitars by Yamaha and SoloEtte work in a way that's similar to the string instruments just described. The SoloEtte can be disassembled to fit into a small carrying case.

- **Brass:** A silent option for brass instruments—Silent Brass from Yamaha—consists of a pickup mute that is placed in the instrument's bell. The mute has an internal microphone that picks up sound and is connected to a processing unit which sends the sound to headphones so the musician can hear, while others can't.

- **Woodwinds:** The EWI, an electronic instrument made by Akai, is played while connected to a computer on which software can be downloaded so that the keys on the EWI use fingering modes for different woodwinds—saxophone, flute, or oboe. Clarinetists can use the EWI because its saxophone fingering matches that of a soprano sax, which is similar to a clarinet's. If the EWI is connected to headphones, it plays silently.

- **Drums:** An electronic drum kit consists of a group of drum pads placed on stands in a layout similar to an acoustic drum set. As the player strikes a pad with sticks or hands, the pad creates an electronic signal that is transmitted via cables to a processing module to make a sound. This unit can be attached to headphones or to an amplifier.

- **Play-along option:** What trumpeter Lorne Wald likes most about the Silent Brass mute for his trumpet is that it has several jacks: an output jack for plugging in headphones, an input jack for the mute, and an additional input jack which lets him connect to another sound source, such as a computer or MP3 player. This allows him to hear recordings of pieces he's learning through his headphones while he plays along. Yamaha Silent models for strings and guitar have this same capability. He had tried playing along with recordings before getting his Silent Brass. "But it was often hard to hear the music over my own playing (it is a trumpet after all). Silent Brass allows you to balance the input coming from the mute to the volume coming from the computer/CD player in such a way as to either blend in, fade into the background, or go almost solo," he explains. "My wife insists that she is delighted that I've gotten involved with music, but she did seem particularly pleased when I suggested that she could get the Silent Brass mute as a gift for me."

- **A different feel:** Playing these electronic instruments feels different than playing the acoustic originals and requires some adjustment. New York publisher Ron Sharpe, who plays in a community orchestra as well as in jazz and bluegrass groups, uses his electronic violin "exclusively for practicing, not for performing. I don't really like the sound. When I need amplification in a performance, I have an inexpensive pickup for guitars that I attach to my acoustic instrument that gives a more natural sound." Sound preference is a matter of taste. Some professional musicians, such as avant-garde artist Laurie Anderson, have embraced the electronic violin sound, but it may not fit as well with classical repertoire. Rowe Grandy likes his electronic drums. "The only thing I don't like about them is the cymbals. You don't get your true cymbal sound. You don't get rim shots either," says this percussionist who for many years played with Army and USO bands, but is now a union shop steward in Baltimore. "Most of the time I use an amplifier with my electronic drums, but sometimes I use earphones to practice." Occasionally he plays drums at his church but mostly he plays at home because a lot of his spare time is taken up with shepherding his young cellist son to lessons and youth orchestra rehearsals. "My wife bought me the electronic drums for my birthday because she knew I missed playing."

- **Chops concerns:** Saxophonist Steve DeMont uses his EWI mostly for practicing. "I'll practice for an hour or so late at night on my EWI with headphones on," he says, so he doesn't wake his wife. "I take it to practice sessions in my jazz class on occasion, especially for playing a fusion tune when I plug it into an amp. I'm beginning to explore the possibilities it has to offer. The feel is a bit different from a saxophone in how you transition from one octave to the next. It has a series of rollers that your thumb rolls over to hit high and low octaves. This takes a bit of practice. One of the reasons I don't play the EWI as much as I might like is I take my saxophone embouchure (mouth position) seriously. It's not an easy thing to acquire, takes a lot of time to develop, and years to maintain. I'm concerned I might lose my chops."

How Parents Manage

Many parents on our advice panel waited until their children were in high school or beyond before resuming music-making. Others have kept on with music while raising young children. It all depends on the family situation, the competing demands of a budding career, parents' tolerance for schedule juggling, and sometimes the health of the children. One team member put music-making on hold for several years because one of her children was disabled and had special needs.

For those who continue with music while their children are young, having a good support network is essential. For some, that support network involves a helpful spouse. For others, especially single parents, it also includes a helpful circle of friends or nearby grandparents, as well as youngsters who sense that it's important to be cooperative about letting parents do music.

Brandon Ray with his daughter after singing in a holiday concert of the
Choir of the Sound in Shoreline, Washington.

"When we decided to have a child, we both decided to maintain our own interests.
My husband is avidly involved in softball. So he gets to do softball and I still get
my music," says Jamie Doyle, a Boston research scientist who resumed playing in
two orchestras shortly after her first child was born. Bassoonist Mandy Ray and her
husband made a similar arrangement. "We agreed that band night was the one night
I would be completely relieved of baby care so that I could de-stress," she says. "I
kept playing until a week before my first child was born, although I lost a lot of
stamina from decreased lung capacity. I resumed band rehearsals one month later.
Sometimes there are tough decisions to make in terms of what gets priority, but
when you realize how much better a person it makes you, you make time for it."
When her husband has a choral rehearsal, she covers for him.

Not all mothers went back to music-making as soon after childbirth as Ms. Ray. Sarah Wright started practicing violin again when her son began sleeping through the night at age seven months. "Until then I was too exhausted to do anything after his bedtime," she observes. Others waited until their youngsters were in school, as Ms. Sogge did, who notes, "It was so important to reclaim some of my own passions and interests that did not center around my children and the home." That's why Joan Herbers' husband encouraged her to keep on with violin. "When my second child was born, I was feeling overwhelmed," she explains. "I told my husband I needed to simplify my life and would quit orchestra. He said, 'No, find something else to cut back. Orchestra is too important to you.'"

It isn't only mothers who need support or whose free time is eaten up by childcare. Mr. Backus settled into a regular twice-a-day practice routine on piano only after his daughters were grown. "When the kids were young, it was a challenge. I'd help with homework and dinner and then at 9:00 p.m. go practice, but then my wife and I wouldn't have had any time to talk," he recalls. He tried getting up early, but that had drawbacks, too.

Julie Puntenney's ex-husband pitched in so she could keep playing cello in a Cincinnati community orchestra while her daughter was a toddler. "He would come over and stay in the house for the few hours I was gone for rehearsals. Then I'd come back and he'd leave and go back home. I started bringing my daughter to rehearsals when she was in first grade," says this banker. The youngster would sit in the back of the room where the orchestra rehearsed. "She'd sit quietly, eat a snack, and stay in my sight. She did fine getting up for school the next day. She enjoyed it. Maybe that's why she chose to do music, too."

Sheneka Lett, another single mom, receives help from members of her Virginia church when she brings her young daughters to church choir rehearsals and performances. "With my choir, we're like a family," says this teaching assistant and former music major. "So many people at church know me. We help each other out. It's good to have a community of people, whether family or friends, to help when you need it." When Ms. Lett joined the church's choir, her daughters were ages 3 and 8. She had instilled in them a love of music, by singing together with them every day at home and encouraging them to join the children's choir and dance group at their church and play instruments, too. The girls were good about tagging along to their mother's events. "You kind of train your kids, saying, 'Okay, I need you to sit down and not act up while Mommy is up here singing.' During rehearsals, they do homework, bring a book, or I let the younger one play on my phone. When I sing at services, I put them in the closer pews where I can see them until the children's service begins. On weekends when I have to sing and they are dancing in the Kid's Street service for children across the street, the dance teacher comes to take them over to their service."

Sheneka Lett (third from left, second row) and the Alfred Street Baptist Church choir she sings with, while it was on tour in Houston, Texas.

Other team members who have brought children to rehearsals have usually waited until the baby stage had passed, although Ms. Ray notes that she has seen musicians bring babies. "But it's rare," she says. "They put the little ones down on a blanket next to them. It only works with children who are very easy-going. I would never try that with my daughter, although my husband has been bringing her to his choir rehearsals since she was two years old. I think it has to do with the volume of a band rehearsal vs. a choir rehearsal."

More Tips for Music-Making Parents

- **Long-range plans:** "I have to plan things carefully with my husband, as he also plays in his spare time," says Arabella Lang. "We look ahead at the year, decide which concerts we want to play, and then negotiate to make sure we have enough but not too much, and try to alternate." Alice Model chose which orchestra to join as a young mother based on which evening it rehearsed—to be sure it was a night her husband could babysit. This retired suburban New York special education and Suzuki teacher has kept playing into her 80s.

- **Babysitting options:** For ensemble rehearsals and performances, Ms. Lang says, "Most of the time, my husband and I take turns, with one playing while the other looks after our wee one. Occasionally we play in the same thing, in which case our neighbor or an aunt babysits." Ms. Lang usually practices after her son is asleep, but on weekends she and her husband take turns practicing, with one practicing while the other keeps their toddler busy. Sofia Axelrod arranges for the babysitter who cares for her children during the workday "to stay an extra hour one day every week so I can have a voice lesson." Her husband helps when he comes home.

- **Close to home:** Marion Berghahn kept up with music when her kids were little by fitting in spare half hours of piano playing at home. Others arranged for their chamber groups to meet at their homes so that no babysitter was needed.

- **Low key:** Ms. Ray's community band "plays easy music and I don't have to practice." Ms. Doyle doesn't do as much practicing as "before being married with a kid," but she adds that "having so many years of built-up skill allows me to learn pieces a lot quicker now."

Sarah Wright with her son, then age 20 months, and the tiny violin she bought for him to pretend to play "after he started wanting to play with mine," she says.

- **Involve the kids:** Ms. Doyle has a toy violin for her toddler to "play" alongside her at the start of a practice session. Once she starts practicing in earnest, her husband escorts the little one out of the room. Ms. Lang lets her son bow her violin with her. He also has a small ukulele that he puts under his chin to pretend to play like a violin. The Rays started early bringing their first child to each other's performances, although sometimes they each missed some of the music if their daughter started crying and had to be taken out of the room. "We kept trying and she learned how to behave. It turned out to be worth it because she's so supportive now and eager to join us," says Ms. Ray.

- **Music to go:** "Once I had kids and made the commitment to stay home with them, the combined isolation and loss of my sense of self increased my desire to express myself artistically," says Laurinda Karston, who has since gone back to work as an occupational therapist. "I had played guitar before and decided to return to it because of its portability and so I could play it quietly if needed while kids napped. I managed the practice time challenge by getting up early to practice and taking my guitar wherever I went with the kids. I was practicing in playrooms, sitting on the sidewalk, in parks, at friends' houses. After a few years I bought a SoloEtte silent guitar. It changed my life! I can practice without disturbing anyone at home and can work through new pieces at the park without the public suffering through mistakes." Dr. Darlene Ifill-Taylor did her singing practice on the go. "When my kids were little and were in their car seats, I would rehearse while taking them to school in the morning before going on to work. All three of them sing now," she recalls. Linda Rapp would practice flute sitting in the car with the windows rolled up when she waited to bring her kids home after their soccer practices.

- **Understanding teacher:** "Find teachers and classes that understand your current roles and time constraints," advises Ms. Karston. She says one teacher "would reprimand me if I did not have time to practice. My current teacher respects my schedule and ability to fit in practice or not."

- **Life stages:** "I felt guilty about not playing violin much after my child was born," says Ms. Wright. "A good friend who plays in the National Symphony Orchestra reminded me that it is totally okay to be in another season of life, and that the strong foundation I had acquired would serve me when I chose to go back to violin more seriously." Being aware of life stages helped Ms. Doyle deal with issues that arise at orchestra rehearsals. Most of the other players don't have young kids and don't realize what a challenge it is for a working mom to cope with a last-minute decision to start rehearsal an hour earlier. "I say, 'I'll be there regular time.' Sometimes the conductor can get frustrated but he values me being in the orchestra and realizes I have a family and full-time job. It's good to set boundaries. Otherwise you can easily get overwhelmed."

Setting Limits

"I go to music class one night a week. I go to jam another day. I go to an open mic once or twice a week," says Ms. Billingsley. "If I go see a friend's show or do anything else, I'm only really home two nights a week and I usually go to bed early because I'm so tired. I wake up early to practice guitar in the mornings. At least with the morning practice, I start the day off doing something to better myself and if the rest of the day is down the crapper, I still have had that time to myself." But despite the hectic schedule, she feels it's worth it. "Without music, a

> CLOSE UP: LINDA RAPP, FLUTIST, MATERIALS ENGINEER
>
> "From the time they were born, my kids learned how to go to sleep hearing a flute playing somewhere in the house," says Linda Rapp. "They were always in bed before I started. Practicing is something I do every night." Her kids also grew up thinking it is normal to have live chamber music in the house. Ms. Rapp joined a weekly chamber music group as soon as she moved to upstate New York to start an engineering job, before she was married or had kids. By the time the kids arrived, the group was meeting at her house every Thursday night. When her children were little, she recalls, "They'd get into sleeping bags and pretend they were worms on the floor. They would lie there, watch us, and listen, sometimes giggling." After the "music friends," as her kids called them, finished playing, everyone—kids included—gathered in the kitchen for chocolate cake. Her kids wound up playing instruments: clarinet for her son, and violin for her daughter. Her son stopped after high school. Her daughter stopped during art school but later joined a fiddling group.

normal day would be work, commute, dinner, TV. Tiny improvements in my playing that only I would notice feel worthy of celebration. I can't get that anywhere else."

Others of our team members also feel overwhelmed at times by the sheer number of their musical activities. Ms. Rosado reports feeling exhausted after a long day at work and an evening rehearsal or class, but has kept going because "I love performing. I really feel like I am in my element," she says.

Violist Julia Moline also came to have mixed feelings about her busy musical lineup. After just two years of living in Washington, DC, she became so much a part of its vibrant community of amateur music-makers that in one month there were nineteen days when she had an orchestra or chamber music performance or rehearsal. "That was wonderful in one way in that I was in the best playing shape of my entire life," says this violist who works for FEMA, the Federal Emergency

Management Agency. "It was stressful. I was burnt out. When you start playing in a regular quartet and a regular quintet and want to do readings with people and somebody wants to put together a small chamber orchestra, you don't want to say no to any of these things because the music sounds amazing and the people are amazing and you're flattered that somebody asked—and you don't want them to stop asking! But you have a life, and a job, and there are other parts of your life, like family and friends and dating."

So she set some limits. "I've already said no to a couple of things. I am starting to feel more confident that if I do say no to something, it won't be the last opportunity I'll have," she says. She and three friends, all in their 20s and 30s, joined together to form a string quartet that has begun getting gigs. That has let her realize that if offers don't come her way, she now knows how to pull together a group to play music she would like to perform. "You start to recognize what you like and what you don't. You have to prioritize. With my quartet, we're friends in addition to playing together, so it's easier to commit to them because it will be socially fulfilling as well as musically fulfilling." After all, as so many of our team members note, making music you love with people you enjoy being with is a big part of what they like about being musicians.

Violist Julia Moline (third from left) with her quartet when they performed at a fundraiser for the organization her father leads, the Interfaith Alliance.

Joe Guttentag at a piano lesson with Lois Narvey, his teacher at Levine Music in Washington, DC, preparing pieces he plans to perform at a recital for his upcoming 90th birthday. "Here I am," he wrote about this photo, "still practicing and taking lessons and making time for music. Still playing that Beethoven Sonata, incorrectly labeled 'facile.'"

7 Instructional Options

"WHEN I WAS a child, I was ambivalent about having lessons. I was intimidated by the teacher and very worried about making mistakes. The experience is completely different as an adult. I collaborate with the teacher, actively bring questions and concerns. My teacher focuses a lot on interpretation, touch, and relaxation. I am now very committed to practicing," says piano returnee Jonathan Pease. He is one of the many members of our advice panel who has been pleasantly surprised to discover that studying music as an adult can be more collaborative than it was as a youngster. This is true also of those who had more positive experiences with childhood music lessons. In this chapter, our panelists describe these new collaborative relationships and how the various kinds of instructional options they have used have enriched their musical lives.

"This relationship, though still one of expert and novice, has a more collegial dimension. My ability to ask questions that clarify confusion is something I don't think I could have brought to the teacher-student dynamic as a child," says Polly Kahn, commenting on the private cello lessons she has been taking recently. She had studied piano and clarinet as a youngster and began studying cello earlier as an adult, but then she put cello aside for thirty-two years.

Advice-team members who study in group classes have also encountered a new kind of teacher-student relationship. Dr. Susan Reeder, who made her return to guitar via group classes at a music school, observes, "When I was a child, the teachers seemed to be more interested in their own agendas. My teachers now have a plan but are also interested in what the students are interested in learning and will adjust the classes accordingly."

One factor in shaping the new instructional relationship is the awareness on both sides that it is the adult student who pays for the instruction. "As adults, we have the ability to have a give and take with the teacher," says cello returnee Peg Beyer. "If the teacher doesn't give you what you need, we also have the ability to change teachers."

Adult education researchers—in music and other fields—have found that a collaborative process works best with adult students, according to University of Minnesota education researcher David E. Myers. In addition to noting the importance of interactive teaching methods, his studies also support the findings of the neurological studies described in chapter 2—that adults are capable of learning new skills throughout the lifespan.

Music educators interviewed for this book are on board with this collaborative philosophy, as they explain later in the chapter. They are aware of the feelings of self-doubt that adult students may bring with them to lessons. Many are particularly careful not to scare away potential students with the "R" word—recitals—those public displays that caused so much anxiety for so many during childhood. Instructors have come up with a variety of ways to handle the recital issue, as will be described in more detail later in the chapter. Such strategies seem to be working. For whatever reason, nearly a third of the questionnaire completers on our advice team like recitals now. About a quarter tolerate them as being useful, 10 percent still hate them, and the rest say they either refuse to do them or don't have to do them given how they are involved with music now. Judging from our team members' experiences, fear of recitals need not pose an insurmountable obstacle to having music lessons.

Other issues, however, have kept some on our advice team from pursuing instruction. Only about half of the questionnaire completers were studying with a teacher when they filled out their questionnaire. Many without a teacher had studied with one earlier in their adult years, although a few never had a teacher as an adult. Those who didn't have a teacher cited three main reasons: no time, too expensive, or not feeling the need. All three concerns are addressed in this chapter.

For help with finding time, advice-team members offer flexible scheduling suggestions. For cost concerns, our team members suggest some money-saving tips. As for the benefit that instruction can provide, most who have studied with a teacher during adulthood are pleased with what they have gained, including those who are quite accomplished musicians but have made new discoveries while working with a teacher or coach. Laurel Kuxhaus, the very busy oboist described in chapter 3, explains, "I take lessons from time to time with a teacher who identifies and fixes problems that I didn't even know I had." Didi Correa, a New York registered nurse who is quite serious about piano, keeps on with weekly lessons with a teacher who is helping her move to a new artistic level. She appreciates that this teacher "is detail oriented in the artistry of the music and emphasizes the importance of listening, helpful in order to play technically challenging pieces." In the following pages our team members describe qualities to look for in searching for teachers and coaches who can both encourage and inspire.

The New Relationship

"My teacher is very flexible and understands that adult students have different goals and priorities than kids. I have much more control over the lesson content now as an adult. I usually choose the repertoire and what aspects to focus on. We do less technical work and it is less rigorous than my childhood instruction," says Dr. Lili Barouch, who returned to violin after a gap of fourteen years. Dr. Elizabeth Nevrkla appreciates that her teacher doesn't have a set roster of solo cello pieces for her to study but "is happy to work on whatever music I am preparing to perform" in chamber music groups or community orchestras. In contrast, Dr. Alvin Crawford is eager to focus on technical polishing in the lessons he has with a clarinetist from the Cincinnati Symphony Orchestra. Dr. Crawford's goal is to maintain his ability to play fast passages "without blurring them" so that he can keep his position as lead clarinet in his community band. "Each year there's someone better that comes in and I want to be able to hold my chair," he reports.

Dr. Alvin Crawford playing clarinet with Cincinnati's Queen City Concert Band.

Others have different goals—to master jazz skills, play more expressively, expand their vocal range. They have managed to find a mentor willing to tailor the instruction to fit their needs. Goals may change over time, as does the role an instructor plays. Marilyn Reichstein, a retired New York graphic designer, likes the teacher she has now, who is "encouraging and supportive." But she is also still grateful to the teacher who helped change her whole approach to music when she returned to a serious pursuit of piano during her late 50s. She explains that the earlier teacher "changed my life. I learned to listen better, play more expressively."

Many team members are glad that their teachers realize, as Bill Freshwater's does, that "we are adults and have other demands on our time. The teacher needs to be able to change a lesson if you were not able to learn the assigned piece. I am lucky that my teacher could do that. We shift to sight-reading," says this Washington accountant who returned to piano after a gap of more than thirty years. John Warshawsky is glad that his viola teacher understands "that there are times when work gets in the way of playing. She is very positive. I never feel that I've been a slacker, and I strive to play better with her."

"Someone who teaches adult amateurs has to be prepared for a lot of questions and to deal with the student's frustration," observes Dr. Nancy Bridges, a Maryland physician who has asked a lot of questions since starting cello in her 50s. Carol Eisenbise, a newcomer to double bass, notes that some of her questions arise because "the teacher may assume adult students know more than they do. I have to keep reminding my teacher that I don't know about that technique or that I need help on fingering or that I never heard of that famous jazz bassist because this is the first time I've played jazz." Michelle Billingsley speaks up during her voice lessons to ask questions "instead of worrying that I'm doing something wrong." But she advises, "I don't ask until I've tried to figure it out myself. Private lessons are expensive and every minute counts."

Charmarie Blaisdell's vocal teacher anticipates her questions by explaining "why we are doing certain exercises. As a kid, I was never exposed to how to improve my singing voice." This retired professor is pleased with the progress she has made in the lessons she has been having since joining a Maine community chorus when she was in her 70s. Her teacher has helped her realize that "I have a better soprano voice than I thought I had!"

Julia Steinmetz's singing lessons helped her learn that she is a better performer than she thought she was. Before starting voice lessons—which she won in a silent auction at her children's suburban New York preschool—she had only been singing informally around the house. After that first batch of lessons, she kept on with the teacher for a few years and discovered that she has a flair for performing. "We started with Italian arias, but when I got into rock and roll, he helped me with that, too," says this stay-at-home mom. She now sings lead vocals with a band she put together that plays at open mic nights. "It's worth it to take lessons," she notes. "You may think you sound one way in your bathroom, but to actually perform is another skill set. The singing part came easier. I had to work with him on the performing."

Several team members who are seasoned musicians enjoy working with teachers who use a method that encourages students to be in charge of adjusting their own technique. French horn returnee Paul Seeley says his teacher stresses that it's important for a student to "listen closely to every detail of your music-making, forcing you to decide what musical effect you want to produce. When you're younger, your teachers are more directive: 'Do this. This is the right way.' Now, I need to figure out myself what sound and musical effect I want to produce and the right way to produce that." Kathy Fleming experiences something similar with her viola da gamba lessons. "My teacher is careful not to discourage my thought processes or to correct fingers and bowings as I play through something, even if I'm not exactly correct, because she wants me to think and she trusts me to figure it out."

Less of a focus on the one right way to do things appeals to many of our team members. "When I was a kid, there was a lot of pressure, from my parents and my teachers. Now playing music is more lighthearted and relaxed. My teacher is easy going and understanding of what I am trying to get out of my music. He knows that I am doing this for fun but that I also want to improve," observes Sarah Monte, a Tennessee clarinetist and jeweler. Carol Katz's bass guitar teacher encourages her "to keep going even if I make mistakes" and to think of mistakes as "an improvisation or a solo. It's pure enjoyment without stress because as an adult I don't have to worry about exams or being marked. Positive encouragement works best with me and bolsters my self-confidence," she explains. Bette Pounds has also seen a lessening of perfectionism in her music-making, partly because she is learning to play jazz saxophone now in a New Horizons ensemble. "I studied classical music formally as a kid. My piano teacher was very rigid," recalls this New York psychotherapist. "Now I study jazz on the alto sax. I've had to conquer my wish to play all the 'right' notes since this is all about being informal and expressing myself within the structure of jazz theory."

CLOSE UP: DR. DEBORAH EDGE, DOUBLE BASS PLAYER, RETIRED PHYSICIAN

"I re-started playing double bass in my 40s when I had a full time job, two young children, and a wonderful supportive husband," says Dr. Deborah Edge. She began taking lessons with a teacher "who changed my approach when he beat into me: 'Whenever possible, play beautifully.' No one ever before had suggested that bass playing could be beautiful, and that I could do it! He would ask why I played a passage the way I did or what kind of a sound I was trying to make. He is the first person who challenged me to think critically about my playing." He has retired and she has a new teacher now, who is also terrific. "Often when practicing or at rehearsals, I will hear that first teacher's voice, 'Why are you playing this way? How can you make it sound better?' He gets a lot of credit for inspiring me to play more."

Educators on Board

The educators interviewed for this book report that they have adapted their teaching methods to fit the needs of the increasing number of adult students they are teaching. "When you teach an adult student, you have to come at it with a different attitude than when you're teaching younger students," says Louise Hildreth-Grasso, a violin instructor who teaches both kids and adults at Peabody Preparatory in Baltimore. "With adult students it's, 'How can I help you learn what you really want to learn?'" As she noted in chapter 5, adult students require more encouragement than kids. "Especially those who start as adults. The ones who started as teenagers pretty much say, 'I know I can play—how well can I play, what's the hardest piece I can play?' But with beginners, it's all about encouraging them not to give up." The skills she teaches are the same as those she teaches to children, but not the approach. "One of the biggest impediments with adults is that they have jobs. With an adult student, I am not going yell at you that you haven't practiced when you had to do three surgeries that day. The point of the lesson is different. If they haven't had much time to practice, that's okay. Come to the lesson and at least you will have practiced once—at the lesson. Let's work with what we've got. Just keep showing up. That's the key thing. I play a lot of duets with my adult students. They record them to show their families. The recording sounds good, to make them feel they're progressing."

"My approach is to teach people first. Teach music second. Assess where they're at and what they're going to need," says Mark Dvorak, guitar and folk music instructor at Chicago's Old Town School of Folk Music. Patrick O'Donnell teaches piano and serves as a vocal coach for adults at Levine Music, a community music school in Washington, DC. His goal is "to create opportunities for the students wherever they are, to help them get better. I want them to enjoy doing music at whatever level they want. I help people find a level where they can enjoy it and maintain that enjoyment and not have it turn into a chore." He spends time in lessons showing a student how to practice, how to approach a tricky passage in different ways. "They understand that if they don't put in a certain amount of work, they won't get results. I try to help them figure out what that amount of time is and how to get the most out of it. They're busy adults. I try to help them with time management. They will get better gradually."

Finding Instruction

Of the questionnaire completers on our advice panel who study with a teacher, about half found their instructors as a result of a recommendation from a music-related colleague, such as a fellow ensemble member or someone they met at a summer program. Other recommendations came from former teachers. About one-fourth contacted a local music school and chose among its roster of faculty, or they asked for recommendations from a music store, college music department, or a professional orchestra. A few searched online. Others asked to take lessons with someone they had seen perform, had performed with themselves, or had observed leading a master class.

Several members of our advice panel study with professional musicians, as Dr. Crawford does, but a few team members warn that being a professional musician is no guarantee of being a good teacher. Max Weiss learned that the hard way. Shortly after graduating from college, she began taking lessons with a young cellist in a professional orchestra. "I had always taken cello lessons and I couldn't imagine life without them. He didn't understand why a 21-year-old woman with no aspirations to be a professional would continue taking lessons. Looking back on it, I realize he was dead wrong, but at the time I thought, 'Huh. Why am I taking lessons? To what end?' So I stopped," explains this Baltimore magazine editor. She joined a community orchestra for a while, but then became too busy at work to continue and put cello on hold for several years. She finally came back when her sister, who had become active in chamber music, urged her to start playing again.

That insensitive teacher put a damper on Ms. Weiss's enthusiasm for music for quite a while, illustrating why pre-lesson screening is a smart idea. Several team members had a sample lesson or signed up for only a limited number of lessons to be sure the teacher-student relationship would work before making a longer commitment. Marilyn Hanna-Myrick conducted careful research when she decided to start clarinet lessons again in her 70s, after not having had a teacher during the many years she had played in a community band and with chamber music groups. "I wanted to improve my technique, to play in a more advanced ensemble," says this retired librarian. "I asked my band director for references, went to hear the teacher perform, checked out her credentials, had an introductory lesson to see if we were a good match and if she would cover what I wanted to learn. My teacher knows that I am mainly taking lessons for fun and structures the lessons to achieve that goal." The trial lesson worked out. "I am still enjoying the lessons."

Dr. Morris Schoeneman shopped around for teachers when he returned to violin. "I experimented with several music schools and teachers until I found a teacher with whom I could bond. This teacher understands and can work with some of the difficulties older students have. She also is willing to work with me on genres other than classical music, such as klezmer," says this retired physician. Sofia Axelrod also believes in searching carefully, after having been discouraged initially with teachers whom she felt had "no idea how to teach singing. It was frustrating to look for a teacher to help me with my technique who would not harm my voice," says this singer/neuroscientist. She eventually found a teacher who "is able to teach me how to sing wonderfully. She can play the piano so she can accompany me during the lesson. She is a warm and supportive person who makes me feel like I can do anything."

Pre-lesson discussions with a potential teacher can help make sure that teacher and student have similar goals for the instruction and that the teacher understands the constraints on the student's time. Also important to discuss are physical issues that the student might have and what strategies the teacher has for lessening the risk of music-related strains and pains. For singers, otolaryngologist Dr. Robert T. Sataloff suggests a few warning signs to look for in screening voice teachers. "Singing teachers who know what they're doing, start with exercises. So if you go to a teacher and all you get are songs, you're not working with a pro who knows how to train and build a voice," he says. "If someone is hoarse at the end of singing lessons or if singing the way the teacher advises causes pain, that's another warning sign about the teacher." The next chapter discusses ways to avoid injuries and how to cope if they should occur.

Even after finding a terrific teacher, there may come a time when the student decides to shop around again. Several team members report that this happened when teachers spent too much time chatting, eating up valuable lesson time minutes. Violist Dr. Marc Mann notes another reason for making a change. "I learned a lot from each of my earlier teachers but when I stopped getting better (or the teacher ran out of ways to help me get better) then I moved on," says this Connecticut physician. Guitarist Joseph Arden explains why he likes to sign up for classes with different teachers at the music school he attends, "It provides a nice breadth."

One-on-One Lessons

Most of our questionnaire completers who receive instruction study with a teacher one-on-one. A prime benefit of this approach is receiving personalized attention geared to a student's individual needs. The majority of these private lessons aren't done under the auspices of a music school, although in some cases the student may have first made contact with the teacher through a music school, but for various reasons, the lessons moved off-site. Those who study with an independent teacher may prefer the potential for flexible scheduling and not being tied to a set semester plan, as well as the possibility of negotiating lower fees than with a school. Sofia Axelrod has voice lessons in her own home or in a music room where she works, a time-saving benefit for this working mother of two. Her teacher also agreed to lower the per-lesson fee so Ms. Axelrod could afford to have two lessons a week.

There are also advantages for those who choose to have their lessons at a music school because of all the extras a school can offer, such as courses and ensembles that students can participate in along with the lessons. Harriet Rafter feels that becoming involved in the life of her school, San Francisco Community Music Center, has helped her stick with violin lessons, rather than quitting as she did in the past whenever she grew discouraged. She is in the school's certificate program. This provides a structure for her learning, with benchmark recitals that give a sense of accomplishment and supportive feedback. Certificate program students must take a music theory class and an ensemble class in addition to one-on-one lessons. She also writes book reviews for the school newsletter. "I value and feel connected to the organization and somehow that makes a big difference," says this retired administrative assistant. Rufus Browning, the octogenarian composer, attends this same San Francisco school and makes the most of its resources. He takes weekly lessons in voice and composition, and a music theory class, too.

Most team members have one-on-one lessons on a regular schedule: once a week, every two weeks, or once a month. Others have them on an as-needed basis, which is Roland Wilk's choice. "I have a lesson with the principal bassoonist of the Canadian Opera about once every three months, whenever I run into challenges," he explains. "I heard his solos in Mozart's 'Magic Flute' and wanted to play like him. He is encouraging as well as critical. He focuses on helping me achieve my own potential." Alex Jones does something similar, having a lesson with a clarinetist in the Pittsburgh Symphony Orchestra "when I'm working up something significant, like a solo with an orchestra," he explains. Ms. Steinmetz doesn't take regular lessons any longer with the voice teacher who helped her find her way with singing, but "if there's a song I'm having a problem with, I would go back and have a lesson," she says.

What if the carefully selected teacher moves away? When that happened to Dr. Henry Wang, he continued having violin lessons online with that teacher via Skype, an online video conferencing service. "It's easier to communicate physical things and difficult fingerings in person, but for now with my busy professional schedule, Skype is perfect, when sketchy Internet service is not getting in the way," he explains. Dr. Jeff Alfriend uses some technical tricks to improve the weekly Skype clarinet lessons he has, connecting online from his home on the Hawaiian island of Maui to his teacher's home in New Jersey. On a visit to New York City several years ago to buy a new clarinet, he asked the store for recommendations of clarinet teachers who would do Skype lessons. "I'm kind of it for clarinet on Maui," says this retired veterinarian. That's how he started Skyping with a clarinetist from the New Jersey Symphony. "For the teacher to get better vision and sound, he puts himself on no picture, just sound. I can't see him, but he can see me. We can both hear each other. When I do a passage that needs to be in strict tempo, I put on the metronome so he'll hear the clicking and can tell if it's a Skype

Dr. Rena Johnson had been singing in a Washington, DC, church choir for several years, becoming one of the cantors who lead the congregation's singing. Her choir director thought her voice was too soft, not big and brassy like others in the choir. "I like it soft because love is soft, gentle, and kind. Love is what I want the congregation to hear," says Dr. Johnson. Nevertheless, she had her voice analyzed and began voice lessons at Levine Music with Charles Williams, an opera singer in his 70s who still performs professionally. He is teaching her how to protect her vocal cords while she develops her own particular voice. She explains that he tells her to " 'Play *your* instrument. Don't try to imitate someone *else's* sound.' He is showing me that I can have a classically trained voice and still do jazz and Broadway. It takes time, but something special happens when you allow your voice to develop. It's nice when someone in church comes up and says, 'What you sang really touched me. I've never heard a voice like that before.' "

delay or my playing that is uneven. He turns the camera on if he needs to demonstrate something. Sometimes he asks to see out my window, to see what Maui looks like. It's fun for me to see snow in New Jersey."

Group Classes

Nearly a quarter of questionnaire completers who were receiving instruction when they filled out their questionnaires were doing so in group classes. They were generally enthusiastic about the supportive environment of the group experience, as well as the lower cost of group lessons compared to private instruction. A few pointed out an inherent problem with group classes, however. Progress may be slowed if some members of the class aren't keeping up with the others.

Not all group classes take place at a music school. Christine Anderson-Morehouse and her friends in Maine organized their own group class by hiring a teacher to help them learn to sing. Janet Howard took a group ukulele class through an adult education program called OLLI (Osher Lifelong Learning Institute). OLLI classes, which are geared to students age 50 and over, are inexpensive and are sponsored by the Bernard Osher Foundation at more than a hundred US colleges and universities, including at the University of Kentucky where Ms. Howard took her class. Course topics depend on whatever someone in that community wants to teach. "I really like the uke," says this retired schoolteacher who has played piano off and on since childhood, but not ukulele until this OLLI class. She and some classmates have joined a uke ensemble—Hot Cookies of the Bluegrass—that plays at retirement communities. The next few sections describe the main kinds of group classes that our team members have taken.

Music is in my head all the time now. I like that.

—Janet Howard, ukulele player, pianist, singer, retired schoolteacher

Single-instrument Classes

Lydia Zieglar joined a group cello class taught by one of the cello teachers who had been working with her son at Peabody Preparatory. "I love the low stress environment," says Ms. Zieglar, noting that the teacher "never makes us feel bad if we haven't been able to practice much during a particular week. She's good at explaining technique and adapting her explanations to the particular student. It's actually instructional to observe her helping a classmate." Ms. Hildreth-Grasso, who teaches both private lessons and group violin classes at Peabody, points out that "some adults want a group class because they feel more comfortable when everyone is having as hard a time as they are. When everyone sounds terrible, you don't feel as bad. Finding support is important. The group class is also a good taster. It's less expensive than private lessons. They can rent an instrument so that the outlay is not particularly high and then figure out whether they actually want to do this."

Some group students later move to private lessons. "The further they go in their playing, the harder it is to teach them in groups because each one would develop certain technical problems and I do not have the time to tailor the teaching to each student's problems," explains Bai-Chi Chen, who is Ms. Zieglar's group cello teacher. Deborah Wythe started with a group piano class and then went on to study privately with the group class instructor. "I miss the group experience, but my teacher's students meet together two or three times a semester for workshops, master classes, and recitals, so that helps meld us as a group," she reports.

Digital Piano Classes

The group classes that Ms. Wythe took involved small groups of students learning to play on acoustic pianos, with two Steinway grands to a classroom. These classes were part of the evening division of the Juilliard School in New York. Other schools use digital pianos for group classes, sometimes with multiple digitals linked together in a piano-lab set-up. The students often wear headphones so that everyone in the class can play at once, working on whatever song the teacher is presenting.

Group piano instruction with digital pianos is often referred to as Recreational Music Making, which is designed to make pianos seem accessible and fun. The goal is to prepare students to play for their own enjoyment, not to become concert musicians. Yamaha Clavinovas are often used in piano-lab classes. They have a built-in audio player that can play audio files of a song that's being learned. Hearing background accompaniment as the students play can help them keep to the right rhythm. The soundtrack can be slowed down as needed. In addition, the piano's output can be altered so that what the student plays can sound like other instruments than piano, adding an element of fun.

Rebecca Bellelo offers piano-lab classes at her school, Piano Pathways, in Baton Rouge, Louisiana. Her group classes range in size from three to six students, all wearing headphones while playing Clavinovas. The pianos are linked together to a central system so everyone can work on the same piece at the same time, while wearing headphones. "I can see and watch everybody's hands as they play and can tell when we need to stop and work on something," she explains. "Or we can take our headphones off and just play out loud." For students who have acoustic pianos at home, using the digital piano "can be a little adjustment initially," but they are able to adapt. "They do notice the differences though, like the weight or actual touch of the keys, the shape and edges of the black keys. But I remind them that they would have to adjust for any piano they play on other than their own piano at home."

There's a difference of opinion among music educators about digital pianos. Some teachers and schools prefer teaching with acoustic pianos because they believe that the sensation of pressing down on the keys of a digital piano is too different from an acoustic piano, offering a less nuanced range of tones that pianists can create by altering how they press on the keys. Those teachers feel that too much is lost in terms of expressivity with digitals. Rebecca Bellelo feels that high-quality Clavinovas can work well for students "for some time, for developing correct technique. If a student seems to be advancing extremely quickly or has a special goal in mind, I have a discussion with the student about different instruments and I might suggest something different." For private piano lessons at her school, she uses both acoustic and digital pianos. She feels that piano-lab classes using digital pianos "work best with groups that start together as beginners. Returnees can be placed in a group class, but typically opt for private lessons because they are used to that lesson format. If people have played piano before, it can be hard to fit them into a group because they play at a different level than a beginner with absolutely no musical experience." One of our advice-team members, Philip Knieper, takes private lessons with her, practicing at home on a hybrid piano that can switch from acoustic to digital, as noted in chapter 6. Marvin Bishop, a retired computer administrator who earlier taught himself to play recorder and dulcimer, is a piano-lab student at this school. The class size is small enough so the teacher can "work with us on our own level," he says. "Piano is the hardest instrument I have ever tried to learn. It has been challenging but rewarding."

Rebecca Bellelo (left) teaching in a piano-lab classroom of her school, Piano Pathways, in Baton Rouge, Louisiana. Advice-team member Marvin Bishop is at one of the Clavinovas.

Learning-by-Ear Classes

Several of our advice-team members attend classes at Chicago's Old Town School of Folk Music, which specializes in teaching by ear, in the folk tradition, rather than by using sheet music and scores. These are the classes that helped Steven Duke become a more confident guitarist and gave him the courage to sing. He explains the process used in those classes: "The two teachers play through a song a few times to get it in our ears. Then they have us join, and they call out the chord changes. Then they stop calling the chord changes, and start lining out the words. After we've got a pretty good handle on that, they demonstrate a harmony or two and break us into groups to play or sing the melody or a harmony. Then they bring us all back together to put the parts together. It's a great way to learn. I've been taking this same eight-week class over and over for more than three years."

Mr. Arden has taken both private and group classes at this school but prefers the group arrangement because "it gives me the opportunity to play along with others in a safe environment." Communications consultant Lizabeth McDonald prefers the learning by ear that she has done at Old Town School as an adult with guitar, banjo, and fiddle, rather than the score-based instruction she had as a child on flute and cello. Learning by ear "is focused on telling a story, getting people to join in, without so much polish or formality, to touch people at their core. It's magical, more free and accepting," she says. "I am more confident as a musician."

Realizing that it is possible to learn by ear can remove another roadblock that may keep some adults from getting into music—those who feel that because they never learned to read music as a child, there is no hope for them musically. As students of guitar have discovered, not all music is notated the way music is for piano, strings, woodwinds, brass, and voice—those five-line staffs with little black notes and symbols. Notation systems for guitars are more pictorial. A guitar tab (tabulature) is a chart with six lines representing a guitar's six strings, with numbers placed on the lines showing whether to press down and, if so, on which crossways fret line on the guitar's neck. Written scores for rock drummers are also rather easy to master, as drum newcomer Janet Blume discovered. There are no symbols noting what key the piece is in, no sharps or flats to remember. "It just says to hit this drum or that one, how hard to hit, and the time signature," she says. "I'm fairly tone deaf, not knowing whether things are in tune or not. So drums work out well for me."

Ensemble Classes

Many music schools offer ensemble classes that give adults a chance to perform with an instrumental or vocal ensemble while having teacher or coach guide the group and offer instruction during rehearsals. These classes are particularly helpful for those who don't feel confident enough to join a community band, orchestra, or chorus. "I take an ensemble class that is exactly at my basic level," says Harriet Rafter. "We get along quite well. We have a good teacher, too. The warmth between the four students makes the experience particularly welcoming." The concert band, jazz band, and rock band ensemble classes that Philip Koch has taken at Seattle's Music Center of the Northwest have helped him regain his trumpet skills after not playing for about fifty years. "It has been more challenging than I thought it would be, but I have persisted and am enjoying playing in three bands. The instructors are very patient with our rate of learning, and very clear with instruction. I plan on playing as long as I keep improving," says this retired aeronautical engineer.

In addition to her ukulele classes, Ms. Howard also signs up regularly for the OLLI chorus at the University of Kentucky. "Our director is a retired high school choral teacher," she says. "He loves teaching and working with our group. He challenges us and praises us. It's great."

Emily Chen, who has played violin since childhood and plays in a community orchestra, has for several years been taking the music theater class at the Old Town School of Music. A lawyer who is staying home while her children are young, she had taken her kids to that school for a toddler's music program. "When I thought about taking a class to get me out of the house more, I zeroed in on this one, as I am a lifelong musical theatre 'nut.' I had no singing experience going into this class, and it didn't (still doesn't) matter. We perform a forty-five-minute showcase each term. These are always enjoyable because they are the culmination of sixteen weeks of hard work and great collegiality."

Jeremy Castillo, who teaches rock band classes at Levine Music, feels ensemble classes at a school offer an advantage for students, instead of them trying to form their own bands by connecting online with people to jam with, who may or may not show up as promised. "We try to be as organized as possible, giving them charts to take home and learn, having a schedule, an organized rehearsal, and a space to rehearse, so they know that every Wednesday for the next sixteen weeks, they'll have band class. I want people to play what they've always wanted to play. I try to make every song we do to be a student request. We have a live performance at the end that becomes the motivator to practice and get everything together. We go to a bar or other local venue and all our bands play in public for the other bands, family, and friends, or whoever is walking by."

New Horizons

With New Horizons beginner-level bands, orchestras, and choruses, instruction takes place not only during rehearsals but also in pull-out group teaching sessions in which newcomers receive basic instruction on how to play their instruments. As newcomers become more skilled, they can move up to more advanced New Horizons ensembles. Roy Ernst, now an emeritus Eastman School of Music professor, founded the New Horizons International Music Association in 1991. He not only saw a need for finding a way to involve the growing demographic of older adults in meaningful, stimulating, and engaging activities, but he also realized that lifelong learning was possible. As noted earlier, there are more than two hundred New Horizons bands, orchestras, and choruses in the United States, Canada, and a few other countries. Geared primarily to those age 50 and over, but often including younger adults as well, these groups are sometimes connected with music schools and the instruction is provided by the school's faculty. For other groups, the instruction is given by experienced musicians in the community. Membership costs are modest.

All of the members of our advice team who play in New Horizons ensembles are pleased with the ensembles and the instruction they receive. "I had never dared to play music with others before because I learn rather slowly. I never felt I was precise enough in keeping tempo and observing dynamics," says Brenda Lee, a retired educational counselor who plays saxophone in the Montréal New Horizons Band, which has links to McGill University. Earlier she had taken lessons sporadically in a variety of instruments—guitar, saxophone, piano, and ukulele. Joining this band has made her feel committed to really mastering tenor saxophone so she can hold her own in the band. "I seem more confident now. There are teachers and coaches available during the New Horizons rehearsals and sectional practices. I do both the beginners' as well as the intermediate band practice. Playing with a group is helping me recognize rhythms more easily and I am more aware of dynamic markings. I don't ignore them anymore. It is fun and uplifting to even play a scale beautifully, believe me!"

Some New Horizons members sign up for private lessons in addition to the support they receive in the group sessions. Some also play in ensembles that aren't part of New Horizons. Joyce Richardson continues to play in the recorder ensemble she joined many years before starting to learn to play euphonium with the New Horizons Band of New York's Third Street Music School. She supplements the euphonium instruction she receives in that band, with one-on-one lessons every two to four weeks with a teacher she found through another music school.

Uneek Lowe receives violin tutoring from one of the music students who helps with the New Horizons String Orchestra sponsored by the University of Cincinnati's College-Conservatory of Music (CCM). "I have a neurological disorder and at times the instructions in rehearsal are too fast. One-on-one tutoring after the group class helps," says this retired health insurance technician. "I don't let my illness stop me from learning and enjoying my violin."

"About sixty percent of our members are beginners. About forty percent have played a string instrument before or some other musical instrument," says BettyAnne Gottlieb, the music director of the CCM New Horizons strings program. She uses Suzuki learning-by-ear methods as well as note-reading instruction while working with the beginners' group. "When they are ready, they move up to the more advanced group. Their main issue is getting over the need to be perfect. Adults have been engrained with the idea that if it's not perfect, we don't want to share what we've done. We use a light-hearted approach so there's no stigma in doing something wrong when they play together. We don't call them 'mistakes.' We call them 'interpretations' or 'composing' and laugh about them. We talk it through and get them to release that need to be perfect. I give them a practice plan to take home with ways to practice. I feel that everyone is capable of learning. They can learn to play and to match pitch, too."

"I spend about twenty minutes or more in each rehearsal on vocal pedagogy, basic music skills, although a fair amount of teaching is going on during the entire rehearsal," says Juli Elliot, conductor of the New Horizons Chorus at the Eastman School of Music in Rochester, New York. "Most have had some experience with choral singing, but about ten percent have never been in a chorus before. I give them vocalization and breathing exercises to do at home. There's no pressure. We're not a competitive show choir. We're a chorus that is about continuing to grow, having a lot of fun, and giving back to the community by performing at YMCA's and senior centers."

The Cincinnati New Horizons String Orchestra's first members, including two on our advice team in the first long row: cellist Amy Dennison and violinist Uneek Lowe (third and fourth from left). Program director BettyAnne Gottlieb kneels in front with a viola.

Coaching

About half of the questionnaire completers who were receiving instruction did so with coaches, often in addition to other ways they were interacting with teachers. Many worked with coaches in the summer programs they attended. Others enrolled in chamber music workshops and classes that are offered by music schools or other music organizations.

TV reporter Magee Hickey found her way back into flute by enrolling in a chamber music class at the Lucy Moses School in New York City. "I had always been playing a little bit with friends, frustrated, and often out of tune. So I made a commitment to practice more," she says. She was nearing her 60s and realized "you're not going to be here forever, so if this is what you want to do, you better go do it." She thought the chamber music class would give her a reason to practice, and it has. Through the class, Ms. Hickey formed a trio with a pianist and with clarinetist Sarah Monte, another member of our advice panel. They took the class together for more than three years, performing at the class's recitals and elsewhere. "I don't want to do solo playing. It's the collaborative part that is so much fun," says Ms. Hickey. She studies privately now with the class's coach and tries to practice an hour or more a day. Having a coach helps keep the trio together. "We're all at different levels. We need a coach to tell us who is getting off the beat, how the intonation is. Sometimes she conducts us." Meghan Carye, who teaches chamber music classes at New England Conservatory in Boston, agrees that the coach-as-mediator is an important benefit of these classes. "If students are working on a piece that is slightly above their range, it's more attainable with having a guide along the way," she says.

Sometimes people form their own chamber music group and enroll in a class together. Pianist Dr. Stephen Kamin teamed up with a clarinetist, violinist, and cellist to be coached in a chamber music program at Rutgers University. Flutist Heather Rosado has enrolled in this same program because she wanted to perform more difficult repertoire than she plays in her community band. She found her playing partner, a guitarist, through the class. "I would normally never get to play with a guitarist," she says. Bassist Daniel Savin enjoys chamber music classes because "the faculty pick interesting pieces, my fellow musicians are highly motivated amateurs, and I don't have to organize anything."

Others of our team members connect with fellow musicians on their own to play chamber music. These independent groups sometimes receive coaching, too, by signing up for chamber music workshops together, or by reaching out on their own to professional musicians whom they hire to coach their groups.

Ms. Weiss now relies on coaches for her instruction, having recovered from her earlier misadventure with that cello teacher who didn't understand her goals. "I now fully believe that the young professional cellist who didn't understand lessons for lessons' sake was wrong. Making music is something that enriches my life, so why not continue to learn more about it? That being said, with all of my work commitments, the occasional coaching model works better for me now. I sought out a great professional cellist I know to give me coaching on a solo cello piece before a concert," she says. She plays in a trio with her sister, a pianist. When preparing for a performance, "we like to have at least one coaching session. My sister has great connections in the amateur music world and is my point person to find coaches. Some are better than others. When we do ensemble work, we love someone who talks about the big picture and helps us shape the piece musically, as opposed to someone who focuses too much on one instrument."

Ellen Tenenbaum has found another way to receive coaching for piano pieces she is preparing. "I have been taking a group class called Piano Performance at Levine Music for more than seven years," she explains. "Every month, a different faculty member teaches, as a master class. Each of the four students will play something and get coaching from the teacher and input from the other students. It is so helpful to hear these other voices." Music schools and other music organizations often offer

Professional violist Korine Fujiwara coaches clarinetist Georgiana McReynolds and violist Maggie Speier in Mozart's quintet for clarinet and strings at the Bennington Chamber Music Conference summer program.

master classes that are open to the public. In master classes, audience members watch a professional musician or noted teacher offer comments on performances that a few students do during the class. There is much that audience members can learn from a master teacher's comments even if they play different instruments than those featured in the class. Some master classes by well-known musicians are available on YouTube, such as the ones by James Galway that Ms. Rosado enjoys or those by Jascha Heifetz that Dr. Schoeneman likes.

Ensembles and choral groups often provide coaching, either during rehearsals or in separate sessions that the ensemble arranges. Summer programs, which often offer coaching, are discussed in chapter 9.

Music Theory and Sight-Singing

About half of our questionnaire completers have taken courses on music theory or sight-singing. Music theory involves learning the language and structure of music—the nuts and bolts of how music is put together. This includes the music notation system, rules of harmony, common rhythm patterns, chords, and so on. Sight-singing is an aspect of music theory that involves becoming familiar with how the basic intervals in music sound—such as what it sounds like to go from the first note in a scale to the third note, or from the first note to the fifth. Training the ears in this way allows someone to be able to identify and sing those intervals just by seeing the notes on the page. One aspect of sight-singing involves learning the solfège system in which each note is sung using its musical name in a scale—do, re, me, and so on. The notes are also identified by their numeric position in the scale. Some team members received music theory and sight-singing training during high school or college. Others have explored these topics during their adult years through classes, online courses, books, or as part of their regular music lessons.

Most feel that learning about music theory and sight-singing has been worthwhile. "It has helped me to transpose, to figure out a song by ear, and to try to sing on key by recognizing that there are patterns and intervals that commonly occur and can be decoded," says guitarist Ted Dawson. Jazz saxophonist Steve DeMont says the Jazz Improv Theory class he took has been "a real foundation for me, although I try not to think about it too much while I'm improvising, to empty my mind of all that, but it's very helpful when you're practicing and working through a tune." Phyllis Kaiden took a class in music theory as an adult not long after she started on viola and found that it "filled in gaps in my knowledge and helped me understand musical structure. I can now recognize musical patterns that help with phrasing and playing musically."

"I did not have any training in sight-reading or music theory until I was in my 30s and found two community music schools in Chicago that offered classes at night and on weekends," says Mark Sherkow, a university office manager who sings in a community chorus. "I have trouble recognizing keys, intervals, and modulations automatically. The teacher of one of the sight-reading classes suggested the idea of writing the solfège numbers above the notes on a score. These numbers show more clearly the intervals that needs to be sung, as well as patterns that might repeat such as, for example, 1-3-5 and then 2-4-6. This helps me while working on a piece in rehearsal and also allows me to practice silently, so I can work on music on the bus or during lunch at work."

Sight-singing isn't only for singers, however. Violinist Laura Rice has taken three sight-singing classes given in a music school's evening division. "So very helpful," she says. "Excellent training in rhythm and ear training." This kind of training can also help those who want to compose new music or transcribe music that they hear, such as transcribing a jazz solo heard on a CD.

Sight-singing classes make it easier for singers to audition for high-level choruses. At first, Eloise Bensberg didn't realize that sight-singing is different from the sight-reading she could do on piano. With piano sight-reading, she looks at the score to see which piano key to press and then hits the key. With sight-singing, after seeing a note on the page, she has to pull a tone out of thin air to sing—much harder, as she discovered during her first chorus audition. "They give you the starting note and then you have to figure it out. That's what led me to sight-singing classes. Now I am able to pick out the tune on my own," she says.

A few team members find music theory boring or overwhelming. To make it seem more accessible, several students recommended an engaging online introductory theory course taught by Berklee College of Music professor George Russell, Jr. that is offered on the Coursera and EdX websites. "His enthusiasm and caring reaches right through the computer screen," says Mr. Duke, who has also taken a more advanced course on Coursera that was more challenging, but useful as well.

Handling Recitals

As noted earlier, some of our advice-team members have mixed feelings about recitals, whether the standard kind involving a private teacher's students or the end-of-semester performances that group classes and workshops hold, or performances that occur after a week or so of a summer music program. "I think recitals are great to have something to work toward, but the actual event is very stressful. Although after it's over, it gives me a great feeling of accomplishment," says Ms. Monte.

A few team members feel so stressed about performing in a recital that they take medication—a low dose beta blocker that can counteract the adrenaline rush caused by the hormone epinephrine that makes people feel anxious. Even without taking the medication, many team members found that the more you do these performances, the easier it gets. "The first couple of years in my group piano class, I shook every time I had to play," says Ms. Wythe. "But playing in front of a small group every week in class and before the larger studio several times a year helped." She also eventually tried beta blockers. A low dose "made performance less stressful and more satisfying. I can now handle performing and even look forward to it. It's as much part of the study as learning the music." There is more about beta blockers in chapter 10.

As noted earlier, about one-third of our questionnaire completers actually enjoy recitals. Mezzo soprano Suzanne Epstein has organized her own recitals at private homes. "I get nervous, but I love them. I want to communicate music to others. I hope to do more," she says. Dr. Barouch is another recital fan. "I like showing off my new repertoire at the adult recitals at my music school and in the talent show at our synagogue's annual retreat," she says. She also enjoys performing at one of her daughter's piano recitals each year, playing a mother/daughter violin-and-piano duet. Her daughter's piano teacher encourages students to play some chamber music instead of only piano solos at one recital a year and parents who are musicians are invited to participate.

Dr. Lili Barouch (left) with her teenage daughter after they played a violin-and-piano duet at the daughter's piano recital.

Linda Bauch performs in juries, a kind of recital during which students receive feedback from some of a school's teachers. The first time her Levine Music teacher suggested doing a jury, she refused. "He didn't push it. But the second time I thought, 'Why not? What are you afraid of? It's only two teachers and they're on your side. He wouldn't let you play and make a fool of yourself. If you get too nervous, you can say you can't do it today. But at least you tried.'" She did a jury and found it wasn't as bad as she feared. "The comments from the teachers were very helpful," says this retired trade association issues manager. "They pointed out the positives and areas where I had a problem. I go over the comments with my teacher. As long as you're not afraid to take a risk, you're not really old yet."

Some team members want nothing to do with recitals or juries. "I hate them. I am playing for myself and will not do them," says Mr. Freshwater. Many teachers make recitals optional for adult students. Levine Music offers an alternative for adults who don't want to do a jury. They can take a music theory class that day instead. Mr. Freshwater took the theory option and loved it.

Although Ms. Zieglar finds recitals are "too much pressure," she doesn't mind her cello class's group "play-ins"—low-key group recitals that give students a chance to see that they really have made progress. "The teacher who runs the adult violin program holds an adult 'play-in' once per semester where the cello and violin students play in an ensemble together," she says. "We sign up several weeks in advance, she sends out music, and then we get together to play together for one session. It's a low stress commitment."

Other music schools cope with recital aversion by making recitals for adults optional or by turning them into parties, as Rebecca Bellelo does for her private piano students. "We have some adults who just come to the parties to be social but don't play," she notes. For her group classes, she asks everyone to play the same tune together at the same time at a semester-ending wrap-up that they call a "jam" session. "We make it a fun, party-type atmosphere." The Old Town School has called its semester-ending performances the "big gig," and holds them in a real performance venue, such as at a blues club, with family and friends cheering the student ensembles.

Miriam Jackobs did a clarinet recital a few years ago that went well because "there was no plan to have all the music memorized. Therefore it was doable." Educators interviewed for this book report that memorizing shouldn't be a requirement for an amateur recital. "If a piece can be memorized, great, but that's not why we're doing it," says piano teacher Patrick O'Donnell. "We're doing it to make music, enjoy it. We need to take away a lot of those 'shoulds.'" Professional pianist Adam Kent, who has several adult students, notes, "Well-known pianists like Richard Goode have started to use scores in their public performances. It's not considered scandalous for a pianist to have a score in a concert now. The prohibition against that is softening." (There is more on memorizing in the next chapter, and more on performance anxiety in chapters 9 and 10.)

Cost Concerns: Instruction

Nearly all of our questionnaire completers who are receiving instruction feel that the cost is fair, although several have had to do some belt-tightening in their overall budgets. Here are cost-saving suggestions for instruction, followed by savings tips for supplies and instruments. Guitarist Mike Alberts points out, "Music is much cheaper than golf, which I used to be into. I have spent a lot on equipment. It is what I like to do. So I don't regret it."

- **Spread out the instruction:** "I take lessons only every other or every third session at the music school," says guitarist Dr. Larry Lindeman. One strings teacher lets students who register for a semester space out that number of lessons over a whole year. Some team members take lessons only now and then, on an as-needed basis.
- **Scholarships:** "Ask for scholarships," advises Ms. Lowe. Many schools offer financial aid or a sliding scale on fees but may not feature that prominently

in their catalogs. If you ask, you might receive tuition assistance, as Ms. Lowe did. The chamber music association ACMP has a grant program to help members hire a coach for a chamber music group.

- **Senior discounts:** Dr. Reeder benefits from the discount seniors receive at music schools. Seniors-oriented New Horizons and OLLI programs are often less costly than music school classes.
- **Share:** "I split my flute lessons with a friend. We share the same time slot," says Andrea Elkrief, a New York nursery school teacher. They alternate weeks, so that each one has a lesson every other week. Ms. Ten Cate reports that when her chamber music groups sign up for workshops to receive coaching, "we'll distribute the cost unequally if cost is an issue for some members, or we'll apply for funding from ACMP."
- **Freebies:** By registering for flute lessons at the music school she attends, Ms. Elkrief can add on two chamber music classes for no additional cost. Other schools may also offer this option.
- **Volunteer:** "Volunteer at the school and reduce the cost of classes that way," says Mr. Dawson. Some schools offer this kind of discount.
- **Group classes:** "Group lessons are generally less expensive than private lessons," says Dr. Reeder.
- **Comparison shop:** "The cost of instruction is unrelated to its quality. I simply don't work with expensive people. Find the right, reasonably priced teacher," says Ms. Axelrod.
- **Barter:** "I have been able, in the past, to exchange voice lessons for services that are in my area of expertise—graphic design," says New York choral singer Nicole Ryder.
- **Play for tips:** The string quartet that violist Julia Moline formed with friends has played a few gigs, starting at a wine bar owned by a friend of the cellist. "After the gig, he handed me a sandwich bag full of twenties. It never occurred to us that this was something we would do for money. We also got paid to play for a yoga class and a podcast launch party. We spend a lot of it on music. We use most of the rest to get a coach."

Other Money Savers

- **Free scores:** "The IMSLP, a free public domain Internet site, is a godsend to classical musicians," says Mike Tietz. "The editions are usually older and not the most up-to-date, but the site makes it possible to find all sorts of music in the public domain (not under copyright) that would otherwise be inaccessible or unaffordable." IMSLP stands for Internet Music Score Library Project, also known as the Petrucci Music Library. Many of our team members find scores to use for practicing or performing via IMSLP, although Ms. Epstein notes, "Of course IMSLP is one way to save money, but I am happy to pay for scores so that there will be music publishers, and I often prefer to because of the quality of the printing." Others save money by borrowing musical scores from libraries. The Musopen.org website offers some free sheet music. Other sources of free scores are listed on the companion website for a book that several advice-team members found helpful, *The Musician's Way* by Gerald Klickstein. Those doing non-classical styles can find music, chord sheets, guitar tabs, and lyrics free online, or may figure out how to play a tune simply by listening. Bob Weaver recommends the St. James Music Press's website. For an annual membership fee, this site provides access to "a large collection of anthems and organ pieces which can be downloaded for free," he says. Music reading apps for iPads or tablets may make purchasing scores and sheet music easier, such as ForScore, PiaScore, MusicReader, and Henle Library. Websites for all the money savers mentioned here are listed in the resources section at the end of the book.

- **Savvy shopping:** Many team members found good deals on used instruments on such websites as eBay, Craigslist, and Keys44Kids. Sophia Jimenez got a free keyboard through the Freecyle Network, a reuse and recycling organization. Philip Knieper negotiated with a music store for a below-market price for his new hybrid piano. Beth Chapple recommends waiting for sales to buy supplies, as she does for trumpet valve oil. When starting on a new instrument, it's wise to rent first, using a rent-to-buy plan so rental fees can be applied to the purchase price later. When ready to buy, Mr. Alberts recommends, "Buy a decent instrument. It's less costly than continually upgrading." Liz Sogge agrees. "It made a huge impact on my playing and enjoyment when I traded up from a clunker violin to a more expensive one," she says.

Do It Yourself

The great majority of our questionnaire completers did some learning on their own, either instead of or in addition to formal instruction. YouTube and other online resources offer many instructional videos, a vital resource used by more than half of our team members. "I do online lessons fairly frequently," says Baylor Fox-Kemper.

Primarily a keyboard player, he has been teaching himself to play guitar and bass, which he had some basic training on during high school. "It's easy to find lessons online that are at the right level." Many online instructional videos are free.

While many of these instructional videos are geared to beginners, Ms. Rosado notes, "Once in a while you can find videos for more advanced students." Those have helped her learn specific flute techniques, as have master class videos, such as ones by flutist James Galway. Ms. Ten Cate, an accomplished cellist, says she has found "quite enlightening" a series of instructional videos on YouTube by professional cellist David Finckel.

"I watch performances of flute soloists on YouTube to see their technique," reports Ms. Rosado. "If there is something that I want to do better, I look at famous soloists to see how they do it." Dr. Dwight Campbell does the same to improve his French horn skills. "There is no end of things to be learned from close observation of professionals playing via YouTube or other sites, such as the Berlin Philharmonic's Digital Concert Hall—breathing, phrasing, blending with the orchestra, embouchure," says this retired orthopedic surgeon.

> **Our progress may be slower than a teenager's. Assess your progress in months/years not days/weeks. The goal is to play better every year.**
> —Dr. Deborah Edge, double bassist, retired physician

Audio recordings of pieces can be found on other sites, such as Amazon, Classical Connect, CyberBass, iTunes, Musopen, Spotify, Piano Society, or the website of sheet music retailer J. W. Pepper. Some team members play along with online recordings, often using technological options to "slow down" the piece, as explained in chapter 8.

About 10 percent of our questionnaire completers have taken more formal music courses online, some of which charge tuition and are taught by university-based faculty on such topics as music theory, music composition, musicianship, and music history. About a quarter have also used instructional DVDs. More than half turned to books and magazines for instructional advice, using methods books for specific instruments, music theory workbooks, books about famous professional musicians, or memoirs of amateur musicians. Online blogs and e-newsletters are also sources of advice on practice and performing. There are too many methods books, instructional DVDs, and books about professional musicians to list, but the bibliography does list memoirs of amateur musicians, some general books about practicing that team members found helpful, as well as blogs and e-newsletters. The resources section lists online links for many of the options noted in this section.

Composing and Arranging

About a quarter of the questionnaire completers on our advice panel have done some arranging, composing, or songwriting. Some ventured into these areas to help an ensemble they were in, such as the arranging John Vishneski does for his Barristers Big Band. "Sometimes I cannot find a chart that matches our instrumentation so I need to translate parts," he explains. "Or I get charts for a small band and expand it for the Big Band." To help in preparing arrangements, many have taught themselves to use notation software programs, such as Finale or Sibelius, which have free trial versions. There are less-advanced notation programs, such as Garage Band and Noteworthy Composer, or more advanced ones, such as Pro Tools. "Music notation software is a huge resource," says Ron Sharpe, who uses it to make arrangements of pieces for his community orchestra, and chamber music and jazz groups, being careful not to violate copyright restrictions.

Others use notation software to make it easier to create their own original compositions. South Carolina architect Emil Henning had been writing music off and on for years, but experienced a fresh burst of creativity when he taught himself to use notation software. "It is fairly easy," he says. "I had resisted learning it before because I thought it would be harder." For retired Maine speech pathologist Cherrie Waxman, discovering notation software "opened a world of possibility. I've recently started composing and arranging," she says. "The fun factor is huge."

The songwriters on our team tend not to use notation software. Catherine Kasmer says her songwriting starts by playing guitar and deciding on a chord progression. "Then I create a melody," she says. Next comes writing words for the song on paper, after which she returns to the guitar to create an introduction, ending, and solo section. "When the song is complete, I record a video of myself playing it. I will write a guitar tab of the guitar part and use chord charts as well." Walt Meder also creates his tunes without benefit of notation software, but his inspiration begins with the words. He has been writing poetry since childhood. "I took up guitar at 55 to give life to the words that I constantly put on paper," says this Chicago insurance broker. He has recorded three CDs of his songs, available on iTunes.

Many of the composers on our team have had composition instruction at a music school, as Mr. Browning has, or by taking online courses, as Mark Dalrymple did to learn how to create electronic dance music. Doug Campbell took music composition courses in college and had considered a career as a composer, but decided against it because he felt that the tunes he liked to write wouldn't be commercial hits. He became a businessman with a recording studio in the garage of his Tennessee home, where he uses notation and recording software to write songs in his free time. "I made a decision not to monetize my musical efforts. It's amazing what you can do when you unshackle yourself from the market and go whole hog after any creative impulse," he says. "I have written and recorded more than 1,500 songs." He finds inspiration in unusual places, writing songs for each element on the periodic table or putting teenagers' poems to music (more on this in chapter 11). When inspiration fails him, his wife, an artist, "makes up album covers and puts titles of songs on the cover. I write songs for her titles," he says.

Mr. Bishop, mentioned earlier as a digital piano newcomer, has used notation software to write pieces for his recorder ensemble, which have been performed by other groups, too. Mr. Weaver did a little composing for the church and community choirs he sang with during his career as a mathematics professor in Massachusetts but says that "only in retirement have I been able to devote the kind of time to this work to allow me to get some things published." He collaborates with Bill Pasch, a retired English professor in Georgia. Because they use the same notation software program, they can share their composition files, making their long-distance collaboration possible.

Dr. Eugene Beresin has made music throughout his child psychiatry career by playing piano in folk, rock, and blues bands, including a band he started that plays at psychiatry conferences. He recently started composing by creating piano and guitar pieces that he performs. They are used as the music for informational podcasts and films for the Clay Center for Young Healthy Minds, which he heads at Massachusetts General Hospital in Boston. An audio engineer helps with the technical details.

The springboard for Dr. Jonathan Newmark becoming a composer was the more than thirty years he spent playing viola and piano in summer chamber music programs. Going to conservatory at age 60 to earn a master's degree in composition "was a massive and welcome change," he says, from many years as an Army chemical defense expert. The transition would not have been possible, he says, "if I hadn't been involved in the chamber music community which sustained my musicianship and provided me with a huge number of people willing to try anything I write."

Conducting

A few team members have taken on the challenge of conducting their ensembles, mostly figuring out what to do on their own. Two have received instruction in conducting. "Since my retirement, I've taken conducting workshops and private lessons to improve my skills and give my orchestra players, and me, a better music-making experience," says Mr. Tietz, who conducts a community orchestra that he founded. Shannon Polson took a conducting class before beginning to direct a chorus of girls and women in the small town in eastern Washington state where she lives. "This has been a ton of fun and challenging, a lot of learning for me. I look forward to doing more of this," says this writer, who has been singing in auditioned choruses for years.

Learning from Fellow Musicians

Just as popular with advice-team members as learning online is the more personal approach of learning from fellow musicians. "I learn to improve through playing with friends, especially those who are better. I don't have the time or finances to commit to lessons," says guitarist Bob Gronko. Bruce Gelin had private lessons for a while to refresh his skills after returning to clarinet, but now he learns mainly through the playing he does in Boston-area community orchestras. "The direct experience of rehearsing and performing with good players and good conductors is the most valuable thing at this point," says this chemical specialist. Violinist/violist Joan Herbers, who plays in chamber music groups and a community orchestra, agrees, "I am getting better just by playing."

Ron Sharpe and his violin. Marilyn
Hanna-Myrick on clarinet, with her
husband on bass clarinet.

8 Smart Practice

"AS A KID I didn't really know how to practice at all and what little I did do was directionless and odious drudgery. Practicing is now a delightful intellectual game and something I really look forward to. The two experiences are so fundamentally different that it is difficult to even think of them as being remotely the same thing," recalls Ron Sharpe, who returned to violin in his 40s, having played violin and a few band instruments briefly as a youngster.

Many of the musicians on our advice team agree with Mr. Sharpe that practicing is a more positive experience than when they were kids—and not just because they're not being forced by parents to log in a certain number of minutes each day, although that's part of it, as clarinetist Marilyn Hanna-Myrick notes. She expresses a sentiment shared by many when she observes, "Now I practice because I want to and enjoy it, not because my mother is making me do it."

Just as important in forming a new attitude toward practice is realizing how it can enhance the music-making experience. "I now realize that I enjoy playing much more if I've had a chance to practice beforehand," says violinist Arabella Lang. John Warshawsky sees practicing viola as a way to become more deeply involved in music.

"As a young player, I focused on simple mechanics. Now I think more about what it takes to produce better sound and music. I think more about what I am trying to accomplish when I practice."

Even those who had good experiences with practice as youngsters find it more fulfilling as adults. "I have always liked to practice and learn new pieces as far back in childhood as I can recall," says pianist Didi Correa. "But as an adult, I am more disciplined and structured with my time to practice. I love the process of learning, the development of good sound. It is also cathartic in expressing emotions I cannot articulate in words." Dr. Lili Barouch shares that view, noting, "The interpretation of the music makes more sense and comes much more easily to me now than when I was studying violin as a kid." Cellist Lydia Zieglar mentions another change that others have also noticed in their practicing: "I understand how to practice better than I did as a kid. My practice is more productive." Making practice more efficient is especially important for her and other team members who are long on enthusiasm but short on time.

This chapter explores some of the strategies our team members use to turn practice into an activity they are willing to make time to do. In addition, health-care professionals offer advice on injury-free practicing, along with suggestion for what to do if physical issues arise. How much time our team members set aside for practice was discussed earlier, in chapter 6.

Practice Phobia

Not all of our team members are fond of practicing. Although the great majority say they do some practicing each week, about 5 percent say they usually don't practice at all. "I hated practicing as a child and I hate it now," says trombonist/bassoonist Mark Dalrymple. His terrific sight-reading skills help him keep up with the repertoire of his many community ensembles. "I'm into music for collaboration and performance. Sitting at home playing is completely unappealing. I don't practice, save for the half hour at rehearsal before the rehearsal starts. If I have a really tough lick, I might get the horn out at home," he explains. Lynn Malnekoff also prefers keeping up her violin skills by playing with others, noting, "I don't like to practice by myself, but rehearsing with a group is no problem."

Among those who do practice, most have a regular routine for their efforts. However, a few take a more loose approach. "I don't really have a routine," says banjo and guitar player Steven Duke. "Some days I practice specific techniques or specific songs. Some days I simply play tunes I'm familiar with to enjoy the sound of the music."

Ellen Shepard isn't sure whether what she does with music at home would be regarded as practicing. "It depends on what you mean by practice. I'm always singing and playing around with my voice. In terms of structured practice, lately I'm awful about it. Lack of time, too stressed out. When I'm doing something musically that I love, the time seems to make itself. I'd clear just about anything else off of my schedule for it. When it's just rote practice or something else that's not that fulfilling, other parts of life take over. I wasn't good at creating structure for practice when I was a kid, and I'm still not," says this nonprofit executive director who plays guitar and banjo, while also singing with a Chicago choir and performing with folk and jazz ensembles "For me, the best strategy is to get excited about a song and learn technique through learning to play that song. The joy of it takes over."

Ellen Shepard with her guitar.

Some team members actually object to the term "practice." Although guitarist Joseph Arden spends time at home most days playing his guitar, he says, "It's not 'practicing.' It's making music. It's meant to be fun. I pick up the guitar throughout the day and just pick some songs to play and sing, improving on what I currently know, or adding new songs to my repertoire. I don't spend much time trying to learn new techniques."

A few educators shy away from using the word "practice" with their students. "We use the word 'play.' We say, 'Play what you love and love what you play,'" reports Will Baily, who teaches group piano classes in Nebraska. Karen Mitchell, who is making her return to piano via group classes in Florida, also prefers the word 'play.' "Practice brings back memories of my hour of practice every day as a kid. It was like a dirty word to me," she explains. However, she isn't just playing around when she sits down at her piano at home. She gives herself a pretty rigorous workout. "I do scales and technique exercises, then do whatever I'm working on for the next lesson.

Then I play whatever I like. That's when time gets lost. I relax and have fun. I find it difficult to stop and time flies."

The word "practice" seems to shut down some very musical people, making them feel they are not quite measuring up, despite all the very musical things they are doing. Some have a similar reaction to the word "recital," as noted earlier. Both words carry leftover baggage from childhood battles. Perhaps using another word, as Ms. Mitchell does, can let the fun of learning new tunes rise to the top. So can finding ways to add musicality to tasks that might have seemed tedious or rote when team members were kids, as some of them describe doing in the next section. Others explain how they insert elements of fun into their at-home sessions, to counter the aspect of practice that professional trumpeter and composer Wynton Marsalis notes in his book *Marsalis on Music*. In describing why practice has such a bad reputation, he writes, "You have to spend time on things you can't do, which makes you feel bad about yourself." That's why some team members make sure to include in their practicing things they can do well. These and other suggestions from our team members and expert advisors in the following pages may help make whatever time is spent doing music at home a more positive experience, no matter what you call it.

Musical from the Get Go

Many of our team members start off their practice sessions with a short warm-up period that includes running through a few scales, arpeggios, études, or other technical exercises before plunging into working on a piece. Those warm-ups can help loosen up fingers and voices while also serving as a bridge from the bustle of everyday life to the stress-reducing world of music.

Several have found that by focusing on the musicality in those scales and études—rather than seeing them as something rote to speed through—the musical enjoyment begins right away, making limited practice time feel more fulfilling. "I had to change my bad attitude from childhood when I did not even attempt to make scales and études sound musical. I thought that they were just annoying, required exercises to build dexterity," says violinist Liz Sogge. "Now, I always try to find the music in everything I play. This change in attitude makes quite a difference." Ms. Lang agrees, "I always start with the same exercises, then play some unaccompanied Bach or Telemann if I have time, before moving on to the pieces I'm working on. My warm-up exercises are amazing at making me feel I'm much more in practice than I actually am! If I don't do them, then all the rest of my practice is much harder work." Violist Paula Washington adds, "At this point in my life, scales and arpeggios are both meditation and physical therapy. They pay great dividends in all other music, so about half my practice time is spent on them."

Brass and woodwind players often include in their warm-ups a few minutes of playing long tones, which saxophonist David Inverso describes as follows: "I play a note for a full minute, crescendoing and de-crescendoing, trying to keep the tone and pitch the same." For clarinetist Bruce Gelin, "My long-tone warm-up, with its slow regular breathing, is a little like a yoga session where you try to forget about everything else and just focus on what you're doing." Bassoonist Lauren Hill adds, "I always have a better and more efficient forty-five minute session if I take the time to properly warm up and work on intonation for ten to fifteen minutes before I practice difficult passages. It's not much good to just jump in cold and try to get challenging

Steve DeMont playing in a jazz class recital at Seattle's Music Center of the Northwest.

runs under my fingers." Trumpeter Beth Chapple ends practice sessions by coming back to playing "long, low tones, a form of cooling down that makes me play better the next day."

Saxophonist Steve DeMont lets jazz inform the way he plays scales in his warm-up by "running a specific chord progression and lick through a few turns. I've been working to have a progression memorized so it's more reflexive." That will help him later when he needs to use that chord progression while improvising. Pianist Marion Berghahn has a different strategy for getting into a musical frame of mind at the start of her practicing. "I mostly play some older pieces just for fun and then focus on the current ones," she says.

A Moving Warm-Up

Medical experts recommend another kind of warm-up—a brief period of stretching. "You are athletes of the small muscles," says Dr. Alexander Pantelyat, a Johns Hopkins neurologist and amateur violinist. "You should treat yourselves as such. Just as a football player needs to stretch before every practice and game, this is important for musicians to keep in mind, too." He made those comments in a 2014 lecture on wellness for Peabody Institute music students, as part of that conservatory's Music and Medicine program. In a follow-up interview for this book, he notes, "Stretching is important for amateur musicians, too. As we get older, muscles are less supple. What we want to avoid is the Weekend Warrior situation that happens to athletes who don't play during the week but on the weekend dive in, exposing themselves to injury and pain." To keep that from happening to amateur musicians no matter when they practice—weekdays or weekends—he feels that some stretching is "crucial."

Professional pianist Vivian Weilerstein agrees. When asked what advice she would have for amateur musicians who want to keep on making music throughout their lives, this New England Conservatory professor notes, "I can't underline strongly enough how important physical movement and exercise are! It is important to understand that all parts of the body are related, to feel flow through your whole body, and to relate that to rhythm and musicality. When applied to playing the instrument, it can help dramatically. It also helps keep the brain alive." She uses the Feldenkrais method, but there are other programs that also teach "awareness of the body through movement," such as Alexander Technique and yoga.

Deborah Wythe is one of several team members who have taken lessons in Alexander Technique to "learn how to use my body better, fix aches and pains, and avoid new ones," she explains. Oboist Karen Greif regularly does some stretching, but doesn't link it directly to a practice session. She starts her day each morning doing yoga and Alexander Technique exercises. "Then I'm good to go for the rest of the day," says this Pennsylvania biology professor.

Not many advice-team members report that they include stretching at the start of practicing, but those who do find that it helps. Several do stretches because they have experienced practice-induced injuries. "I use hand and arm stretches to warm up," says Joanne Fekete, who injured her left hand when she returned to playing guitar in her late 30s. The injury occurred when she tried a fingering technique that was too hard for her small hands. "I use different fingerings now, try to sit properly, and take frequent breaks," says this Pennsylvania church secretary and choir leader. Cellist newcomer and retired Ohio librarian Mary Novak does stretches recommended by a physical therapist who has helped her deal with her practice-induced aching back and sore shoulder. Mike Tietz, who has had finger and arm issues, sometimes warms up his fingers in hot water and then does stretches before playing cello. He often applies ice after playing.

Physical exercises help singers, too. As otolaryngologist Dr. Robert T. Sataloff notes, "Singing is an athletic activity" that requires "physical and aerobic conditioning, abdominal and back muscle strength." Aaron Polley, an Army resources manager and cousin of professional singer John Legend, makes physical exercise part of his plan for maintaining his singing voice. He sings in a Virginia church choir and does yoga "to strengthen abdominal muscles and develop breath control," in addition to his regular vocal warm-up of singing "the musical scale using vowels."

What kind of stretches are good to do? Dr. Serap Bastepe-Gray showed a warm-up video with examples during a lecture she gave at a Peabody Health and Wellness Seminar. In the video, student volunteers start with large general motions, such as reaching arms up and out sideways, first to one side and then the other. They follow that with movements that mimic those used in playing a particular instrument, such as having hands and fingers curve over and down as would be done in playing piano. In the video, the exercises are performed to a jazzy beat, as if it were a musician-oriented Jane Fonda-type exercise video. The point of the warm-up is to increase local blood flow to the specific muscles that will be used in music-making, to "increase tissue temperature, which increases tissue flexibility," says Dr. Bastepe-Gray, a physician who also teaches guitar at Peabody. As she told the students, "If you come up with a good warm-up design and you keep doing that every day before practice, it becomes a psychological anchor so once you do that warm-up, you feel ready for successful practice or successful performance." Links to YouTube videos of her and Dr. Pantelyat's Health and Wellness lectures are listed in the bibliography, as are books and informational articles on musicians' health-related issues.

**I can't play as fast as I used to do, but I think I bring more understanding
and feeling to my playing.**

—Marilyn Hanna-Myrick, clarinetist, retired librarian

Healthy Practice

All this talk about practice-induced aches and pains may seem concerning, but
Dr. Pantelyat notes that by following some common-sense guidelines, "Prevention
is possible." If aches and pains develop, he advises, "Treatment is available." Here are
suggestions from our medical advisors for healthy, injury-free practice. Many of our
team members have already been using these approaches. Later in this chapter there
is advice on how to proceed if aches, pains, and other health issues arise.

- **Take breaks:** "Don't play longer than twenty to twenty-five minutes without
  taking a five-minute break," advises Dr. Michael Charness, a neurologist,
  pianist, and director of the Performing Arts Clinic at Boston's Brigham and
  Women's Hospital. Short breaks help keep the mind from wandering, backs
  and necks from getting stiff, and music-making muscles from growing tired
  and strained. Dr. Pantelyat notes that there's some evidence that practicing or
  studying in twenty-five minute time blocks improves productivity. It's often
  called the "Pomodoro Method," named for the tomato-shaped kitchen timer
  that an Italian neuroscience student used when he developed this plan for
  productive practicing. It's a pretty easy rule to follow for those who rarely find
  more than half an hour of practice time. But as Dr. Charness points out, "Many
  amateurs play incredible amounts of time on the weekend because they don't
  have time during the week. The irregularity of the practice schedule that a lot
  of amateurs have and the large fluctuations in the amount of playing they're
  doing hold their own special risks. We see so many musicians in our clinic,
  especially amateurs, who play for two hours without taking any break. It's not
  surprising they get into trouble." Dr. Pantelyat also advises against excessive
  repetition of music that's beyond your abilities or outside your range.
- **Stop if it hurts:** "Stop if there is a significant amount of pain," warns
  Dr. Pantelyat. "Playing through pain is a bad idea. Pain is an evolutionary
  mechanism that tells us that something is wrong." This applies to singers
  as well as instrumentalists. Pain in the throat or hoarseness while singing
  are signs that a singer may not be using good technique and could benefit
  from instruction in how to lessen tension in the throat and use breath
  better to support the singing voice, according to Dr. Sataloff. "The voice

gets hoarse because of a problem with the vocal folds. Singing under those circumstances is how people develop injuries that lead them to offices like mine," he says. For instrumentalists, Dr. Charness notes: "Musicians who play a lot may develop an ache in one part of the body and the next day it's gone. That's less worrisome than people who develop a consistent symptom of pain, which suggests that one part of their body may have been injured and needs to be looked at to find the best way to recover. It could be bad technique or a sudden increase in practicing. The pain may arise from nerves that are being compressed. Continuing to play may lead to loss of strength or sensation. When problems persist for some time, seek medical advice."

- **Hydration:** "It's important to keep hydrated," advises Marlene Riley, an occupational therapist and hand therapist at Maryland's Towson University. Muscles that aren't well hydrated "move at slower speeds. As you get older, you're less aware of feeling thirsty and dehydration can occur," which can lead to music-making muscles not working well. She recommends keeping water bottles handy during practice and rehearsals. This is especially important for singers. Vocal cords, also called vocal folds, "vibrate better when they are wet," says Dr. Jayme Dowdall, an otolaryngologist at Brigham and Women's Hospital. She recommends that serious singers "sleep next to a small portable humidifier." Dr. Sataloff notes also that some medications, including over-the-counter allergy medications, can dry out the vocal folds.

- **Plan ahead:** "Avoid sudden increases in practice time," says Dr. Pantelyat. Plan ahead for special events, such as a big performance or before attending a summer music camp where participants generally play or sing for more hours than usual. Gradually increase practice time before these events, instead of binge practicing at the last minute, which can lead to stress and muscle strain.

- **Watch your posture:** "Proper body alignment—posture—and correct physical technique are essential," adds Dr. Pantelyat. Concern about posture led some of our team members to buy chairs that offer better support for the sitting position needed to play their instruments.

- **Specially for singers:** "Take care of your voice like it's a Stradivarius," says Charles Williams, voice teacher and professional singer. Although he encourages his students to sing every day, he advises, "If you are sick, have a sore throat, and your voice is not functioning, do not sing." Dr. Sataloff warns against misusing the speaking voice as well, which can harm the singing voice. Shouting, straining to be heard at noisy gatherings, whispering, or excessive throat clearing and coughing can damage the vocal folds. He recommends also that singers warm up their voices first thing in the morning, even if they're not planning to practice singing at that time. "They can run scales in the shower or in the car. Even five minutes of scales if done correctly can make a huge difference in placing the voice before beginning a day of speaking," he says. Team member Theodore Sapp does that. His early morning routine involves "waking up the voice doing some arpeggios or I hum familiar tunes. Throughout the day I try to speak very deliberately, focusing on the words spoken and how they sound." In the evening he warms up his voice again and begins practicing. More tips on protecting voices can be found in Dr. Sataloff's book *50 Ways to Abuse Your Voice*, listed in the bibliography.

Listening Counts

"For learning new music, God bless YouTube," says Sofia Axelrod, who likes to listen to and watch other singers perform new pieces she is learning on YouTube. Nearly all our questionnaire completers use this strategy when working on new pieces. They also use CDs, MP3s, iTunes, Spotify, and the website of music retailer J. W. Pepper to hear performances of new pieces. For classical music, the Classic Connect website offers an archive of recordings to listen to for free.

Trumpeter Bruce Burgess doesn't just listen to the performance. He also reads along with the sheet music for his part so he can pinpoint difficult passages to focus on during practice. Rey Forrest often listens to several versions of a new piece her choral group is singing. "Then I take the sheet music and bang it out on the piano. I learn it best when I play it myself. I concentrate on learning the notes and the words; so when I go to rehearsal, I can concentrate on how the music director interprets it," she says. Mr. Warshawsky looks at the whole orchestral score while listening to new pieces his community orchestra will play "to gain a greater understanding of how my viola part fits into the work." He downloads the score from the free online classical music library IMSLP.

Eloise Bensberg does her listening on the go. "I listen to recordings of good performances of a piece in the car, at work, or at home while in the kitchen or cleaning. That gets the piece in my ear," she says. Flutist Judith Grubner notes that when working on a solo for her community orchestra, "I listen to a recording of the piece so many times that my husband says I hum it in my sleep." All that listening is especially helpful for those who don't have good music-reading skills. "My sight-reading is poor, but if someone plays a passage for me, I can usually replicate it immediately. Listening to music is a critical part of my preparation," says violist Jay Choi.

For choral singers, there are websites designed to help them learn their parts, such as CyberBass, which several of our team members use. It's a free online service that has recordings of many major choral works using digital sounds. The recordings offer a chance to hear individual parts while the rest of the piece plays in the background. It's possible to slow down the recording to make learning easier. Some choruses provide singers with similar types of recordings, made either by professional recording companies or by people connected with the chorus, such as the practice tracks that Sean Fleming makes. He is the assistant conductor of a chorus that many of our advice-team members sing with, Midcoast Community Chorus of Rockport, Maine. He uses notation software and a computer to make MP3 recordings of all four voice parts for a piece, either by playing each part on an electric piano or by him or his wife singing each part while a recording of the whole piece plays on another track. The MP3s are uploaded to the chorus's section of Wikispaces, a file-sharing site. Chorus members go online to listen to their parts, slowing down the recording as needed.

Many of our team members play or sing along with recordings of pieces they find online. "I sing along to see which parts I really need to work on," says Liz Langeland. Then she goes to her piano to play through the tough passages "and do them more slowly. Once I know them well enough to speed up the pace, then I practice singing along with the recording again until confident." Trumpeter Lorne Wald, as noted in chapter 6, uses the audio input option of his Yamaha Silent Brass mute to play along with pieces he is learning, something that is possible also with Yamaha's electronic strings and guitars.

Some team members use special software programs to slow down recordings without changing the pitch so that they can play or sing along before they are comfortable enough with a piece to go at full tempo. Programs they have used include Amazing Slow Downer, Anytune, Audacity, as well as Capo for guitars. Ms. Novak has found another way to slow down recordings, by using a Zoom recorder to tape pieces she has found on YouTube.

In addition, several team members have used play-along programs that may not have the exact pieces they are working on, but can be good for developing skills and having fun. These programs include the Music Minus One series, mainly for classical music, which lets you solo while an orchestra plays backup; Jamey Aebersold Play-Along series, which does the same for jazz; SmartMusic student software, which keeps track of errors as you play; and the Cadenza app by Sonation that adjusts the speed of the accompanying orchestra to keep pace with your playing. For singers, there are a variety of karaoke and vocal warm-up apps.

Some team members also listen to recordings they make of themselves practicing. "I advocate using a simple tape recorder to monitor how the practice is going. Do not wait to be 'ready' to record. Use it as a tool for the process. Record only little bits—the spots you are working on. Later, do the whole thing," says

The Midcoast Community Chorus of Rockport, Maine.

violinist Laura Rice. Clarinetist Jeff Alfriend does this, too, and advises, "Listen to the playback with unbiased criticism." Mr. Choi uses a microphone to listen to himself while practicing. "I set up a microphone at various distances from me, and listen to myself as I practice though a pair of in-ear monitors that isolate the sound so I only hear what the mic picks up," he explains. "It has given me useful clues as to how my instrument sounds from the audience, which is very different from what I hear!"

About a quarter of our questionnaire completers tape their private lessons to help with remembering suggestions the teacher offered. The record function on smart phones makes doing these recordings fairly easy. Choral singer Bob Weaver sometimes does this so that when he practices at home, he can practice exercises he did during his singing lesson, as well as hear the piano playing of the accompanist who sits in on his lessons and plays the piano part for solo pieces he is studying. There's another kind of listening, of course, that helps: Listening to any kind of music deepens an appreciation for how to bring out the musicality in your music.

Woodshedding Basics

Volumes have been written on ways to practice. A few books and blogs that offer practice tips are listed in the bibliography. Here are some basic strategies that members of our advice panel have found useful.

- **Tough spots:** "I don't keep playing through a piece like I did when I was younger, if I need to work on one passage," says flutist Andrea Elkrief. Many of our team members agree with her that the way to get more done in less time is to focus on the troublesome spots. If not, as pianist and architect Emil Henning warns, "When it comes time to play with or for people, that one place you avoided really learning will rise up and smite you." Many put a mark on the side of the score for passages they stumble over during rehearsals or in earlier run-throughs, as a reminder of what needs work. Then, as Ms. Rice says, "I jump into the tough spots, figure out the exact nature of the problem, then work at training my mind and body to do the right thing."
- **Practice tricks:** Team members use a variety of tricks to tame those trouble spots. Flutist Kathy Dockins explains: "If you're struggling with a section, change it up when practicing. Keep the same notes, but play them slower or faster, or as triplets instead of sixteenth notes (or whatever) so you

remember the fingering kinetically rather than musically. Then your fingers will remember what to do more easily." Other tricks to help the brain and fingers pay closer attention to what notes need to be played involve playing a passage backwards or in a different rhythm. Clarinetist Jeff Alfriend finds that singing his clarinet part helps. For singers, practicing tough spots by singing using just vowels or the notes' solfège numbers lets the mind focus on the notes and intervals, without being distracted for a while by the words. Then once the notes are solid, words are re-introduced.

- **Slow down:** "Practice difficult parts slowly until they're right. Then gradually speed up and fit them into the broader musical line until it all works," says Mr. Tietz. As a musician friend once told saxophonist David Inverso, "First you get good, then you get faster." He follows this advice with the help of a metronome. "I slow a new piece down and when I get it under my fingers at that speed, I click the metronome up two notches until I master it there and then up two more, and so on." Metronomes may not have been a hit with some team members when they were kids, but the great majority of the questionnaire completers on our advice team now see their value and say that they use them. Flutist Dr. Karlotta Davis waits to move her metronome up a notch for a tricky part "until I am able to play it perfectly five times in a row." Pianist Dale Backus returns to slow practice even after having mastered a piece at full speed. "If you can't play it slow days before your performance, you don't know that piece well enough," he warns. There are metronome apps for smart phones, which can make this age-old clicker seem more cool and up-to-date. Peg Beyer makes her digital metronome even cooler by hooking it up to an amplifier so she can hear it better as she plays her cello. Jacking up the volume lets her really "feel the beat."

- **Chunking:** Many do slow, careful work on a new piece section by section, waiting until one section is set before moving to another. Some start at the end of a piece to master later sections before moving forward. Always starting at the top can lead to later sections being neglected. Plus, as Linda Bauch has found, "Some pieces get more difficult as you get toward the end." After working section by section, it can help to try to pull them all together and play through the piece as best as possible, even if everything is not totally fixed. A coach advised violist Carol Davidson at a summer music camp: "Don't worry about the bowings and fingerings—just let the music flow as if you were singing this melody."

- **Time out:** "If you're struggling on a spot and start getting angry, stop. Then come back to that part later, slow down, and play it successfully slowly three or four times. Don't leave the piano on a bad note," advises Mr. Backus. Violist Dr. Marc Mann has found that slow practice may not solve the problem in one practice session. "I work up complicated passages slowly and speed them up over the course of several days." He adds that often the problem improves "after I've had a chance to sleep on it."

- **Lessen perfectionism:** "While it's good to have high standards, don't let that take away from your enjoyment of the process," advises pianist Hamadi Henderson. It took him a while to lessen the grip of perfectionism, as noted in chapter 4. "When I was younger I often felt discouraged to practice because I felt that I could never become a piano virtuoso. Now that is not something I worry about. I like that there isn't the same pressure to be perfect."

- **Mental practice:** Thinking through a piece without actually playing or singing it counts as practice. As noted in chapter 7, Mark Sherkow learned a practice strategy from a sight-reading class that lets him practice his choral music mentally anywhere, anytime. When he starts working on a piece, he writes the solfège numbers above the notes. Those numbers show the intervals that need to be sung. Seeing those numbers lets him "sing" the intervals silently in his mind while sitting on a bus or during lunch at work. Going over a song silently helps singers keep working on a song without causing voice damage from over singing.

- **Fun stuff:** "If things aren't going well, find something to play that you can play well and take pleasure in," says French horn player Paul Seeley. Others make a point of regularly adding fun elements whether practice is going well or not. Kathy Fleming tries to end that way. "I try to leave time to play through something at the end I'm curious about or for the joy of it," she says about her viola da gamba practicing. So does guitarist Dr. Larry Lindeman, who says that after he does the hard stuff, "I spend ten to fifteen minutes just horsing around. I try to feel the music and play the music, not the notes."

- **Gear:** Besides digital metronomes and metronome apps, there are other technological versions of standard practice gear that may make practice easier for the technologically inclined, such as digital tuners and pitch pipes for smart phones. Score reading programs that let you load scores onto an iPad or tablet can be convenient, such as ForScore, PiaScore, MusicReader, Henle Library App, and others. Singer Sophia Jimenez uses a "virtual keyboard" program on a computer or smart phone "when I just want to check a note without dragging

CLOSE UP: DR. KEITH C. CHENG,
PIANIST, RESEARCH SCIENTIST

"The thought process I use in music is almost exactly the same as I use in science," says Dr. Keith C. Cheng, a pianist and chief of the Division of Experimental Pathology at Pennsylvania State University. "In music and art, you imagine an ideal. You constantly do experiments on the instrument to get to this ideal, which you never reach. Most of the experiments fail. It's good to learn how to practice to aim at a high goal but to allow failure to teach you. Every failure is an experiment that tells you what to do next. It's the same in science. You aim at an ideal and you try to get there. We constantly miss. At times you get close." He aims high in his piano practicing—to learn all thirty-two of Bach's Goldberg Variations, inspired by the famous 1955 Glenn Gould recording.

my keyboard out of the closet." Mr. Seeley recommends another accessory—a low-tech notebook or a higher-tech computer file— in which to "keep a log of your teacher's recommendations. Reread them regularly."

Memory Issues

"As a youngster, I just played and that was enough to instantly memorize. Our brains were so absorbent then. Now I don't trust myself to play anything from memory," says pianist Leslie Vieland, who plays chamber music with family and friends. About half of the questionnaire completers on our advice team say that learning new pieces or trying to memorize them is harder than when they were younger. "Surely it's the normal aging process," observes clarinetist Dr. Alvin Crawford. Indeed it is, according to neuroscience researcher Brenda Hanna-Pladdy. "We all peak at age 25," she says. "We all get age corrections in variable degrees. Every person is a little different." Although the brain remains capable of learning throughout the lifespan, "for older people learning takes a bit longer," says neuroscientist Aline Moussard. "The first few times you do something new, the older brain is going to be a bit lazy and say, 'Let's see if we are really going to use this.'" You have to keep having the brain do the new tasks, "be persistent to provoke changes in the older brain." Thus the value of regular practice.

Memory and learning challenges haven't deterred our team members from learning new music. Quite a few of our team members report that even though memorizing may be harder, other aspects have improved. "It is definitely easier to learn a new piano piece. I've got more tools in my arsenal. I know more music, so I'm not trying to figure out a style at the same time as learning the notes," says Ms. Wythe.

Others cope with memory issues by opting out. "I don't even try," says Dr. Mann. He plays chamber music and in community orchestras where it is perfectly acceptable to use sheet music, even while playing solos. Violinist Yoel Epstein reports, "I played a lot of concerts last year of solo pieces, which I played with the music, something I would never have done twenty years ago." This retired Israeli computer consultant plays in several chamber groups and gives recitals with a pianist at retirement homes.

Some of our team members, however, do manage to memorize their pieces, something that's often expected of solo classical singers or those singing or playing in rock, jazz, or folk bands, or at open mic nights. Trumpeter Catherine Getchell, blind from birth, reports, "I have memorized all my music since I began to play. I have it down to a science now so I can memorize things quickly." She never learned to read music in Braille, which would be tricky for trumpeters because they generally keep both hands on the instrument while playing. She learns her pieces by ear, listening to recordings she finds online or to recordings she makes of another trumpeter playing her part.

Janae Miller, another visually impaired member of our advice panel, memorizes all the music that she plays on piano or that she sings with the Harmony Project chorus of Columbus, Ohio. She listens to recordings of pieces she's learning on piano and to the recordings she makes of her piano lessons. For choral music, she listens to the practice tracks that her choral director makes for everyone in the Harmony Project chorus, all of whose members learn the music by ear, as noted in chapter 5. This chorus paired Ms. Miller with Jen Robinson, a sighted fellow singer, who stands next to Ms. Miller at rehearsals and performances, tapping her leg. Ms. Miller explains that the taps "tell me whatever the music director is doing, whether we're holding out a note or repeating a line, or changing the rhythm. The tapping system changes for each song, and sometimes changes right before a concert if he's doing something different in a song at the last minute." She has been singing with this choir for more than six years. "This is the first choir I've been in where I'm seen as a valuable person, never left out. In the past in choirs, I always had to find the help. Here, the help comes to me."

Harriet Rafter tries to memorize her beginner-level violin pieces, because "once you know the notes you can start to 'play' them. You can't make sure the bow is well-positioned if you also must look at the music." Mr. Backus, an accomplished pianist who has entered several amateur piano competitions, reports, "I do my best performances without the music. But I don't have a photographic memory. I don't memorize very well." He laments the fact that with a full-time engineering job he can't put in the long hours of practice and memorizing that professional pianists do. He feels extra practice time might make memorizing easier.

However, professional pianist Adam Kent, who practices quite a lot, notes that memorizing new work has become harder for him, too. "Every professional colleague

Janae Miller (right) singing with her choir partner, Jen Robinson, in a performance of the Harmony Project chorus of Columbus, Ohio.

I speak with seems to find this. We have to learn a different way to memorize as we get older. When you're young, you have an unconscious way of learning and absorbing music, through sheer rote. You don't even pause to analyze how you remember it. Over time, memorization becomes more deliberate. You have to intellectualize it more—how is it structured, how does one part relate to another part—and activate other parts of your brain in trying to remember. That's one of the great things about continuing to do it, because it forces you to know a piece more profoundly. Even if you elect to play in a concert with the music, as some professionals are doing, the effort of memorizing is a useful part of learning. I love and feel music more deeply. That's the gift of growing older."

Several team members succeed in memorizing new pieces using the same strategy as Mr. Kent—analyzing the music carefully. Pianist Bill Freshwater observes, "I don't memorize note by note, but look for phrases, repeats, intervals. I enjoy it." Guitarist and singer Michelle Billingsley has found that learning a new tune by ear makes memorizing easier. "If I learn a song by hearing it, or working it out myself on guitar without resorting to looking at the tab, it is easier to remember."

Professional pianist Ursula Oppens, when asked how to keep making music despite the inevitable declines of aging, including those that may make memorizing harder, advises, "Keep learning music that is new to you. Do not just go over what you have played before. And allow more time for everything."

Memorizing tunes at age 60 keeps my brain fit—keeps it from turning to mush.

—Steve DeMont, saxophonist, technical writer

Tips for Memorizing Lyrics

- **See them as poems:** Dr. Mary Lane Cobb studies a song's "lyrics as a poem, practicing reciting them, writing them down repeatedly, and then fitting them to the melody. If the melody is complex, I might do the reverse—get comfortable with the tune first."
- **Write them out:** "When learning the words, I write them on paper, then I type them on the computer, create the pages into a 'Poetry Book of Songs,' and carry them in my purse to look at," notes Eileen Greenberg. A highlighter helps, adds Julie Terray, a retired Maine customer service supervisor. "I highlight buzz words on my index card word sheets, or the first word in every line, or if there are repeating stanzas, I write down the words that change within the stanza," she says. Mary Schons brings her lyric sheets with her to performances "so I can glance down at the page from time to time," a plan she developed after forgetting the words for "The Rainbow Connection" that she was singing at a funeral. "I fumbled my way through the song and left in an ashamed daze. I now know the song by heart."
- **Down-time repetition:** Ms. Billingsley says she "spends time repeating the lines to myself in all sorts of situations—waiting in line, on the bus, at work— until I can do it without thinking." Bob Gronko reports, "I memorize songs on long road trips, listening to it over and over, taking a break, and going over it again until I get it."

When Aches and Pains Arise

"I often overdid practice, stressed out my hands, developed tendonitis, played through pain which I would not do now," says pianist Jonathan Pease. "I am much more calculating about what I am trying to accomplish and work within my limitations. I am not as hard on myself when things are not going well. I focus on slow practice, mindful of sensations of overuse. I cannot play as long without getting sore. When I am having tendonitis, I rest." Other team members have experienced pain while playing and nearly all have learned to manage as Mr. Pease has done by stopping when pain arises and tailoring their music-making to avoid the triggers that cause pain.

Dr. Mary Lane Cobb singing at a Juneteenth service at Community Unitarian Universalist Congregation of White Plains, New York.

"This is not unique to amateurs," says Dr. Charness. Of the more than three thousand musicians with music-related injuries he has seen in his Performing Arts Clinic, most are professional musicians. About a third are amateurs. "The amateurs are in good company. The injuries and disorders are the same. The amateurs are just as devastated as the professionals when something happens that compromises their ability to play." One of the first things he does when evaluating musicians' complaints is to watch them play their instruments. He tries to identify any technical problems that may be causing the difficulty, looking at how they hold their instruments, how they sit, if there are unnecessary muscle contractions that add tension such as raised shoulders, neck twisting, gripping the instrument too tightly, or wrists bent at the wrong angle, which "may lead to muscle spasm and reduce the fluidity of movement in adjacent muscles."

Using tension-free technique may help. So may modifying the ergonomics of the playing situation, such as changing the chair, wearing a wrist support, or altering an instrument. For example, placing extenders on some flute keys can make them easier to press without overextending the wrist. Attaching a cello-like endpin to an English horn helps Ms. Greif so that her arms don't have to hold up this heavy instrument. Putting less pressure on arms, hands, shoulders, backs, and voices in other aspects of life helps, too. Ms. Riley, a hand therapist, suggests sleeping with arms extended, rather than bent in the fetal position, especially if sore arms and tingling have developed from keeping elbows bent too long playing an instrument. "Keeping elbows bent close to the body while sleeping puts stress all night on the ulnar nerve at the elbow," she explains.

Joy Procida had a special trumpet holder built during college to enable her to continue playing trumpet when her muscular dystrophy, diagnosed at age 7, had progressed to the point that she could no longer hold up the trumpet. Before then, she had been propping up her right arm on the back of a Wenger chair turned sideways. But playing in this position made it hard to use her lungs fully and interfered with her playing. This Pennsylvania musician contacted a trumpet teacher in Texas that she had read about in an article in *Instrumentalist* magazine. He had built a trumpet stand for a student that clips to the side of a chair, enabling his student to play in a way that didn't interfere with air capacity. "He sent me the plans for how to build it. The father of a friend in college owned a mechanics shop and was able to build it," says Ms. Procida. Her sister, Jill Procida, who also has muscular dystrophy, uses the arms of a chair to enable her to keep playing saxophone. "The alto sax rests on my chair seat. I rest my arms on the arms of the chair to hold up my hands," she explains. Both sisters have been playing in community bands in western Pennsylvania for more than thirty years and recently started their own swing band that performs for dance concerts.

Sometimes the physical changes of aging call for a change of instruments. Retired engineer Fritz Hessemer used to love playing an open-hole wooden flute for Baroque chamber music. "Its sound matched the other musicians and didn't overwhelm them," he notes. In recent years, however, he has switched to using only his modern closed-hole silver flute for the Baroque music he plays with friends at his Maine retirement community. "Peripheral neuropathy in my fingers made distinguishing the open-hole locations impossible. I can't feel the ends of my fingers. That's the way it is when you get to be 95. But no matter where you hit the key on a modern closed-hold flute, it closes the hole."

Fritz Hessemer (far left) with the friends he plays Baroque chamber music with each week in his Falmouth, Maine, apartment.

To discover the cause of aches and pains—or hoarseness and wobbly voices in the case of singers—a musician could ask a teacher, coach, or fellow musician to watch them play or sing, looking for signs of tension, poor technique, or instrument issues that might be the culprit. Playing or singing in front of a mirror can help for self-analysis. As noted earlier, if pain or hoarseness persists, it's wise to consult physicians or physical, occupational, hand, or voice therapists. Our team members who have done so have generally had good results.

Here are suggestions for dealing with common music-making health issues.

- **Stiff fingers:** Most of the older instrumentalists on our advice team who complain about having stiff fingers attribute the stiffness to arthritis, in many cases osteoarthritis, the most common kind for people as they approach their 60s. Studies have shown that finger movements used in playing an instrument can be good for osteoarthritis, as long as the playing pauses when a joint starts hurting. However, it would be wise for newcomers to arthritis to check with a doctor about what kind of practicing they should do. "The developing arthritis in my fingers means that it is hard to play for long periods without a break. I take ibuprofen and shake my hands out when I can," says flutist Judith Grubner. Pianist Marilyn Reichstein has made modifications to cope with arthritis in her right pinky. "It has limited my ability to play music with many chords," she says. "I sometimes drop notes or change things around so I can play without injuring myself. I also play pieces that fit my hand better—Mozart, Haydn, rather than Brahms, Liszt." Dr. Jack Light, a retired dentist in his late 80s whose arthritis made it hard for him to lift his guitar, worked with therapists in Ms. Riley's department. They helped him find adaptations in his technique that made it possible for him to resume playing guitar again. "I manage as best I can now," he says.

- **Rheumatoid arthritis:** A few team members suffer from a different kind of arthritis—rheumatoid arthritis, an immunologic disorder in which the body's immune system attacks healthy joints, causing inflammation and swelling. For rheumatoid arthritis, medications given under a doctor's supervision can control the swelling. "My rheumatologist is very much in favor of my violin playing," says Dr. Barouch. "My rheumatoid arthritis has been under control most of the time after the first year, although it does flare up once in a while. During those times, I play easier repertoire and practice only a few minutes at a time. When I play, my fingers feel very good afterwards. The exercise helps my hands stay healthy in the long run." Rheumatoid arthritis can vary in severity and affect other joints besides in the hands. Heather Hostetler, a health policy analyst, stopped playing piano because of "rheumatoid arthritis and hand surgery that made proficient playing impossible." She uses piano now only to "plunk out" notes to help her learn music for a Baltimore choral society." Her arthritis has also led her to "sit on a tall stool instead of standing for choral concerts when there is no intermission or opportunity to sit between movements."

- **Reflux:** A few team members feel that acid reflux has made their singing voices so unreliable that they have given up singing. "I am emotionally impacted by people who stop singing for these reasons because there is so much that can be done," says Dr. Dowdall, an otolaryngologist who sees many singers in her practice. "There's a lot of misinformation out there about reflux." Reflux can occur when acids from the stomach back up into the throat and cause trouble. That can lead to excessive throat clearing and possible damage to the vocal folds. She notes that there are other reasons for excessive throat clearing or hoarseness besides reflux. She feels it's smart to see an otolaryngologist or other physician to understand "what's really going on. A lot of people will self-treat with over-the-counter medications, but there are side effects to those medications, especially if taken for a long time. The medications do not actually stop reflux. They just change the pH of what's coming up. We don't want people to be on medications that they don't necessarily need." There are a range of treatments that physicians can offer, including making dietary changes. "We recommend the book *Dropping*

Acid as a good place to start," says Dr. Dowdall. "The dietary exploration can have a high impact and low side effects." This book has advice and recipes for lessening the amount of acid in the diet. Suzanne Epstein took the diet approach after months of laryngitis that was finally diagnosed as caused by reflux. "By observing strict dietary restrictions, I have brought it under control and am back to singing," she says. "My doctor sent me to a wonderful voice therapist." A voice therapist helps get the voice back in good working order rather than teaching specific vocal techniques, as a voice teacher does.

- **Vision issues:** "It's a bit harder to see now. Getting glasses that are perfect for reading music at a cellist's distance is tough," says cellist Sally Long. As a result, she has been cutting back on the playing she had been doing with orchestras and chamber groups. Ophthalmologist Dr. Teddy Tong solved that problem for his own violin playing by having a separate pair of glasses made just for when he plays violin. "Measure the distance to the music stand so an ophthalmologist can come up with a lens that would be optimal for seeing at that distance," he says. He recommends getting progressive lenses, with one section of the lens perfect for music-stand reading, while the upper part would be calibrated for seeing a conductor at a distance.

- **Hearing loss:** "I have potentially a minor hearing loss. That is a problem we need to address throughout the music community," says clarinetist Alex Jones. Dr. Charness agrees and notes that one way to avoid music-related hearing loss is to wear earplugs, as many professional musicians do, such as those who sit in front of the brass section and get blasted, or flutists and violinists who hold their instruments right next to an ear. "Ear plugs allow them to hear the subtleties of what they're doing without causing hearing loss," he says. If there is hearing loss that requires a hearing aid, Dr. Dowdall recommends having it fitted by an audiologist who works with a doctor's office. It's important to let the audiologist know what kind of music you do. "Hearing loss is not a one size fits all diagnosis," says Dr. Dowdall. There are different kinds of hearing aids that can be adjusted to fit different situations, although she warns, "It takes a while for your brain to get used to the new sound mix that's coming in." Rufus Browning had so much difficulty adjusting to the sound mediated by his hearing aids that he stopped choral singing, focusing instead on singing solo. Ms. Miller, the visually impaired singer and pianist described earlier who sings with the Harmony Project chorus, also has hearing loss in both ears. She has a hearing aid in only one ear (the left one). She has adjusted to it quite well so that she can both play piano and sing in the chorus. Each situation is different. The website and blog Grand Piano Passion features articles and reviews of books and documentaries on making music with hearing loss.

Carrying On

"It's slightly harder to sing now than when I was younger. My voice is a little less fluid. But I'm much better at interpretation now. Age, wisdom, and experience really add to the flavor of my singing. Also, I'm much less afraid to make a fool out of myself than when I was younger," says Ms. Shepard. Dr. Dan Brook has reached a similar conclusion. "The arthritis does not help, so I am physically less able, but this is less important than the improvement in my musicianship," says this New York physician and lawyer. "I am a much better pianist than when I was younger. I just push through and play anyway, as best I can."

A few of our team members developed physical issues that unfortunately couldn't be solved no matter how hard they tried. They didn't give up on music. Instead they changed the way they engage with music. Ms. Epstein bounced back from what must have seemed like a devastating obstacle. She had played cello since childhood but as an adult developed a severe hand injury while rehearsing a particularly challenging piece. Her situation didn't improve despite rest and treatment by physicians and physical therapists. She switched to singing, which she is loving, as described in chapter 5. Mitchell Frizzell, a science writer who sings in a Delaware choir, developed a serious jaw problem that forced him to stop playing bassoon. Luckily it doesn't interfere with choral singing, his main focus now. When various physical injuries sidelined Dave Perlman from playing a series of instruments he had played during his adult years—flute, cello, and harp—he too joined a chorus, even though he hadn't sung with a group for fifty years. "I find the chorus much more fun to be with, much less stressful than playing in an orchestra, as errors aren't as audible," says this retired Chicago IRS revenue officer.

CLOSE UP: JUDITH SEUBERT, RECORDER PLAYER, RETIRED LAWYER

Judith Seubert didn't find her instrument until she was a young mother, raising two children, while also attending law school. She wanted an instrument whose music would be easier to master than the complicated piano pieces she played as a youngster. She settled on recorder, taught herself, and before long was playing duets with her husband, a lifelong avocational violinist. "I practiced when and where I was able and used opportunities to make music with my husband and with my kids as they grew up. It was only after we retired and moved to Oregon that I've consistently stuck to playing music." That's when she began studying with a teacher for the first time. She also joined the Portland Recorder Society and was soon playing in several ensembles. "I try to play some each day, but there have been gaps, such as after having shingles which settled into neuralgia in the ring and little fingers of my right hand. You just practice when you can and try not to obsess about it. Music-making at this stage of life is for fun! Otherwise, why bother?"

Other team members have experienced cancer, mild strokes, broken legs and arms. They have gone to great lengths to find their way back to music. Retired schoolteacher Eileen Greenberg benefitted from many of the extras provided at Levine Music in Washington, DC, when she had to relearn how to sing after a bout with cancer. She gained confidence from the school's voice lessons as well as from doing low-key recitals and performances that the school arranges at senior centers, and has even developed a one-woman cabaret show with her voice coach. Retired New York hospital executive Richard LaVine's return to playing concertina has been especially heroic. He explains that cancer "necessitated the removal of large parts of my shoulder and upper back. I've developed the physical resources to compensate for the loss of function, and my playing is stronger than ever."

"I have focal dystonia in my right thumb so it's harder for me to play the right hand parts of piano pieces than it used to be," says Mark Porter, who teaches English in Japan. Focal dystonias involve involuntary muscle contractions or movements in a certain part of the body. They are relatively rare, occurring in about 1 percent of professional musicians. The cause is unknown but is thought to have a neurological link—"unusual misfirings in the brain," as Mr. Porter describes it. Years ago, he consulted a physician who diagnosed his focal dystonia but had little to offer in terms of treatment. Since then, a treatment has been found—botulinum toxin injections—which have helped professional pianist Leon Fleisher curb his dystonia enough to resume two-handed performing. But benefits from the injections last only a few months at a time. Mr. Porter has decided to just keep doing what he has been doing—adjusting his technique so his spastic thumb doesn't keep him from playing Chopin. "Re-fingering a passage often helps," he says. "Sometimes my left hand takes over a note in the right hand. Because I love the piano so much, I'm able to 'dial down' the irritation and focus on what I can do to play the music I want to play."

When physical problems interfere with music-making, a local conservatory may be able to offer suggestions for how to locate health-care professionals who are knowledgeable about music-related issues. So can PAMA, the Performing Arts Medical Association. Fellow musicians are another referral resource, as Paula Washington points out: "We do not give up. Broken bone? Rotator cuff tear? Tendonitis? We share war stories and support and encourage one another to get through the setback. Ours is a social art. We have a network and a support system full of people who know how important music is to our well-being. They know the doctors and therapists to recommend, and what to say to keep one another's spirits up." The next chapter describes a key element of that music support system—the networks that develop from making music with others in ensembles large and small.

Dr. Deborah Edge in the center of the double bass section, performing in a Baltimore Symphony Orchestra Rusty Musicians side-by-side playing workshop. All the bassists around her are members of the Baltimore Symphony.

9 Making Music with Others

"JOINING A CHORUS has changed my life. I'm so happy to have found a community of singers who support each other, plus we are really very good," says Julie Terray, explaining her feelings about the Maine chorus she joined a few years ago. Kathy Dockins feels the same way about the community band in which she plays flute: "I like the sense of camaraderie and how it's so clear we all enjoy playing music." That's what guitarist Ted Dawson likes about the folk jam sessions he has made time to attend, noting, "I love getting together with friends to play." So does bassoonist Hugh Rosenbaum, who meets with friends to play chamber music. He too appreciates the feeling of connection that comes from these gatherings, adding that "the opportunity to interact with people face-to-face dispels for a while the modern isolationism that technology fosters."

The sense of community and connection that comes from making music with others has been emphasized throughout this book and is central to most of our advice-team members' involvement with music. Three-fourths of our questionnaire completers take part in an ensemble, whether vocal or instrumental, large or small, formal or informal. Many also participate in summer music programs or music workshops, enroll in group classes, or take part in musical theater productions.

A few, however, see music as a personal, private activity to do at home for their own enjoyment. This too is a meaningful way to engage with music. "You can be a wonderful musician and never play for another human being," says Susan Levine, a Seattle psychotherapist who returned to piano in her late 50s after a thirty-five year gap. "I'm not ready yet to play in the presence of a person, besides my teacher," she says.

But for those who do want to connect musically with others, this chapter can be a resource. It describes the variety of group music-making experiences that members of our advice team have participated in, frustrations that have arisen, and suggestions for making the most of the experience.

In addition to providing a sense of community, making music with others can serve a more practical purpose—a reason to practice, so as to keep up with the group and not let them down. Another benefit noted by history professor Kerry Smith: "Finding people to play with really does change the relation to the music and the instrument besides just going to lessons." He started on electric bass in his late 40s, "because I needed something to do other than work." After two years of lessons, he joined a rock band of fellow Brown University faculty members and reports, "Playing in the band has expanded my repertoire really quickly. I have learned a lot." Jürgen Hemm, a German security manager, adds another reason for playing with others: "It's boring to fiddle alone." Plus, research shows that becoming involved socially with others can be good for general health and well-being, and may even lead to a potential delay in age-related memory loss.

Of all the benefits that may arise from engaging musically with others, however, the one that probably spurs our team members to rush through dinner week after week to make it to rehearsal on time is the enjoyment they expect to find there. As violinist Maya Weil, a Washington arts fundraiser, observes, "When you are playing with others and it is going well, you feel as if you are soaring. You are suspended in time and hyper alert. You are moving as a unit and there is a feeling of community."

Large Ensemble Options

"There are groups out there for people of all levels," says flutist, singer, and dulcimer player Laurel Bishow. To find a group that fits their needs, many members of our advice panel did what bassoonist Mandy Ray did. "I found my community band when I did a search online about amateur music in the Seattle area," she says. Other team members found ensembles by phoning a local music school, checking out music store bulletin boards, or asking a musical friend. Once they became involved with one musical group, word-of-mouth took over. Fellow musicians, as noted earlier, are terrific about sharing information on musical opportunities.

To help a newcomer launch a search for musical options—or to provide some extra word-of-mouth input for veterans about possibilities they might not be aware of yet—here are the main kinds of large group music-making experiences that keep our team members busy. About half of those who are in ensembles perform with groups like these. Smaller chamber music groups and bands are discussed later in this chapter.

- **Community orchestras, concert bands, jazz big bands, choirs, and choruses:** There are many kinds of community-based ensembles. Some welcome beginners and rusty returnees and don't require auditions. Others prefer more experienced performers and may require auditions. There are also semi-pro ensembles, with a mix of accomplished amateurs who perform alongside professional freelancers. Some ensembles charge membership fees. A few of the high-end groups may pay some travel expenses. Most groups meet and perform during the regular fall through spring concert season, while others are summertime affairs. Some large ensembles are connected to professional organizations or businesses, such as those sponsored by the Chicago Bar Association or the Procter and Gamble Big Band, made up of company employees, although "the company does not officially recognize us," reports Jeff Spaulding, an electrical engineer and pianist who was the band's music director for many years.
- **Ensembles with a mission:** Some community ensembles have a specific social service mission. Others, while not primarily devoted to community service, often perform at nursing homes or senior centers. There is more about ensembles with a mission in chapter 11.
- **Faith-based ensembles:** Church or synagogue choirs and instrumental ensembles generally welcome beginners, although large congregations may have auditions for higher-level groups.
- **Music school-affiliated ensembles:** As noted in chapter 7, music schools offer a variety of choral and instrumental ensembles for adults.
- **College and university ensembles:** Several team members have performed with instrumental and choral ensembles of local colleges and universities, even though they weren't enrolled as students at the time. These ensembles often welcome faculty, staff, and local residents. Eugene Henry, retired Notre Dame professor of computer science and engineering, has continued playing first trombone in the Notre Dame University Band well into his 80s. Some of these ensembles go on tour, such as the Manhattanville College Chorale that Eileen Shea has been singing with for more than fifteen years. Some colleges have alumni bands and choruses which may also go on tour, as does Sarah Muffly's Smith College Alumnae Chorus.
- **Seniors ensembles:** There are more than two hundred New Horizons concert bands, orchestras, jazz bands, and choruses in the United States and Canada that are geared to older adults, as described in chapters 1 and 7. There are also more

than thirty no-audition Encore choruses for older adults in the Washington, DC, area and in six other states. Both Encore and New Horizons provide start-up help for people interested in forming new groups. Retirement communities and senior centers often sponsor ensembles, as do universities that offer OLLI (Osher Livelong Learning Institute) programs, described in chapter 7.

- **Community musical theater:** Several team members perform in musicals presented by community theaters or light opera companies—either as singers, members of the chorus, or instrumentalists in the pit. "I enjoy immensely the high impact of it all, the focus that needs to be there to recall lines, lyrics, and dances," says Theodore Sapp who often performs in musicals. Some instrumentalists have helped out local schools by playing in the pit for high school musicals. French horn player and singer Dr. Marc Wager notes, "I have gotten to live out my fantasy of being both in the cast and the orchestra of a show."

- **Medical school-related ensembles:** Several medical schools and medical centers sponsor orchestras and choral groups for students and staff that are sometimes open to members of the community. The resources section lists medical centers with ensembles.

- **Once-in-a-while ensembles:** Several team members enjoy participating in sing-alongs that crop up now and then, such as a Messiah sing-along that Ms. Bishow sings in every year. Ora McCreary, a retired IT specialist, has attended "summer sings" sponsored by New York City choruses. He explains, "The sponsoring group provides the music, and anyone can come and sing the designated work for the evening." The recorder society that Judith Seubert belongs to holds large group playing sessions once a month. Other team members have participated in drumming circles that sometimes crop up in public parks during the summer. Amy Dennison leads a monthly lunchtime drum circle at the University of Cincinnati that is open to faculty, staff, and students. "We drum for an hour as a way to relax and reduce stress. People who like this end up getting their own drums," says this professional oboist, music educator, and cello newcomer.

- **Professional orchestra-related ensembles:** Several professional symphony orchestras have programs that give non-pro musicians an opportunity to play side-by-side with the orchestras' professional musicians. The Baltimore Symphony has two programs: BSO Academy Week, a week-long summer program; and Rusty Musicians, a one-day event. Canada's Edmonton Symphony Orchestra offers its own versions of both of these programs. The Buffalo Philharmonic's BPO Fantasy Camp is a five-day summer program with side-by-side playing. The Pacific Symphony Orchestra, offers a side-by-side playing opportunity called OC Can You Play with Us (the orchestra is based in Orange County). Other orchestras have offered variations on the play-along format: Allentown Symphony, Boston Symphony, Louisiana Philharmonic Orchestra, Richmond Symphony, and Britain's Bournemouth Symphony. A few orchestras have started no-audition community ensembles, including the Detroit Symphony, the Pacific Symphony, and the Kingston Symphony in Ontario. The Cincinnati Symphony Orchestra started a community choir—the Classical Roots Community Mass Choir—that performs as part of the orchestra's annual Classical Roots concert; this choir has also started performing in other concert settings. The Vancouver Symphony Orchestra sponsors ensembles as part of the music school it operates. "In the last ten years or so, orchestras have been looking to play broader roles in their communities, beyond generating attendance at their concerts, recognizing that their sustainability would be dependent upon having a wider set of stakeholders caring about orchestras and wanting to stand up for them," says Jesse Rosen, president of the League of American Orchestras. If music lovers want to encourage their local orchestra to follow the lead of the orchestras just listed, Mr. Rosen feels there might be interest, especially if the programs would be self-funding through participants' tuition payments, as is true of some of those listed here. There is more about summer opportunities later in the chapter.

The Chicago Bar Association Symphony Orchestra.

Picking and Choosing Large Ensembles

In deciding whether to join a large ensemble and which one to choose, Ms. Muffly suggests, "Think about what you want to get out of music: Do you want an interesting way to meet people? To practice your technique? A creative outlet? Or a low-commitment group for fun? Reflecting on your priorities will help you find the best fit." Having been a serious student of voice all through high school and college, she chose an auditioned chorus whose members are in her age group—20s and 30s. It provides an outlet for creativity as well as a way to make friends in a new city. With eighty members, it's a little bigger than she would like, but as a busy young professional, she has discovered an advantage to a large group. "It's not a huge deal if someone misses a rehearsal," she explains.

Large groups also have the advantage of performing major choral and orchestral repertoire. This is why Mr. McCreary auditioned for a high-level, multi-age chorus that books itself into prestigious concert halls so he could "sing with an orchestra and professional soloists several times a year. It's great to sing the major oratorio works," he explains. Big choral works attracted writer Shannon Polson at first, motivating her to join the Seattle Symphony Chorale when she settled in that city after years in the military during which she sang with community choruses wherever she was stationed. Soon she realized, "I preferred a more varied repertoire and the challenges of a cappella performance." So she auditioned for Seattle Pro Musica, which specializes in a cappella works. She continues to sing with that choir even after moving to a small town a four-hour drive away. Mr. Rosenbaum likes both big choral works and early music and so he has joined two groups—a small a capella choir and a large ensemble that does big works with orchestra and organ.

Repertoire influenced Ms. Ray's decision-making, too. As a working mom, she opted for a band that plays relatively easy music so she doesn't have to do a lot of at-home practicing. Ms. Terray needed to find a chorus that didn't require members to be able to read music, something she has tried but failed to learn, possibly, she thinks, due to her dyslexia. Her chorus provides everyone with practice tracks to listen to at home and is fine with her learning her parts by ear.

Attending a group's performances can also help in making a decision, which is what Mr. Rosenbaum did for the two choruses he joined. "I went to listen to them and didn't hear any warblers or bellowers and decided they would be okay. The conductor was an important part of that decision. So was whether they reached any quality pianissimos. That one feature differentiates amateur choirs from each other." Attending rehearsals helps percussionist and baritone horn player Dana Schwartz choose an ensemble. "I choose whether to join after attending a few rehearsals and judging the atmosphere," says this retired Maryland computer programmer. "I stay in groups when I know I am making a clear contribution to the group's sound, and am appreciated."

Emily Chen looks for a group that has a spirit of mutual respect. She likes that her community orchestra doesn't do what she hated about orchestras during high school. "There are no auditions, no conductor yelling at you and making you play your part by yourself in front of everyone, no guilt trips for missing a rehearsal because of your job. I like that it's egalitarian; there is no seating by proficiency," she says.

For those who are determined to improve their technique, cellist Dr. Nancy Bridges advises, "Play with people who are better than you as often as possible." But those who are looking mainly for a relaxing outlet and aren't concerned about skill development may prefer a low-key group, as violinist Ron Sharpe does. He has chosen a New York community orchestra whose name defines its level: Late-Starters String Orchestra. Its musicians are either at the intermediate level, as he is, or are beginners. "The focus is getting together and playing, not performance. This really takes the stress away," he reports. However, definitions of relaxation differ. For accomplished bassoonist Lauren Hill, playing in an orchestra "of fellow amateur musicians who are really good at their instruments, playing challenging, exciting repertoire, while we hold each other to high standards, is all very relaxed and fun." To each his or her own.

I love the singing, the inspiration, the teamwork, and the thrill of working hard together.

—Roy Hitchings, choral singer, retired hospital CEO

Ensemble Frustrations

Those who play popular instruments may run into difficulties in finding a group. The orchestra at the university where Ann Rogers teaches already had enough flutes. She joined the university's flute choir instead. Frustrations can also arise after joining an ensemble, ranging from personality clashes to unhappiness with the repertoire or with fellow musicians who don't come prepared to rehearsals. If trying to work through the problems doesn't help, there's always the option that Stephen Lustig uses. "I don't dislike anything about my music-making, except playing for the occasional idiot conductor, but then one simply does not return," he says. A soprano on our advice team took the same approach with a church choir she had been in for years whose music director always gave solos to the same four singers. She left the church choir to audition for a high-level chorus, even knowing she would never have a chance to solo there. "I would rather remain a choir member with no solos in a semi-pro choir where I know the soloists are always hired professionals, rather than be in a community religious choir that doesn't give a chance to everyone who wants to practice and try," she says.

Uninspiring repertoire has soured flutist Peggy Radin on some ensembles. "I would like amateur orchestras to stop programming mostly 'pops' type music. One amateur orchestra I play in did Mahler's 9th Symphony; what an incredible experience! I wish for more of that. I wish for more contemporary music, too," she says. Repertoire negotiating may be possible because some of our team members' community ensembles do play ambitious repertoire and even program music by contemporary composers. "I am a strong advocate for music by composers who are underperformed or unjustly forgotten, and whenever I can I try to entice my friends to perform something from this largely untapped body of work," says cellist Ken Williams. If persuading orchestra leadership to experiment doesn't work, check out the final section of this chapter about team members who started new ensembles to play the kind of music they prefer.

"The ideal group has camaraderie, stretches you musically, has a director that makes good musical choices, also teaches well, and protects our voices," observes Kathy Fleming, who performs with choirs and early music instrumental ensembles. "I've not found that perfect combination yet. Each group has its foibles. We weigh options always, but this is an imperfect world."

The Chicago Bar Association also sponsors several small ensembles including the Fair Use Wind Quintet that features several members of our advice team: Judith Grubner on flute, Katherine Erwin on bassoon, and John Vishneski on clarinet.

Chamber Music Groups and Small Bands

"I got involved in some large community orchestras, but did not like the lack of connection to the other musicians. Smaller ensembles are so much more intimate and rewarding for me," says Daniel Savin. He switched to playing bass in smaller settings—chamber music groups, jazz combos, and a band he organized at his synagogue. Violinist Arabella Lang does some orchestral playing, but she too prefers small chamber music get-togethers with friends. She explains that she likes "being part of a group that's small enough for me to feel everyone is making a real contribution that can be heard, appreciated, and responded to. I especially like working on quartets, quintets, etc., where everyone has an equal voice."

Advice-team members who are into rock, folk, and jazz often play in small bands, such as the jazz improv band at his music school that saxophonist Steve DeMont plays with, or the jazz band that trumpeter Arthur Carvajal has joined, a spin-off of the Chicago Bar Association's big band. Mr. Dawson formed his own jug band, which won a prize at Chicago's Battle of the Jug Bands. Guitarist Dr. Brad Reddick has a folk/rock group that began as a shared musical interest with a few friends at his church.

About three-fourths of our questionnaire completers who make music with others perform in small chamber music groups and bands, although about half of them also perform in large ensembles. The genres of music played in small groups differ widely, but the way that pianist Leslie Vieland describes what she loves about chamber music seems to apply to the playing that non-classical groups do, too. "It is very intimate," she explains. "You must listen to every instrument and play with them, sometimes adjusting to them and they to you. Chamber music is all about communication: expressing yourself through the music and fitting this with the other musicians' expressions and working together to present our best understanding of the composer's intent." She came to chamber music as an adult, having played only solo piano as a child. After a thirty-five year break, she came back to piano in her 50s in order to accompany her teenaged son on clarinet and her husband on cello. "I have spent the past fifteen years learning the piano chamber literature and exclusively play chamber music now. It's a joy," she says. Here's how others of our team members became involved in small musical groups.

- **Finding partners at schools:** Several small groups started when students who met at a music school decided to keep making music outside of class. That's how Mr. Dawson formed his jug band, and how pianist Anne Isburgh found the members of her piano trio. "I signed up for a chamber music weekend course. The organizer put a cellist, flutist, and me together. We had so much fun, we've continued to play together over the years," says this Cincinnati engineering manager. Others have met potential partners through summer music camps or workshops. "I have a four-hand piano partner I met through an annual week-long piano workshop. We get together a few times a year and attend the workshop together. Having a chance to collaborate is great," says Deborah Wythe.

- **Widen the search:** "I've never been able to find people to play chamber music with in the small, rural Wisconsin town where I live," says Eric Godfrey. He broadened his search by participating in a chamber music workshop in the neighboring state of Minnesota. "This has opened doors to all the playing I now do. I play chamber music regularly with a variety of musicians in the Minneapolis-St. Paul metro area, a four-and-a-half-hours' drive away. My son lives there, so I schedule visits to him to include one or two ensemble sessions, and a violin lesson."

- **Large ensemble spin-offs:** Others have found small group partners by first joining a large ensemble. "A community orchestra is a great place to start looking. There are so many people concentrated right there. But it can be scary to put yourself out there. The hardest thing is asking the first person," says violist Julia Moline. She was shy about making plans with two violinists she met through her community orchestra for what to do during a period when their orchestra wasn't rehearsing. They agreed to meet at one of their homes with a cellist friend to read through a quartet. "We had a good time. Then we got together again to read through the same piece. We were so tentative with each other. Finally we decided to be a group and continue to work together." The quartet meets regularly to rehearse and has played a few gigs, as noted in chapter 7. Dr. Mann has his own personal database of people he has met over the years playing in New Haven community orchestras. "I keep track of them," says this violist. When he wants to form a quartet to attend a coaching workshop, he taps into this list to put a group together.

- **Online connections:** Dr. Teddy Tong, the ophthalmologist who returned to violin in his 50s, avoided in-person-asking by finding chamber music partners online. He joined a music Meetup group in Los Angeles which offers online messaging between members. A violist posted a notice asking if anyone wanted to play a Dvorak string quartet. "I love that piece. I said, 'Yes,'" he recalls. The violist recruited two others and they had fun playing through the piece. Then Dr. Tong posted a notice on the email bulletin board of the hospital where he works. "I got a couple of responses from physicians I never knew were musicians," he says. They formed a quartet that practices at the cellist's apartment and performed at the hospital's fundraiser. Chamber musicians have also made connections by using the online database of ACMP (Associated Chamber Music Players). Bassoonist Robert Gemmell found a woodwind quintet via the online site Craigslist. "The quintet advertised and I answered," says this retired Massachusetts software engineer. There is more about Meetup groups later in the chapter.

- **Workplace connections:** Mentioning an interest in music to a colleague helped keyboard player Baylor Fox-Kemper join a rock band of Brown University faculty members even before he arrived on campus to start work as an oceanography professor. He noted his interest in music on a registration form for incoming faculty. Minutes after sending that form by email, he received an email back from a senior associate dean of the faculty, Janet Blume, a drummer, who invited him to jam with her and the school's deputy provost, guitarist Joe Meisel. This rock cover band soon added two more faculty members, including Kerry Smith, the bass newcomer mentioned at the start of this chapter.

- **Friends and neighbors:** Tom Krouse's bluegrass band began when he and a neighbor pulled out their guitars to jam after a neighborhood block party one summer night. They kept playing during that summer, adding more friends. "We play bluegrass songs or songs that were never intended to be bluegrass songs but we play them that way," says Mr. Krouse, who runs an Ohio restaurant company. Julia Steinmetz started singing vocals with a rock band that her neighbor had formed, which led to her creating her own band so she could sing the kinds of songs she likes. "There are lots of people on the amateur rock band circuit and they all know the same 'guy songs.' I'm not singing those and some people don't want to learn new songs. It takes finding someone who is not only good but willing to learn something new," she says. She put together a group through word of mouth, held rehearsals in her basement (with her kids complaining about the noise—a reversal of the usual situation), and arranged for her band to play at open mics at a local bar. The role of band organizer has its downsides, however, from having to provide amplifiers and other gear to coping with personnel issues. "The bass player had a hip replacement and we lost our drummer," she says. Her band went on hiatus for a while and then slowly rebuilt.

- **Long lasting:** The membership chemistry in some small groups has worked out so well that they keep getting together for years. One of Kathe Davridge's many chamber groups, a string quartet, has been meeting biweekly for thirty years, reports this violinist and New York hairstylist.

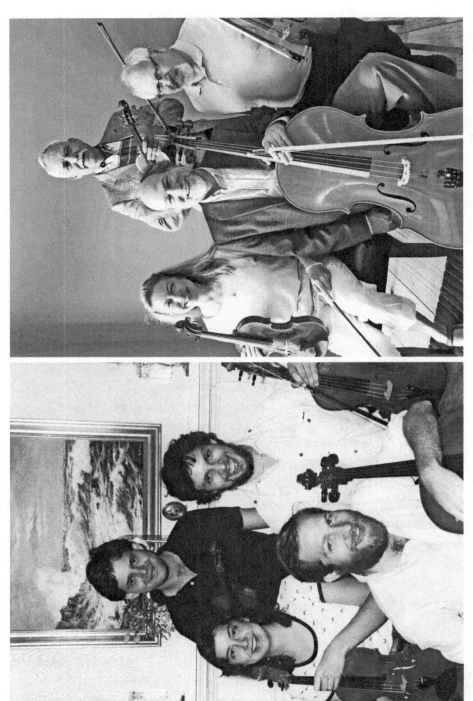

Before and after photos of violinist Liz Sogge's quartet—from when they were undergraduates at the University of Chicago, and at a reunion get-together in 2016.

Nuts and Bolts of Small Group Management

Here are some of the ways our team members keep their small groups going.

- **Where to meet:** Often groups rehearse at members' homes. Ms. Blume's band meets in her basement. Dr. Reddick's church band rehearses at the church and plays at services each week. The band also performs at various venues around town about twice a month, with any earnings going into a fund to buy music and supplies for the group. As noted earlier, Janet Howard's ukulele group practices in the common room of a retirement community. Mary Schons made arrangements with an Indiana art gallery so her band's practice sessions—and the classes it offers—could be held at the gallery in the evening after the gallery closes.

- **When to meet:** Regular rehearsals make planning easier, but isn't always possible. Ms. Vieland's chamber music partners bring along their calendars to schedule their next playing date. Michelle Billingsley suggests using an online scheduler, such as Doodle, through which participants log in possible dates and times so the group's organizer can select the best time for all. Because of rehearsal time scheduling issues and shifting membership, a few advice-team members prefer doing small-group music-making through workshops at a music school so that the school handles all the organizing.

- **Group cohesion:** Some small groups have the same members show up each time. With other groups, the membership is more fluid. In some cases, there's no set membership at all, especially for spur-of-the-moment get-togethers. For ongoing groups that meet regularly, there can be personality problems, as well as musical mismatches. "You cannot expect a good match every time," says Suzanne Epstein, referring to the cold calls she made using the ACMP database when she was playing cello. "You have to be willing to be good-natured about mismatches, whether your skill level is above or below that of the others, and not be impatient or unpleasant about it. You can then call someone else next time." But cellist Rebecca Berg decided to stick with some players who weren't necessarily the best fit "because I just wanted to keep playing. Eventually it sorted itself out according to people's priorities, and some people went in one direction and others in another." Angela Bowman, who has created several bands, has found it best if "everyone has the same motivation." For her Cajun band, she says, "Everyone basically wants to have a good time and get better. It's not that somebody wants to record albums and the others are squeezing this in between their kids and their jobs. We all have similar motivations." The same is true of Janet Blume's band of professors. "We are all totally into it, with the same level of enthusiasm," she says. Bandmate Baylor Fox-Kemper notes, "We're all getting better together."

- **Perform or not:** Some groups look for opportunities to perform, such as the Brown professors' band which plays at campus departmental parties or as the demo band for a course on the history of rock music. Mr. Gemmell's woodwind groups schedule house concerts. But quite a few small groups have no interest in performing. They simply enjoy getting together to sight-read through music without the pressure of polishing a piece to performance level. That is true of the friends who play chamber music with flutist Fritz Hessemer at the retirement community in Maine that he moved to in his early 90s. They gather once a week for two hours in his apartment, which contains a harpsichord that he built, and play pieces from the huge collection of Baroque sheet music that he has accumulated over the years. Earlier, he had a similar group that met at his home in Delaware. He has a knack for persuading people to join him, ever since he returned to flute in his 40s to play Bach duets with his piano-playing daughter, then age 12, with whom he still plays when she visits.

- **Finding scores:** In addition to buying sheet music, classical chamber music groups often tap into free sources of musical scores, such as making use of the music collections at public libraries, or downloading scores that are in the public domain from such online sites as IMSLP (Internet Music Score Library Project). Non-classical groups

---

CLOSE UP: RIVA EDELMAN, VIOLINIST, RETIRED SCHOOLTEACHER

"I have had a quartet for more than forty years," says Riva Edelman. "It hasn't always been the same group. A person will move away or get sick. Then you find another person." She usually uses ACMP to find new players. After returning to violin in her 30s, she played in a community orchestra for a while, but then developed back trouble. "With orchestras, you can't take a break when you need to," she says. So she started playing violin duets with another returning violinist. "We found other players and that was our first quartet." One group broke up after five years when the violist didn't get along with another player. Otherwise, "people have been wonderful. In the beginning we were all working and met in the evenings. Now we are retired and play each Monday from 1:30 to 4:00 in my apartment, with a fifteen minute break for a snack. I always look forward to that day of the week. I have a big library of all the standards. If someone wants something different, they bring it. We have performed, but don't like to. We love playing through a lot of music."

can often find guitar tabs, chord sheets, and lyrics online, or they figure out how to play a tune from listening to recordings, or may even create their own songs. Dr. Deborah Edge, a bassist, has taken a pro-active approach. "There is not as much chamber music for string bass as for other strings," she says. "Some years ago, I purchased the full set of the scores for major works that include string bass so when the chance comes up, I have the music to share."

Collaborative Creativity

All group music-making, no matter the size of the ensemble, involves collaboration, but for small ensembles that don't have a conductor, the experience is especially interactive. "I would rather play with people who understand ensemble thinking than those that are virtuosic but cannot adjust to those around them. With chamber music, it is far more important to listen to others than to play well," says violinist/violist Joan Herbers. In her chamber groups, "our most serious disagreements are on tempo." In one group, they talk through tempo changes before starting. In another group, "we defer to the first violinist. If we have to stop mid-movement, someone will often point out if we were ignoring dynamics, tempi, and the like." In both groups, they talk about the composer and the piece they're playing. "Often we listen to snippets of recordings on an iPad of a piece we just played to understand how professionals interpret the piece."

With rock, folk, and jazz bands, the players often do on-the-spot crafting of a piece. For new songs that Mr. Krouse's bluegrass band wants to cover, "I'll learn the song by ear or if it's difficult, I'll look up the chords online. I'll figure it out on guitar, bring it to rehearsal, and then it turns into something. The creation for us is when we get together to rehearse," he explains. "We'll start playing it and someone will suggest something different to try. We'll incorporate it. Everyone can add an idea. It's a collaborative process. We recently added the Beyoncé song 'All the Single Ladies,' making it a bluegrass tune."

Dr. Reddick's church band uses a similar approach, although sometimes he creates a new tune at home, working out the chord progression and a melody. "I let the lyrics burble up to match the emotion that the melody and chord progression communicate," he says, often with some editing by his wife. "When I introduce it by performing it for the band, they listen and give varied reactions and feedback. Then we play the song together, with all vocalists and instrumentalists adding their own personal part, whatever they feel fits best. Once everyone agrees on the shared co-creative ideas, we record it, write down the lyrics, with block chord notation over the top. Making the song co-owned by everyone is important for their growing with the song, a shared experience in playing the song together."

Group creativity also applies to selecting names for the bands: Grassinine, for Mr. Krouse's bluegrass band; Sunday Union for Dr. Reddick's group; and DFB (Dirty Filthy Basement), a quote from the Rolling Stone song, "Let It Bleed," for Janet Blume's professors' band—a comment, she says, on the state of her basement where the band rehearses.

Jams and Open Mics

"I play and sing at a jam at least once a week. You learn new songs and learn to play by ear and pick up musical cues from better players," says Ms. Billingsley. She and several other advice-team members go to informal folk music jams at Chicago's Old Town School. Jams for folk, rock, and jazz can also take place at bars, art galleries, and other community venues, as well as in musicians' homes. There's a freedom in jamming both in the creative expression involved, as well as in not being tied down to a weekly rehearsal schedule. "I love the informal aspect of it. I love that we all just get together and play music and it doesn't matter if you hit a wrong note while playing a solo or if the group sings flat while trying a song a cappella," says Debra Koran, who takes part in a weekly folk music jam. "But there are times when I wish there was more structure, that we could perfect a few songs." But then it wouldn't be a jam. It would turn into an ensemble rehearsal.

"Jam sessions are a big experiment. You're throwing people together who have not really played with one another before. You're there to try things out. Sometimes things work and sometimes they don't. That's how jam session culture works. You're not there to cut an album," says professional saxophonist and jazz educator Marcus Elliot. He leads a jazz jam session in Detroit that's mainly for professional musicians, but there are other jam sessions in the city that would work for those who aren't yet playing at that level. "A jam session is bigger than the music. It's also a social event. You're making friends, as long as you're respectful and don't take twenty choruses on a song. If you're a jerk, nobody's going to want to play with you. If you go into a situation where you think you might be out of your league, remember why you're doing it, that it's supposed to be fun. The only way to get better is to just jump in, learn from it, and grow from it." An article listed in the bibliography offers tips for surviving at a jam session.

Several of our team members organize jam sessions at home. "Have your friends come over and bring a couple of songs they want to lead. I have a laptop hooked up to our TV and will pull up the chord tabs to songs and everyone can read them from there. It's handy if you don't have a printer at home to make everyone copies," says Ms. Billingsley. Violinist Ron Sharpe started a different kind of jam, called Tap 'n Jam, to bring together instrumentalists to play jazz standards and dancers to tap along to the tunes. "This is something that you can't do in a New York apartment, so we rented studio space and everyone kicked in a few dollars to cover the cost," he says. "If this wasn't New York, I'm sure we could find a place to do this for free." Lawyer Kathy Whisler, a singer who plays guitar and also likes playing rhythm bones and drums in jug bands, sometimes organizes informal jam sessions at home in addition to hosting a monthly sea shanty sing-along in the back room of a Chicago bar. "Participants join in on the choruses," she says. "Ordinarily, I'm pretty shy in social situations. Music is a good way to meet people."

Open mic nights also offer ways to make music with others. These are live events that can take place at bars, music festivals, music schools, or other venues where

David Robinson with his tenor saxophone.

CLOSE UP: DAVID ROBINSON, TENOR
SAXOPHONIST, LAWYER

"I played tenor saxophone in high school and until I was 27, when I began law school. I got busy, sold my horns, and stopped playing for thirty years," says David Robinson. "I'm looking toward retirement and thought I'd get back into music. I joined a beginners' band at Michigan State's Community Music School for two semesters to get my confidence up. Then I joined its New Horizons jazz band. I take private lessons, too. It took effort, but it came back. Music is the simplest and most complicated thing simultaneously. You may not understand the concept today but if you keep messing around with it, what seemed complicated becomes extremely simple. You pick your horn up and do something and another little light comes on and it becomes part of your repertoire. How to put it together with your own signature, your own individuality, it's the most amazing thing. That's why I love music." He attends jam sessions at Detroit clubs, but hasn't brought his horn to sit in yet. But he plans to. "I've got the courage. I've got to get the skill. There is some margin of confidence gathering. I'll get there."

audience members can perform a song or two at a microphone, usually by signing up in advance. "The open mics that I go to are at art galleries," says Ms. Schons, who says her area of northwest Indiana is full of art galleries that sponsor cultural events. "You can spend all weekend going to different galleries to do open mics. Usually at the end of the night there's time for everyone to get up and play together. If someone tells me the chords beforehand, I can usually flail along on banjo. At first I was so nervous, I thought I would pass out. It's gotten better. It has helped me become less nervous playing in front of people and more comfortable making mistakes."

There are also informal classical music evenings taking place in cafes and restaurants in several cities, sponsored by Classical Revolution. These aren't jams exactly, but they feature a changing line-up of musicians. Dr. Sherman Jia and his fellow UCSF Medical Center musicians have performed at one of these events at San Francisco's Revolution Café. To find jam sessions or open mics, check with other musicians and music teachers or search online.

About Support Groups

All the ensembles, classes, workshops, summer programs, jams, and impromptu get-togethers that our team members participate in provide support and validation of their devotion to music, but there are also organizations set up specifically to encourage avocational musicians. Chief among them are Meetup groups that have been mentioned already. These are part of the Meetup social networking organization that provides online support for people who want to meet together in their own communities to explore common interests. There are hundreds of thousands of such groups worldwide on a variety of topics, including more than a hundred for amateur musicians throughout the United States, Canada, Mexico, and other countries. Meetup groups usually hold regular gatherings at which musicians perform for each other. Pianist/graphic designer Glenn Kramer started a piano Meetup group in San Diego called Amateur Pianist that has more than eight hundred members. In addition to offering performing opportunities, it also sponsors a competition for accomplished amateur pianists and has a list on its website of other piano competitions.

A Meetup group helped Daniel Savin find his way in music after he realized that large orchestras weren't for him. A friend invited him to join a jazz trio that was performing at a gathering of a New York Meetup, Amateur Classical Musicians Association (ACMA). Despite its name, this group includes musicians who perform jazz, pop, and world music, too. "I had a lot of fun working in a small group," he says. Through ACMA, he has met musicians with whom he has performed at other ACMA gatherings. The first time he tried playing a solo piece there he found it "very scary," but the next time he played a humorous piece and it went better. "I had a blast, despite several music gaffs," he says. By then he had realized that "music is not my day job, and so I don't have to be excellent at it."

Dr. Edge participates in a support group that isn't part of the Meetup network. She attends monthly Sunday evening meetings of Works in Progress in Washington, DC. "It's a group of about ten adults, mostly pianists, but also two cellists, a violinist, and a singer. Everyone plays something they have been working on. It does not have to be performance ready. You always are appreciated—a great venue to get more confident about solo playing," says this bassist who usually plays a duet with a pianist. Soprano Dr. Mary Lane Cobb receives helpful feedback at the monthly meetings she attends of the New York branch of the National Association of Negro Musicians, at which members present works-in-progress that may be performed later in an annual recital. Flutist Linda Rapp belongs to a similar group in upstate New York that has been around for more than sixty years, the Musical Society of Kingston. Its roughly twenty-five members include amateurs as well as professional musicians, along with a few who come just to listen. Each monthly program has a theme. "There's no criticism. It's all for enjoyment," she says.

For Ellen Tenenbaum, her "lifeline" when she came back to playing piano was another Washington support group, the Adult Music Student Forum (AMSF). It has about a hundred members and offers a different kind of performance arrangement, with eight levels of performances. Some are for beginners; others are for intermediate or more advanced performers. "A performance provides a goal," says Matthew Harre, the piano teacher who started AMSF about thirty years ago as a way to encourage his adult students at a time when there weren't many performance opportunities for avocational musicians. "After people perform a piece, they play better. It gives them a vested interest in what they're doing," he says.

Starting a Support Group

- **Amateurs in charge:** Even though Mr. Harre, a teacher, founded AMSF, he realized that having music teachers run the organization and attend performances added unneeded tension. He is no longer in charge, although he serves as a consultant. "I don't even want teachers to go to the more protected recitals. It's hard for teachers not to comment. As soon as teachers start critiquing, people become intimidated," he observes.
- **Appreciation only:** "At first we tried having people from the audience give feedback after someone's performance. Some people were too brutal in their comments," says pianist, conductor, and business analyst Alberto De Salas, who founded the ACMA Meetup group. "It introduced a level of tension that wasn't helping. We needed to set the mood that it's okay if you make a mistake, the world's not going to end, we're all friends here, it's not a contest of who did best." Dropping audience feedback helped make the gatherings less stressful.
- **Nonprofit status:** ACMA, AMSF, and Mr. Kramer's Meetup all went through the legal process of obtaining 501(c)(3) nonprofit status, which allows them to solicit tax-deductible contributions to help grow their programs. This status also takes tax pressure off the group's founders so that any funds the group takes in aren't taxed as the founders' personal income. Nonprofit status requires setting up a board of directors, who can help with managing the group. "Nonprofit status gives us more legitimacy and visibility," says Mr. De Salas. There is more on nonprofit status later in the chapter.

Summer Programs

"I began to attend CAMMAC—Canadian Amateur Musicians Association— summer programs in my early 40s. I took courses on guitar, recorder, choir, jazz improvisation, and musical theatre. I also made good friends. I came home each time a better musician and was in a good mood for weeks. These experiences got me through the harsh Montréal winters," says Carol Katz, who plays guitar, bass, and percussion. Violist Phyllis Kaiden is just as enthusiastic about the Puget Sound Chamber Music Workshop that she attends year after year. "It is the highlight of my summer," she says. "The wonderful amateur musicians who assemble there have become my musical family." She credits another summer program that she attended several years earlier—Midsummer Musical Retreat in Walla Walla, Washington—as "the catalyst for my musical involvement now. I was exposed there to the world of adults making music together and having immense fun doing so, working together to be the best we can. It was life changing."

Dr. Marc Wager feels that he has earned "the equivalent of a master's degree in chamber music" from more than thirty summers at the Bennington Chamber Music Conference in Vermont. Clarinetist and saxophone enthusiast Dr. Alvin Crawford reports that a week he spent at a Jamey Aebersold summer jazz camp with his teenaged son was "one of the best weeks of my life." Eloise Bensberg loves singing huge choral masterworks each summer at the Berkshire Choral Festival, where she also takes classes on vocal technique and auditioning.

Carol Katz having a blast at the New England Adult Music Camp in Sidney, Maine.

Some summer programs are geared to experienced musicians, but others welcome newcomers. Anna Pope was practically a beginner when she first attended the Sonata piano camp in Vermont at age 60, having had only two years of lessons many years earlier. She has kept going back. "Each time was a revelation. I learned so much from the teachers and other people who attended," says this San Francisco lawyer. "Now I play duets twice a month with a friend I met at the piano camp." This camp also offers workshops throughout the year.

Half of the questionnaire completers on our advice team have participated in summer music programs, whether they are weekend events at a music school, retreats for faith-based ensembles, or week-long programs that are in many ways reminiscent of sleep-away camps for young people. The level of enthusiasm among summertime participants is amazingly high. There seems to be something magical about getting away from everyday pressures to focus on music for a week or two, even if the sleep-over programs involve elements of roughing it. As flutist Dr. Karlotta Davis explains, "My vacations are centered around making music—attending Interlochen Adult Chamber Music Camp and also the Baltimore Symphony Orchestra Academy. I return to work energized, inspired, and at peace. The perfect vacation. Camp food, lumpy beds, and music from 9:00 a.m. to 9:30 p.m.—what could be better? The generosity and kindness of the professional musicians at the Baltimore Symphony Orchestra Academy is astonishing. I smile from the moment I arrive until the moment I leave."

The professional musician mentors are enthusiastic, too, according to Jane Marvine, the Baltimore Symphony's English horn player who helped create and serves as an advisor for the orchestra's summer Academy Week program. "It's incredibly rewarding, the experience of bringing people into your world," she says. "The participants are so interesting and successful in their own life and somehow manage to keep music going in their life. They have such a passion for music and such respect for us. We cheer people on, encourage them to do the best that they can, and be happy, even if it's not technically perfect."

John Warshawsky recalls that initially at his first Baltimore Symphony summer program, "I felt overwhelmed by how skilled everyone else was (including the other amateurs). But as the week went on, I gained confidence, and I ended up having a great time." Some may not be keen on the roughing-it aspect or the lack of sleep that may occur at summer programs, with participants not wanting to miss a minute of after-hours jamming. Ms. Bowman found the lack of sleep musically beneficial. "The sleep deprivation broke down my defenses so that the music seeped into me a lot more quickly," she says of taking part in Cajun and Creole Week, one of the many folk-music oriented festivals at Augusta Heritage Center in Elkins, West Virginia.

"Attending chamber-music courses is something I have only been able to do since my children became independent. I now go once or twice annually," says cellist and pianist Dr. Elizabeth Nevrkla. Flutist Linda Rapp started attending the Bennington chamber music program when her children were young by activating her family support system—her husband and parents. "My parents came that week to help take care of the kids," she says. She has been going to that camp most summers ever since.

Before signing up, it's wise to speak with someone who has participated in a program to learn more about it. There is no central website with a comprehensive listing of summer music programs for adults. ACMP, AMSF, New Horizons, and Encore have lists on their websites of some programs. Websites of music associations may have suggestions or may sponsor programs themselves, such as the early music summer programs that Ms. Fleming has attended, organized by the Viola da Gamba Society of America. The resources section of this book lists summer programs that advice-team members mentioned on their questionnaires. No vetting has been done to assess the programs; individuals could use the list as a starting point to investigate further.

> **How much I love it. I wish I had not waited so long.**
> —Anna Pope, pianist, lawyer

Audition Advice

Some community orchestras, bands, choruses, and summer programs require auditions. Team members who initially could never have imagined themselves as part of an auditioned group were surprised to find that in a few years, they were ready to give auditioning a try. Bruce Gelin played clarinet through college and for a while after, but then put his clarinet away for more than twenty-five years. After about a year of refresher lessons, he joined a community band that didn't require auditions; the next year he joined a higher-level group that also didn't have auditions. Finally, the following year he was ready to try to audition for a semi-pro orchestra. He prepared well, did well at the audition, and gained a spot in that ensemble—three years after returning to clarinet. His "no-lose" attitude toward auditions helped. "If I don't get the part or the seat, I still have my regular groups to fall back on," he says. "I try to see auditions as opportunities, not burdens."

Ms. Bensberg learned how to control audition jitters in a workshop she took at the Berkshire Choral Festival. "One of the things that was most helpful was when they said that if you're not nervous about an audition, you're not human. Even professionals get nervous. Don't get bothered by that. It's normal. Also realize that the people who are listening to you are not sitting there waiting for you to fail," she says.

"It's like jumping into a swimming pool," says choral director Stanley J. Thurston. "You have to be fearless and realize that everybody gets nervous. If you're using your body in the right way, the sound will be produced even if nerves are involved. For singers, a lot has to do with the way you use your jaw. If you're bringing tension into how you use your jaw, your voice isn't going to sound warm. Think about how to relax from your jaw down to your neck and use the muscles in the lower part of your body to support the sound."

"I tell my students to do what I did when I auditioned for the Metropolitan Opera," says Charles Williams, a voice teacher and opera singer in his 70s. He aced that audition by not treating it as an audition. Instead he thought of it as a performance. "I wasn't coming to ask for something or to get someone to like me," he explains. He sang as if he already had the job. "Go out on stage and perform. Have fun. It will be a better audition."

In addition to the audition tips that follow, there is more on jitters control in the next chapter.

- **Pick a piece you know:** Sometimes there are pieces that auditionees are required to perform. If not, choose wisely. "I prefer pieces I know really well rather than the most difficult ones," says J. David Brown, a government economist and violinist who auditioned successfully for two community orchestras the first year he moved to Washington, DC. Performing an easier piece with musicality and confidence makes a better impression than stumbling through a more challenging piece. Ms. Bensberg reports, "I've been at some auditions where they say if you don't have a prepared piece, sing 'God Bless America' or 'America the Beautiful' so they can hear how you sing." Mr. Thurston recommends choosing a song that is in the style of music done by the group you're auditioning for. He suggests bringing sheet music for the song so you can sing with piano accompaniment. "When you sing in a choir, you have to sing with others," he explains. "Music directors are looking to see how good your ear training is. It's not enough that you can sing a song." They also want to see if you are checking to make sure you're in tune with something else—in the case of the audition, the piano.
- **Know what's up:** Find out what you will be asked to do during the audition. If sight-reading or sight-singing are on the menu, practice doing them. Here's where having taken sight-singing, solfège, or music theory classes helps. "I practice by picking up pieces of music that I don't know and giving

them a go," says Ms. Fleming, a singer and early music instrumentalist. Tenor Stephen Whitner adds, "Know what kind of sound the group usually has and try to match that—big, full-voiced, light, or blended." Patricia Mabry adds, "Bring water." That's good advice for instrumentalists as well as singers.

- **Trial run:** "I have found it helpful to do a mock audition in front of friends," says Mr. Brown. "The more practice I have under audition-like conditions, the easier it is in the actual audition." Wear the clothes you plan to wear at the audition to learn how it feels to perform in that outfit.

- **Mistakes happen:** "In some auditions I've nailed the piece and felt great. Other times I felt like I made a complete fool of myself. I still got into the groups I didn't think I did well in," says Elaine Lee Paoliello. If your musicality shines through, a mistake may be overlooked, especially if you recover well from it.

- **Get a pass:** Word-of-mouth carries a lot of weight. Several team members report that they joined an auditioned instrumental group without auditioning because someone in the ensemble was familiar with their past performances in another group.

Creating New Ensembles

Colleen Schoneveld had no intention of starting an orchestra when she began violin lessons at age 48. She had always wanted to play violin, but never had a chance as a child. As a dressmaker and costumer for musicians, she worked with musicians all the time and decided to join the world of music-making herself. A complete novice who didn't know how to read music, she began taking lessons and made progress. But after several years it leveled off. Discouraged, she stopped the lessons and lost the motivation to practice. Then she read an article about a Scottish orchestra for struggling beginners, the Really Terrible Orchestra (RTO). "I figured I needed either to move to Scotland or start an orchestra here," she recalls. She contacted the director of the Scottish RTO for advice and within a year created her own RTO in Pennsylvania, the first RTO in the United States. Now there are several others.

Another British Isles ensemble inspired Elena Rahona to start an orchestra. A violin newcomer with only a few years of lessons who had never played in an orchestra, she used vacation time from her job as an environmental activist to attend the summer program of the East London Late Starters Orchestra. She had so much fun that when she returned home, she and a friend organized a similar ensemble in New York City.

The orchestra that cellist Mike Tietz started and often conducts is definitely not for beginners. His Broadway Bach Ensemble began more than thirty years ago when he and some chamber music friends put together a small pick-up orchestra of accomplished amateurs to play Bach and Mozart in honor of Mozart's 229th birthday. "The orchestra liked it. The audience liked it. So I said, 'OK, let's do another one,'" he recalls. "Then came the hard work of forming an organization."

A few other members of our advice panel have created large ensembles, including Dr. Jia, who, as noted in chapter 3, started a string orchestra at his San Francisco medical center. Audrey-Kristel Barbeau put together Montréal's New Horizons band as part of her PhD research on music's impact on senior citizens. Joy and Jill Procida, the sisters with muscular dystrophy, created the Glass City Swing Band partly to have fun playing trumpet and saxophone for dances, weddings, and music festivals, but also to help change attitudes about the disabled. Their band hosts a benefit dance each year to raise money for the Muscular Dystrophy Association. Other ensemble creators on our advice panel include John Vishneski, who started the Barristers Big Band as an offshoot of the Chicago Bar Association Symphony Orchestra, and violinist Kathe Davridge who formed a conductor-less group, the Mimosa Chamber Ensemble, after she "had enough of playing in community orchestras with conductors." Her ensemble gives one concert a year in New York City.

Managing a large ensemble, however, "is like running a small business," warns Mr. Tietz. Here are suggestions for those who want to give it a try.

- **Set the level:** Ms. Rahona's first attempt to find musicians for her Late-Starters String Orchestra didn't turn out well. "We put an ad on Craigslist that said, 'Come one, come all,' and that there was no audition. Some people showed up who were super advanced and didn't realize that we didn't have tryouts because we're a beginners' orchestra," she explains. She became clearer in future ads and on the ensemble's website that this is a "teaching orchestra" for beginners or rusty returnees who read music and have studied their instrument for at least a year. It's also important to state whether there's a membership fee and when rehearsals take place.

- **A mission statement:** Ms. Schoneveld didn't write a mission statement for her RTO and ran into trouble when a new conductor came on board whose conducting style didn't mesh well with the orchestra's easy-going atmosphere. Now there is a detailed statement of purpose on the group's website, as there is also for the Late-Starters' Orchestra and for the Procida sisters' swing band. For Mr. Tietz, writing a mission statement required figuring out how his orchestra would differ from the many other high-level community orchestras in New York City. He feels what makes his group special is that its concerts are free, give aspiring young professional soloists and conductors a chance to perform, and often feature a piece by a contemporary composer or an older piece that is not often heard.

- **Auditions:** The beginners' ensembles that our team members created don't hold auditions. Neither does the Mimosa Chamber Ensemble, which is made up of people from Ms. Davridge's wide circle of chamber music friends. For Mr. Tietz's ensemble, newcomers can join on the recommendation of someone who is already in the orchestra. If nobody knows an applicant, he will audition them, or he will play duets with potential string members. "I try not to make it high pressure, but we do want to know how people play," he says. His criteria for someone succeeding in the orchestra is that they "have chops, show up, and be nice."

- **Rehearsal space:** Some groups rehearse in cost-free spaces, such as in the loft apartment of one of the Mimosa musicians, or in the Procida sisters' basement, or a room at UCSF Medical Center. The RTO and the Montréal New Horizons Band use space in a retirement community or senior center rent free in exchange for giving free performances there. The Late-Starters group rents space in a rehearsal studio. Mr. Tietz's Broadway Bach rents space in a church.

- **Finding scores:** Mr. Tietz's orchestra often downloads free scores and parts that are in the public domain from the online site IMSLP. In addition to purchasing scores, Ms. Schoneveld's orchestra has borrowed scores and parts with permission from a local junior high school, and has also shared scores with other orchestras. When the Mimosa Chamber Ensemble wanted to play music that was still under copyright, they contacted the publishers to work out the cost for a performance. Ms. Rahona tries to find arrangements of classic pieces that fit the skill level of her Late-Starters' members. She has persuaded some composers to write new pieces that aren't too hard. "The composers love the challenge and hearing their creations live, as well as enjoying the gratitude of our players who get to experience, even at their level, the creative journey," she says.

- **Nonprofit Status:** Ms. Barbeau received help from the New Horizons organization in setting up her New Horizons band, including a grant for start-up material. New Horizons strongly recommends that all its groups obtain nonprofit status and liability insurance. Obtaining nonprofit status involves filing a lot of complex legal paperwork. Luckily someone who joined her band volunteered to handle the paperwork. Volunteers also helped the Procida sisters and Mr. Tietz with their nonprofit filing. Ensembles connected to nonprofit organizations—such as the medical school and bar association ensembles—can use the nonprofit status and insurance of the parent organizations. Ms. Rahona uses a business called Fractured Atlas, which offers arts groups "fiscal sponsorship." This lets an arts group use Fractured Atlas's nonprofit status to solicit tax-deductible donations. Fractured Atlas offers other services, such as arranging low-cost liability insurance, as does a similar group in the United Kingdom called Making Music. Local law schools may help if they have programs through which law students do legal work pro bono for nonprofits. David Brown, the director of the Harmony Project chorus in Ohio, advises, "Reach out to another nonprofit and ask if you can look at their nonprofit applications, to get an idea of how to structure it." These applications are public documents and nonprofits are supposed to make them available if requested. In addition, the Grantspace blog of the Foundation Center has helpful information on filing for nonprofit status.

- **Delegate responsibilities:** Mr. Tietz recommends putting orchestra members on the ensemble's board and dividing up the jobs of running the group among them, with several dealing with personnel, one handling the mailing list, another handling the website, and so on. A user-friendly website and a presence on Facebook and other social media sites, such as ReverbNation. com for rock bands, can attract members and publicize performances.

- **Rally allies:** Dr. Jia didn't need to do much persuading to start instrumental music programs at UCSF Medical Center. It already had a performing arts fund that he used for both the chamber music and orchestra programs. For organizations where a certain amount of persuading may be needed, Dr. David Shapiro recommends starting at the top. This psychiatrist, who describes himself as "a mediocre Afro-Cuban jazz percussionist," loves music and realized how valuable a music program could be for his medical school. So he helped start the Music and Medicine Initiative at Weill Cornell Medical College. "Get the dean behind it," he recommends. "I got the support of the dean and the chairman of the board and created an advisory board of full professors and department chairs." That made it easier to raise private money to fund the program. "It hasn't cost the medical school a dime." He adds, "Occasionally students will let me sit in on their jazz orchestra."

- **Wider links:** Several community orchestras that our team members play in belong to the League of American Orchestras, which offers its members seminars, workshops, and a magazine. A sliding scale membership fee lets orchestras join for $150 a year if they have an operating budget less than

$25,000. The same rate is offered to community orchestras by Orchestras Canada. Some choruses that our team members sing with belong to Chorus America, which has consultants who can advise member choruses; it offers a $150 membership fee for groups with budgets under $87,000. Choral Canada has a $100 membership fee for community choruses and provides a range of supportive services.

> **Remember: We're doing this to have fun.**
> —Angela Bowman, fiddle player, singer,
> software developer

Ensemble Etiquette

In addition to Mr. Tietz's description of what makes a good ensemble member— "show up, good chops, be nice"—here are a few other ensemble etiquette suggestions, including finding a replacement if your absence at a rehearsal or performance would cause problems for the ensemble. Irene Ten Cate tries to do that if she has "to cancel on a chamber music reading session, in which case I do what I can to find a replacement cellist." That's not always possible and may not be necessary for large ensembles with other musicians who can fill in for the missing musician.

"While playing with others, if you can't play a certain section, don't fake it, because you'll make everyone sound bad," advises saxophonist David Inverso. Going through the motions, air-bowing, or mouthing the words may be preferable to squeaking out an off-key note or messing up the rhythm in a crucial section. Flutist Judith Grubner warns, "If you can't hear the soloist, you're playing too loud." For singers, if a note for a piece is out of range, be sure to speak with the music director rather than endangering your voice. Another basic: Bring a sharpened pencil to rehearsals and performances.

"If you're coughing or you have something that's contagious, you have to be stewards of the rest of the people in the room and not sit in the section and spread what you have," says Mr. Thurston. That's good advice for instrumental ensembles, too. For singers, he advises, "If your inflammation has progressed to the point where it's causing pain, then we would recommend that you don't sing that performance." That's why he has more than one singer learn a solo part in the choruses he directs, to make it easier if someone has to drop out at the last moment. "There's no ownership of a solo. It's not a 'my solo' kind of a thing. You have to build that into the rehearsal process so different people are singing the solo along the way." For situations where solo coverage has not been built into rehearsals, he notes, "This is why it is important to learn to read music. If someone has to step in unexpectedly, you can step in quicker if you can read the music." There are more performing tips and suggestions for managing pre-performance jitters in the next chapter.

The Heritage Signature Chorale whose artistic director is Stanley J. Thurston. Several advice-panel members sing with this chorus: Dr. Darlene Ifill-Taylor (6th from right, third row) and Patricia Mabry (4th from right, first row). Rey Forrest is also in the choir, but is not in this photo.

Ken Williams performing with the Thalia Symphony Orchestra at Town Hall in Seattle, Washington.

10 Performing

"MAKING MUSIC IS about communication. Performing gets to the point of it," says Dr. Nancy Bridges. Fellow cellist Ken Williams agrees: "I believe that performance is the heart of music-making. For me, performance serves two purposes: *first* as the driving force for me to work to make the music as good as I can; and *second*, as an opportunity to present to others something good that they may not know." Both of these cellists perform in several concerts a year, playing with community orchestras and chamber music groups. They admit to feeling nervous before performing. "But only a little," says Dr. Bridges. "I've done much scarier things as a physician. No one is likely to die as a result of my playing, no matter how bad it is."

Any music-making with others involves musical communication—the intense back-and-forth listening and responding that occurs among musicians in an ensemble. Sharing that musical conversation with others by performing in public can heighten the sense of communication. The great majority of our advice-team members participated in public performances during the year that they completed the questionnaire about their musical activities. This chapter focuses on their performance experiences.

A few of our team members seem to be natural performers—not bothered at all by performance jitters. "I love to play and sing. I'm a ham," admits guitarist Ted Dawson. "I'll play anywhere. I've played in front of two hundred people in a big concert hall, at open mics, in friends' homes." Vocalist and fiddler Angela Bowman is another for whom jitters are not an issue. "I loved performing as a kid and I love it now," she says. Cassandra Pettway attributes her lack of performance fear to the positive experiences she had playing clarinet as a child, both at school and at family gatherings. "Family always cheered me on. I enjoyed playing for them," she recalls. Even when she put clarinet aside after ninth grade and didn't play it for more than thirty years, she still had no qualms when she started performing again with Detroit's New Horizons Jazz Band, playing clarinet and tenor saxophone, too. "I just fell right back into it," she says. "It felt natural."

For others, performing does not come naturally. Anxiety keeps them from performing in public. "Currently, I play for myself and family," says guitarist Joseph Arden. "I have thought about doing something bigger, but it makes me nervous." Cellist Susan Lauscher can handle performing for fellow musicians at summer music programs (with the help of a beta blocker) but not in more public settings. "I understand that preparing for performances does raise the level of playing, but I get anxious. I have enough of that in my life already," she says.

Pianist Jonathan Pease prefers not to perform for a different reason. "I don't think I play at a high enough standard to perform. I feel too self-conscious to attempt it," he explains." Another pianist, Dr. Dan Brook, avoids public performances because of "the intense preparation and efforts for perfection that are required." He focuses on informal chamber music get-togethers instead. Charles Stark, who began piano lessons after retiring as a Washington, DC, lawyer, explains that his objective "is entirely personal, not public performance."

Performance fears can be tamed, however, according to many of our team members. Quite a few who used to suffer mightily from performance anxiety have found ways to gain control and feel more at ease sharing with others the joy they find in music. "Now that I've gotten a handle on my nerves, it's easier to perform than when I was younger," says pianist Barbara Napholtz. In the following pages, our advisors describe how they handle their jitters. Additional aspects of performing are also covered, including creating performance opportunities and preparing for competitions.

It's Normal

"You always get nervous when you perform. That never goes away. It's just that you learn how to play while you're nervous." That's the advice professional violinist Joshua Bell gives to kids in the book *The Young Musician's Survival Guide*. This observation can be reassuring for adult avocational musicians as well. The responses from those who completed the questionnaire for this book demonstrate that performance jitters are both common and controllable. The great majority of them—about 85 percent—say they get nervous about performing. Yet about the same number report having participated in public performances during the year before they filled out the questionnaire. Clearly, many of our team members have figured out how to do what Joshua Bell does— perform while nervous.

Some actually like the jittery feeling they have before a performance. "I feel better when I'm a little nervous, especially if I have to sing a solo. I can use that energy and channel it into my performance. If I'm not nervous, something is wrong," says Nicole Ryder, who sings in an auditioned chorus. Flutist Peggy Radin agrees, "Pre-performance jitters can be turned into a positive feeling of excitement." She feels that her career as a law school professor helped her gain confidence in appearing before large audiences. "I've given lectures before lots of students and professors. It's not so scary," she reports. Violinist Emily Chen notes that her work as a lawyer gives her a sense of perspective. "No audience is ever as hostile as an angry client or a mean judge," she says.

Shifting Focus

"Doing solos is stressful. Ensemble work has been more fun," says violinist Ron Sharpe. Quite a few of our team members have made the same observation, that performing in an ensemble causes less anxiety than going solo. An individual's mistakes may not be as evident in a group performance. Choral singer Roy Hitchings knows that fellow choir members "will carry me in the areas I don't know as well. We are all in this together."

A commitment to the group reduces stress by shifting a performer's focus away from himself or herself. Focusing less on yourself can help in solo performing, too. Here are strategies that our team members use to try to stop thinking—and worrying—about themselves as they perform.

- **Focus on other musicians:** "Community chorus really is a shared experience, with everyone pulling each other up and beyond," says Cherrie Waxman. So is playing in an instrumental ensemble. Helping the group succeed let violinist and retired fashion designer Kitty Benton recover from the performance aversion that was left over from her days as a burnt-out music major. After deciding not to pursue music professionally, she insisted that she would not perform in public anymore, but she would play chamber music informally with friends. She finally dropped the public performance prohibition when she realized that "I was letting other people down. I got over it by taking the spotlight off myself and instead wanting to do a good job for the group," she recalls. This transformation occurred when a chamber group she had been playing with planned to give a performance. "The first violin was so good that I wanted him to enjoy it." She did the performance, focusing not on herself, but on helping him sound good. "I am now sanguine about performance." A commitment to the group also let guitarist and banjo-player Steven Duke overcome some of his performance anxiety. At the end of each eight-week group class that he takes, "we go on stage and perform one of the songs we've worked up during the session. I never look forward to these, but I'm getting used to them. I participate because each member of the ensemble is counting on all the others being there and contributing their part. I want to be part of the group, part of the fellowship of musicians."

Steven Duke playing banjo at an open mic event at a fellow musician's Wisconsin barn.

- **Focus on the music:** "The thing to do about jitters is to really know your material well, not think about yourself. Get in the zone musically, " says early music instrumentalist Kathy Fleming. Trumpeter Arthur Carvajal agrees, "I allay any jitters by focusing on the music, assuring myself that I am ready to perform." Violinist Liz Sogge calms her nerves by concentrating both on the music that she is playing and on what her fellow musicians are playing, too. "If you don't focus only on your own part, but think of the parts and the musicians around you, you will blend and 'dance' with fellow musicians, have the courage to keep going at all costs, and not let them down. When the focus is on the musical whole, performances are more musical, whether I am playing in a symphony or with a pianist," she says. If errors occur, woodwind player Roland Wilk keeps the focus on the music rather than on himself by noting that "I never let on when I slip up." Neither does cellist Michael McFadden, who observes, "I try not to panic when I flub a note or two but rather focus on a solid finish, working on the theory that if the ending is good, the audience will tend to forget my earlier mistakes."

Don't beat yourself up when you make a mistake. The audience doesn't have a copy of your music.

> —Barbara Try, pianist, percussionist, retired accounting supervisor

- **Focus on the audience:** "I focus on sharing the music with the audience. It's less about me as a performer and more about the gift of sharing something I love with other people," explains cellist Max Weiss. For this strategy to work, Mr. Carvajal notes that it's important to "remember that the audience is friendly and wants to see me succeed." Dr. Morris Schoeneman has found that to be true in the performing he has done since returning to violin as an adult. "Audiences are happy to see the amateur performer making the attempt," he says. It can also help to see the audience not as stern judges but more like the supportive relatives who cheered on Ms. Pettway as a child, turning her into a confident performer. Actually, a good portion of the audience for amateur performances consists of friends and relatives, who are often enthusiastic in expressing their appreciation. Another way of thinking about the audience boosts Dr. Schoeneman's confidence: "I am comforted by knowing that I can play my pieces better than most in the audience can."

- **Engage with the audience:** Some team members try to ignore the audience, but others have found that it is calming to engage with them. "I often introduce the piece being played. That helps," says bassoonist Hugh Rosenbaum. This allows him to seem like a polished entertainer and musical authority, rather than a timid soul seeking approval. However, Michelle Billingsley uses a different approach. She doesn't engage right away during her open mic performances. "When you start a show, walk out on stage, walk to the mic, and start," she says. "Don't make eye contact or talk at all for a couple of songs. Let a few songs sink in and then start making friends."

- **Focus on the fun:** "When I first started performing again, I felt as if I was going to have a heart attack before getting on stage. Now I am much more calm," says clarinetist Sarah Monte. "I remind myself that I'm doing this for 'fun' and that the audience is looking at us thinking, 'Wow, how do they do that?'" For pianist Dr. Stephen Kamin, the chamber music performances he does now are much less nerve-wracking than the recitals he did as a youngster. "The stakes are much lower now. It is just for the fun and the sharing. Of course, there are always a few nerves, but they go as soon as I start to play." Bassist Daniel Savin likes to spread the fun around now, although as noted in the previous chapter, it took a while for him to become a comfortable performer. "I love making music and am usually grinning from ear to ear when I play a recital. For me music is fun. If the audience sees that I'm having fun, they will enjoy it, even if I don't sound that good."

Preparation Counts

As Ms. Fleming noted earlier, adequate practice is an essential part of jitters control. Here are other pre-performance preparations that can lessen performance anxiety, as can the auditioning tips discussed in chapter 9.

- **Picking solos:** "Not attempting pieces beyond my skill set is key," advises Mr. Sharpe. Pianist Ellen Tenenbaum agrees, "It doesn't matter if you're playing the simplest of pieces. If you play it beautifully, people could be moved to tears." In addition, Ms. Billingsley adds, "You don't always need to show up with a new song. Keep working on an old song. I start my shows and open mics with a great song that I know well enough that I don't get nervous thinking about it or performing it."

Guitarist and singer Michelle Billingsley performs often at open mic nights and jam sessions in Chicago.

- **Trial runs:** Just as trial runs for family and friends can help before an audition, they can also calm fears before other performances. Videotaping yourself playing the piece to be performed provides useful feedback, too. So does studying videotapes of past performances, as Ms. Sogge does. "You will find they are never as bad as you remember. There are lessons to learn for next time," she says. Flutist Heather Rosado does a kind of trial run every time she practices in her apartment. "I attribute my lack of pre-concert jitters to the fact that my neighbors can all hear me when I practice—the good, the bad, and the ugly," she says. "Knowing that you're always performing, even practicing at home, prepares you for performance day. I tell myself that everyone has already heard me play this piece. The people at your performance *want* to hear it, versus your neighbors who don't." Violist Jay Choi does an unusual kind of trial run as part of his pre-performance practicing. "I create simulated stress—wearing a thick winter coat in order to limit shoulder mobility, playing without my glasses in a dim light, intentionally squeezing the neck of the viola too hard, playing after a heavy work out," he explains. Shortness of breath from working out and a stiff shoulder mimic the grip that fear could put on his body. "On the day of the concert, when stress kicks in, I can play my part passably because I have done it before."

- **Finesse the schedule:** If you or your ensemble are one of many performing in a concert, persuade the scheduler to give you a slot that will make you feel more at ease. "If you're one of the last on the program, you can get a little jittery. I'd rather be first (or better still, right before or after the intermission) than last. Too much time to think is never a good thing," says Ms. Weiss. Mr. Sharpe notes that if the schedule places him late in the program, "I avoid sitting in the audience."

- **Performance-day calming:** "I have taken Yoga and Pilates, and most often use relaxation techniques from them for calming," says percussionist and baritone horn player Dana Schwartz. Taking slow, deep breaths is recommended by many. Violinist Dr. Henry Wang notes, "I try to visualize myself in a sphere of 'awesomeness' on stage." Visualization is a strategy borrowed from sports—seeing in the mind's eye a performance going well. He and several other team members learned about this at a workshop during a Baltimore Symphony summer program taught by Noa Kageyama, whose Bulletproof Musician online newsletter regularly offers tips on performance anxiety and practicing. Vocalist Patrick Holland's pre-performance strategy is to "keep myself busy doing things until just before the concert. Chatting with people, to keep from sitting and thinking about how nervous I am." Guitarist Laurinda Karston uses the opposite approach. "I just try to sit calmly and not talk with my ensemble members or mention to anyone that I am nervous," she says. Bassist Daniel Savin is proactive, noting, "I make myself extremely aware of my nervousness so that I control it and not the other way around." For pianists, one way to keep busy and quell jitters is to try out the piano in the performance space to learn about any quirks it may have. As for performance day food, several team members say that having a banana is calming. Some like to have a good meal before a performance, while others don't. Having water on hand is recommended for all, to keep music-making muscles in good working order.

- **Beta blockers:** A few of our questionnaire completers—about 5 percent—suffer from such severe performance anxiety that they use a class of drugs known as beta blockers. These drugs make the heart beat more slowly and help counteract the speeding up of the heartbeat and the resulting jittery feeling that the hormone epinephrine can cause. It's important to use these drugs under a doctor's care because beta blockers can interfere with some conditions and medications. Most who go this route take a low dose, and only while performing. Some find that after a while they don't need the medication any more, as their confidence grows. "A low dose is just enough to let me put the physical symptoms aside and concentrate on the music," says Deborah Wythe, who describes in chapter 7 how beta blockers helped her with piano recitals. "Performance nervousness was crippling when I was young. I've conquered that by hard work, persistence, and now some chemical assistance."

- **Loosening perfectionism:** "When I was young, making a mistake was worse than death," says Ken Williams. "Now I know a mistake probably is going to happen and nobody really cares. As long as I don't let down my fellow players, I'm happy. My method is to be as prepared as I can and to concentrate on knowing I can play my part, and not on all the things that can go wrong." Bassoonist Mandy Ray adds, "People come to your performances not because they seek perfection, but because they seek the shared experience

Deborah Wythe (left) playing four-hand piano at the Kinhaven Adult Piano Workshop summer program in Weston, Vermont.

of music. The experience is there even if you're not perfect. Mistakes are part of life. When you stop worrying about them, you make fewer of them." Mr. Holland adds, "My subconscious has (finally) realized that if I mess up, the world won't end. It has realized this because of the large number of times that I have messed up."

- **The more, the merrier:** "The more performances you have under your belt, the less intimidated you feel," says Ms. Ray. "As a child, even being buried in the back of the band with no exposed parts was nerve-wracking. After decades of doing them, it's just another opportunity to play and nothing to get worked up about. I've played with groups that made major mistakes and ones that had standing ovations, and everything in between. I've embarrassed myself noticeably, but I've also done better than I ever expected (which is exhilarating)." Soprano Sofia Axelrod observes, "When I haven't performed in a while and then have three concerts lined up, the first one is hard, the following one easier, and by the third one I feel completely secure on stage. The solution is to perform often." Dr. Darlene Ifill-Taylor took an unusual approach to rounding up more performance opportunities in order to quell the nervousness she felt as a soloist, despite years of singing in choirs. She enrolled in a community college (while continuing her psychiatry practice) to earn an associate degree in vocal music. "I needed to be in a rigorous school situation where I had to perform before somebody every week to get over the nervousness," she explains. Shortly after earning her degree, she was a soloist with a community orchestra and pulled it off just fine.

CLOSE UP: DR. DARLENE IFILL-TAYLOR, SINGER, SONGWRITER, PSYCHIATRIST

As a young psychiatrist in Washington, DC, Dr. Darlene Ifill-Taylor joined a church choir whose director also had a gospel group. She sang backup vocals for that group on several recordings. After a few years, he suggested she make her own CD. "I'm like, 'Okay, give me some songs,'" she recalls. He replied, "No, you've got to write your own songs." Impossible, or so she thought. But several years later, she says, "I was at the beach and a song came." She recorded it on her cell phone. Songs kept coming. She phoned him and he replied, 'Come, record them.'" She had no idea how to write the accompaniment. She sang for him what she wanted the cello or piano to do. He wrote the score and served as producer for her first CD, now on iTunes. "The songs are inspirational, meant to render peace or comfort in some way," she says. "I spend a lot of time in my medical work trying to empower people to do their thing." She's glad when people say that seeing that she made a CD inspires them to follow their dreams, too. "It's a model for being who you were meant to be," she says. "The songs keep coming."

Creating Performance Opportunities

Many advice-team members feel comfortable enough about performing that they seek out performance opportunities. Pianist Adine Usher volunteers to accompany hymns at her church and to play background music for art exhibits at a New York women's club. She has also volunteered to perform at nursing homes, as have others of our team members. There is more on performing at health-care facilities and senior centers later in this chapter and in chapter 11.

Some create chances to perform by starting their own large ensembles, as noted in chapter 9. Others search out places where the groups they are in can perform. They may do this via work connections, such as the hospital fundraiser where Dr. Teddy Tong's string quartet played, or the performance that Mary Schons arranged for her folk band at the library where she works.

Angela Bowman has engaged in more assertive networking, similar to what a professional band might do, to find gigs for her Cajun band. She started by having her band play at a farmer's market and also at the bar next door to Chicago's Old Town School of Folk Music, where she studied. Then she became more bold, arranging a residency once a month at another bar, and also emailing the person who handles bookings for a major Chicago roots music club. In that email, she described her band's personnel and performance history. To her surprise, they were invited to perform there, too. "The people who come out to hear us are musicians and their friends, and we go to hear them," she says.

A few team members started concert series in which they could perform themselves. Guitarist and banjo player Mike Alberts started two series of monthly performances, one at the Chicago bar next to the Old Town School, and the other at a bar near his suburban Chicago home. For the city bar, he invites teachers at the music school to perform. For the suburban show, he brings in non-pro local bands and singer/songwriters. For each series, he has pulled together a separate "house band" in which he plays that performs as the opener for these monthly performances.

Silas Meredith, another guitarist, hosted a series of concerts that he called The Plunge. He rented space at a poetry club or other informal New York City music venue and invited professional musicians to come "take artistic risks" by trying out styles and techniques they hadn't done in public before. "It was a safe space for musical innovation," he says. "I've been blown away by the enthusiasm of the audiences. I always did a song or two myself. I was the organizer, so I figured that no one had the authority to throw me off the stage. It's one of the most fun things I've ever done in all my years with music."

Clarinetist Jeff Alfriend hosts monthly chamber music concerts in the living room of his home in Hawaii. "I play three or four times a year in the concerts," he says. Attendance is by invitation only, with notices sent to an email list he has put together. He has begun to book professionals for the concerts. "My goal is to do pro-am playing, to get a great cellist and pianist who will let me tag along on something like the Brahms clarinet trio."

Many of these performances are done free of charge. For fundraisers, all proceeds go to the nonprofit being helped. For some performances, such as Mr. Meredith's Plunge concerts, there may be a "suggested donation" which helps cover the cost of renting the venue. For bar gigs, the performers may receive a cut of the evening take. "It's not usually very much," says Ms. Bowman, so there's no way she could quit her day job, which she wouldn't want to do because she likes her publishing job. "Money is not a major factor in performing, but I don't want to play for free on principal. I don't want to promulgate the idea that we're worthless, or to underbid our colleagues who are performing to make money." Mr. Alberts distributes any money his series brings in to those he invites to perform, keeping a little to cover his costs for amplifiers and other equipment that he provides.

Stewart Olsen (far left, short wig) having fun with other trumpeters at a 70s-themed concert of the Energy City New Horizons program in Houston, Texas.

Organizing Solo Recitals

A few members of our advice team have organized their own solo recitals, which have taken place in churches, private homes, retirement communities, nursing homes, and hospitals. Team members describe here the planning that went into their recitals. The next chapter has more about performing at retirement centers and health-care facilities.

- **Karen Meyn** held a free recital at the church she attends in the Maine town where she and her husband have lived since they retired. She spent eight months working on the music she chose to sing—a Schumann song cycle and, for a change of pace, some Harold Arlen songs. To prepare, she worked at times with a coach. "I wanted to make the music a part of me," she says. Her piano accompanist was her Spanish teacher at a local language school. "I made my own postcards about the recital and sent them to everybody I knew. I put up posters in town. I typed out the translations of the Schumann songs for the program." She began the recital by speaking about the Schumann songs, explaining what each song was about. After singing those songs, there was a pause, but not an intermission. "I introduced the accompanist, who spoke about the Harold Arlen songs. After those, we had a little reception. The whole recital took about forty minutes. About thirty people came." It went so well that she plans to do another.
- **Suzanne Epstein** has given several vocal recitals. The publicity varies depending on where she holds the recital. Her recitals at a church were part of a concert series and the series coordinator advertised them via email. The retirement homes had activities calendars that listed the recitals she did for them. Performances in private homes were by invitation only. "I also performed in a fourteen-week lecture-performance course on art song that I organized and gave twice through a local graduate school," she says. "In the course, I performed with lecturer/pianists, covering different repertoire each week."
- **Ellen Tenenbaum** found a second career—performing at retirement communities—after she learned to control performance anxiety through the recitals she did for a Washington, DC, musical support group, Adult Music Student Forum (AMSF). "The DC area is rich in senior living communities and adult education programs," explains this pianist, who gives about thirty senior center recitals a year, each lasting about fifty minutes. "First, I look at a center's website to see if there's a good piano there. I call to find the email for the activity director and email this person, offer to give a concert,

and send a copy of my latest program. They might not get back to me. So I call to follow up." On performance day, she arrives early to check out the piano and make sure the seats are arranged so residents can see the piano's keys. "I hand a written program to each person before the concert. They love having someone give them something with a nice smile, rather than leave the programs on the seats or on a table. I talk about the music briefly before I play a set. After the concert, there are always interesting questions, observations, and recollections." She has received repeat offers from several facilities. On some return visits, they pay her a modest fee, usually about $100, but she still considers herself an amateur. "I am a rank amateur who aims for high professional standards in my performances."

- **Joy and Jill Procida:** "The two of us play at nursing homes," says Joy Procida, the trumpeter with muscular dystrophy described earlier. Her sister Jill plays saxophone. Their duo performances are in addition to playing with community bands and their own Glass City Swing Band. To make their duo performances seem more like a full band is playing, they bring along pre-recorded backup music, using the Hal Leonard play-along series that they have uploaded to an iPod, which they hook up to a sound system that they bring with them. The play-along tracks provide background accompaniment for their trumpet and sax.

> **Just get out there and perform. The more you do the better you'll get.**
> —Bob Gronko, guitarist, retired government employee

Competitions

Very few of our advice-team members have performed in music competitions as adults—fewer than 10 percent of those who completed the questionnaire on their music activities. The competitions run the gamut from high-level international competitions for amateur pianists to barbershop chorus competitions, an Irish fiddle contest, a Battle of the Jug Bands, and a Chamber Music Competition at Levine Music. Catherine Kasmer entered a competition sponsored by *Acoustic Guitar Magazine,* with a Gibson Guitar as the prize. "My motivation was the guitar," she admits. "I ended up as a finalist. Even though I didn't get the guitar, the competition was a highlight for me and boosted my ego and confidence. But I don't really believe in music as a competition." Neither do many of our questionnaire respondents. In fact, some actively hate the idea of competitions.

Even Dale Backus has some qualms about them, although he has participated and done well in several of the major international competitions for amateur pianists.

He was a Fourth Place finisher in competitions in Paris and Berlin and the First Place winner in 2006 in a competition in his home state of Colorado. "I don't like that we have to have a winner. Winning to me is walking out on stage to play this wonderful art form. The judging is always very subjective," he says. He decided to take a break from competitions for more than ten years after his 2006 triumph, although he has joined the board of the Colorado Conservatory that sponsors the competition he won. He can't enter that one again. It is not allowed for winners. Overall, he feels that taking part in competitions was worthwhile. "They were great opportunities in that I took my piano playing to the highest level and was accepted into the crowd of top-level amateurs." That led to his being invited continuously to take part in Pianestival, a traveling festival of accomplished amateur pianists who give summertime performances in international concert halls. In recent years, he has focused on giving occasional recitals for friends in Colorado, but may return to competitions after he and his wife become empty nesters.

Sarah Wright feels that she has grown as a violinist from the preparation she did before entering a concerto competition sponsored by Kenwood Symphony, a Minneapolis community orchestra. As a new mother working full-time as a pharmacist, she had been having trouble finding time to practice, as noted in chapter 6. The announcement of this competition motivated her to start practicing again in earnest. Luckily this happened after her young son began sleeping through the night. She began taking lessons online via Skype with people she had worked with years earlier, partly so she wouldn't have to leave the house to do so and also to work with people "who would be sympathetic to my goals and not make me feel lousy about myself. I was self-conscious and embarrassed about my playing at first." Through these lessons, she received useful advice on her playing and also on handling the "mental battles" that had made her feel insecure as a performer. She did well in the competition and was one of the winners. Her prize: performing as a soloist with the orchestra.

Both of these competition veterans recommend that in addition to focused practice, trial runs are essential. A week before the concerto competition, Ms. Wright performed her selection for a musician friend whose comments "helped me feel like a million bucks and helped me give a confident performance," she says. Mr. Backus likes to give three formal recitals of the repertoire to be played at a competition: one for his family, one at the home of a friend who invites about fifteen others over, and a big recital that Mr. Backus holds in his own home for about fifty people. "The only way to practice for a performance, is to practice performing," he says. "You can't simulate that in the practice room. You need breathing living human beings whose eyes and ears are on you while you expose your soul and heart. You work out your nerves and some of the bugs in the music, too. You don't want those to show up at the competition."

Dale Backus playing at the Sorbonne in the International Piano Competition for Outstanding Amateurs, held each year in Paris.

Serendipity Performances

Shortly after Julie Terray joined a chorus for the first time in her mid-60s, she walked Spain's Camino de Santiago, ancient paths that thousands of people hike on each year. She brought along her "new-found confidence in being a member of an amazing choir and knowing that I could really sing rather well," she says. "While walking, a companion asked me to sing something. So I sang *Dona Nobis Pacem*. A French woman came up the path and started singing with me, as did her companion. It was a pure moment of joy, one that attests to the power of music all over the world." Cornelia Dean experienced a similar moment walking along the lower-level concourse of New York City's Penn Station. A science writer who teaches at Brown University in Rhode Island, she had recently begun singing with the faculty rock band there. She had traveled to New York by train and after arriving, "I was headed to the subway. There was a man near a microphone singing a Rolling Stones song. I sang along as I walked toward him. He asked, 'Are you in a band?' I said, 'Yes.' " Maybe not the kind of band he meant, but a band nonetheless.

He asked her to sing with him. So she did, standing next to her rolling suitcase. "People began filming us. They put money in his guitar case. It was fantastic. We got to the end of the song. I said, 'Thank you, very much,' and got on the subway. When I went back to Providence, I told the band, 'We have to do that song.' We added it to our repertoire."

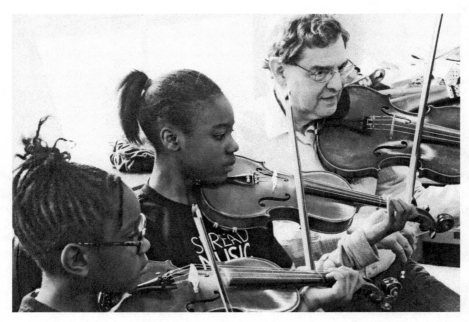
Dr. Marc Mann (far right) rehearsing with students at the Music Haven music education program in New Haven, Connecticut. He helped found the group, served on its board of directors, and volunteers to coach students and chamber music groups.

11 Giving Back, Playing Forward

FOR MORE THAN ten years, Music Haven has provided tuition-free instrumental music instruction and mentoring for children "in the heart of New Haven, giving all kids a chance to play," as the group's website describes its mission. Violist Dr. Marc Mann was active in the planning stages for creating this Connecticut program, served on its board of directors for many years, helped it gain nonprofit status, and has been one of its most enthusiastic fundraisers.

He has also become one of Music Haven's practice coaches, volunteering one afternoon a week to provide one-on-one help for youngsters who are in the program's group classes. He spends a half hour with each of the children he tutors. "We work on difficult passages or straighten out some technical problems," he says. "I also coach a string quartet, using easy string quartet arrangements. You can see amazing progress from week to week. It is so rewarding." Some Music Haven students have performed with one of the local community orchestras in which Dr. Mann performs.

For a while, Miriam Jackobs did something similar with a community group in Cincinnati that offers free music instruction and performance opportunities for children in underserved areas. She was fairly new to strings at that time, having just joined a New Horizons string orchestra. "I told the person who asked for strings volunteers that I'm not very far along and she said, 'You know more than they know. They are beginners.'"

Most of our questionnaire completers have found ways to volunteer in musically oriented community service projects. About a third have have worked with youngsters, as Dr. Mann and Ms. Jackobs have, either coaching music students or giving performances for schoolchildren. Twice that number have taken part in performances at retirement centers, senior centers, nursing homes, or other health-care facilities. About half offer organizational or fundraising help for an ensemble they are in or for other music organizations. Another third volunteer in other ways. Emil Henning plays piano for the chorus at a high-security prison. Arthur Carvajal pulls out his horn to perform as needed with Bugles Across America, "an organization whose mission is to provide a bugler to sound taps for any family who requests it at the funeral of a military veteran," he explains.

Although some of our team members' volunteer efforts have been mentioned in earlier chapters, the following pages discuss these kinds of activities more fully, with suggestions for how to become involved.

Performances at Retirement and Medical Centers

Most of our advice-team members who perform at retirement centers, nursing homes, and other health-care facilities do so as part of a community band, orchestra, or chorus, although a few of our team members have also performed solo in such venues. The performances are usually free of charge. Whether or not a fee is involved, the musicians gain a great deal. The performances provide an impetus to practice and a sense of fulfillment in seeing how much others appreciate the music.

The concerts also benefit the health-care and retirement facilities by allowing them to offer more entertainment events than institutional budgets allow. As noted earlier, some retirement communities and senior centers are even glad to let community music groups rehearse in their facilities as long as the groups promise to give free performances.

"For our community, the residents are involved in choosing the entertainment and this is the kind of entertainment that they enjoy," says Jen Laury, activities director at Luther Crest Senior Living Community in Allentown, Pennsylvania. She regularly books Colleen Schoneveld's Really Terrible Orchestra (RTO), described in chapter 9. "They may be called the Really Terrible Orchestra, but they're pretty good. We have had huge turnouts for the RTO concerts. They don't necessarily have to be the best musicians for the residents to enjoy them. For other concerts, we have to pay a fee." Ms. Laury recommends that a musical program for a retirement community like hers "has to be fun and interactive. Engage the audience with your performance." Ms. Schoneveld's RTO does this by playing a mix of classical and popular music, often pegged to holiday themes. "They tell jokes and share stories about the music to really draw the crowd in and make them part of the experience," notes Ms. Laury. Her retirement community, like many others, also encourages its residents to form their own ensembles and put on performances for fellow residents.

Kathy Fleming plays viola da gamba with an early music ensemble that uses a time travel theme for its performances at retirement communities. The ensemble opens the shows by playing music from far in the past and ends with pieces from a time period that is meaningful to the residents, with tunes that they know. The ensemble uses "anachronistic instrumentation," she notes, for the programs' closing numbers.

Some of these musical performances not only provide entertainment but can also be therapeutic. Retired professor Charmarie Blaisdell performs with a group in Maine called the Solace Singers. They sing a cappella at hospices to help bring some comfort and peace for those near the end of life and their families. Also therapeutic is the pick-up band put together by another Maine musician, Philip Anderson. He works at a residential treatment center for clients with major mental illness, operated by Maine Behavioral Healthcare. His supervisor, Jill Abernethy, notes, "We don't have a designated music therapist." So she is delighted that Mr. Anderson (mentioned in chapters 4 and 5) puts on what they call a "jam" every Friday afternoon, offering the center's clients a bit of informal music therapy. "Phil is the go-getter who organizes this," she says, although it's not part of his job description. He and staff members from this center and from other nearby residential centers get together at these "jams" to perform for a combined audience of clients from each of the centers. "I'm the lead singer and strum a guitar a little, too," he says. Staff members bring their instruments. So do some clients, who are encouraged to join in the music-making. "It is absolutely beneficial to our clients," says Ms. Abernethy. "It's heartwarming to see clients who are quite shy and don't speak much, but when their favorite song is played, they belt it out. Anything that helps them build confidence and self-esteem is beneficial, in a warm and welcoming environment. It's good for everybody."

Mr. Anderson is also the lead singer in another band that performs for free each Tuesday afternoon for residents of an Alzheimer's unit of a nearby nursing home. "We play for the folks, the staff, and whoever is there to visit," he says. When the band missed a week because one member was having surgery, the residents kept asking when the band was coming back. Mr. Anderson notes that sometimes it's hard to tell what impact the music is having. "Some residents don't respond, others tap their feet, some sing and clap wildly. They experience what they experience. We just keep doing it."

Neuroscientist Sofia Axelrod performing in the lobby of Mount Sinai Hospital in New York City where she sings classical songs every few months.

Sofia Axelrod, as noted in earlier chapters, has been singing every few months for several years in the lobby of New York's Mount Sinai Hospital as part of Weill Cornell Medical College's Music and Medicine Initiative. Several local medical centers participate in this initiative, including Rockefeller University, where she works. These aren't formal concerts. She and her accompanist show up in the lobby and she starts singing. "I don't announce the songs," she says, and she doesn't take requests. "I sing for about twenty minutes, classical songs, generally from the romantic, impressionistic era, and also operatic repertoire. It's a wondrous transformation that takes place when the first notes float through the air. The hall has amazing, cathedral-like acoustics. I don't have to sing loudly. Every sound is heard. People stop cold in their tracks, they abandon their smart phones, and stare in amazement.

Nobody expects in such a tense place like a hospital to hear classical singing. I feel like I come from a different world and I take them with me." She has also performed at a nursing home as part of the Music and Medicine program. "It turns out, not surprisingly, that the sick love and appreciate a little musical distraction, especially people who can't go out to enjoy music anymore."

Peter Hung played piano through this same program at New York Hospital while he was a medical student. "On a palliative care floor, there is a clunky old upright piano. A group of musicians put on an impromptu recital, and patients and family mill in and out as they please. Every few months, instrumentalists come for half-hour blocks to the chemotherapy Infusion Center waiting room. We bring a digital keyboard and an amp. I play solo piano—Debussy, Ravel, other quiet classical masterpieces, random contemporary music, or video game songs, whatever feels right."

Quiet, peaceful music may work well in some medical settings, but upbeat music seems to do better for the Alzheimer's unit where Mr. Anderson's band plays. If the band plays music that is too slow, residents tend to fall asleep. Songs that were popular when the residents were in their teens or 20s can help keep them engaged. To take the guesswork out of what to program for a health-care facility, it's wise to meet with the staff at the facility beforehand to learn what kind of music program they feel would work best. That's one of the suggestions offered in a planning guide that the Pittsburgh Symphony Orchestra's Music and Wellness program has created to help its musicians and others who want to perform in health-care settings. Penny Brill, a violist with the orchestra, started this program in 1999 and has created a separate organization called Musacor. Its website also has useful guides for musicians who want to do community outreach performances. The resources section lists links for these planning guides.

CLOSE UP: CELESTE CHAU, VIOLIST, SINGER, ARCHITECT

"I play viola about once a year. I'm an okay singer. I'm much better at organizing. I organize concerts for others who aren't good at organizing," says architect Celeste Chau. After college, she immersed herself in the New York amateur music scene. When one of the groups she was in played for stroke patients, she found her calling. She knows a huge number of non-pro musicians that she can call on to perform for free at nursing homes and other venues. "I look for nursing homes or Medicaid facilities that don't have a budget for a music therapist. They really appreciate us. Better facilities use conservatory students." She also organizes free concerts at an unlikely site: Maple Grove Cemetery in Queens, NY. Its large community room was sitting idle. She persuaded the cemetery's directors to let her put on musical programs there. "My goal is to use music to bring the community together. It brings me joy."

Working with Young People

Violinist Willem van Eeghen has volunteered at several public schools in the Washington, DC, area. He coaches students in much the same way that Dr. Mann does in New Haven. The schools where Mr. van Eeghen has volunteered don't have enough music teachers to give personalized attention to all the youngsters who want to play instruments. In some cases the teacher isn't a violinist, and so Mr. van Eeghen's assistance has been especially helpful. "The teacher works with the students in a group and then I take the students one-on-one and work with them for ten minutes. Often they have developed bad habits because nobody was there to correct them. I try to help the kids, showing them how to hold the violin and the bow, how to put their fingers on the strings. I enjoy doing it. I think the students enjoy it, too. They appreciate the one-on-one attention that they don't get in a big classroom. The teacher is very disciplined. I try to be more of a soft hand, and they appreciate that."

He had intended to do music after he retired from the World Bank, but had no idea that he would become involved in doing so much teaching. By chance, just before he retired, he met someone at a recital who was organizing musical outreach programs. When he mentioned to her that he wouldn't mind working with kids, she put him in touch with the schools where he wound up tutoring. "That's how it started," he says. He still plays chamber music with friends and has a few private students, mostly adults and some youngsters, too. "It's not full time, but it keeps me busy. Basically I try to convey what I've been taught, but students are so different and have such different abilities. I'd like to learn more about the art of violin teaching," he says. He asks friends who are violin teachers for teaching tips. "They give me their input and design specific exercises to use to overcome specific problems the students are having."

Cellist Rebecca Berg has a few students, too, young people and adults, as noted in chapter 4. She has taken formal teacher training courses in the Suzuki instructional method to help with her new teaching role. "Teaching is good for my playing," she says. "I really have to think consciously about fundamental aspects of technique, how not to tense up with your bow, or the position of the left hand." She also feels that her own struggles with perfectionism help her as a teacher. "Having a sense of when to back off, when to push, when someone will stop learning because you're telling them too many things at once. Watching someone go from zero to being able to play is kind of amazing."

Several New Horizons ensembles involve their members in coaching schoolchildren, as Mr. van Eeghen does. Members of the New Horizons Band of the Third Street Music School in New York City interact with much younger students—those in preschool classes that take place at the music school during the hours when the New Horizons band rehearses. "We go into their classrooms and

Dr. Deborah Edge (far right) with the bass section (aka "BassBall Team") of the Capital City Symphony at a Family Concert for children in Washington, DC.

demonstrate the different instruments. Very often they come to our rehearsals on Tuesday and Thursday mornings to listen. They are our biggest fans," says Brandon Tesh, the band's director. The New Horizons Symphony of Las Cruces, New Mexico, has done outreach work by sponsoring a concerto competition for students at a local university. The winners get to perform as soloists with the orchestra.

Saxophonist David Inverso helps introduce youngsters to music by taking part in instrument "petting zoos" that Seattle's Music Center of the Northwest holds regularly "at the beginning of sporting events, at the opera, at community picnics," he says. "Adult volunteers encourage children to make a sound on the instruments. Some really light up after a wounded goose honk comes out of a sax. This experience just might be that little extra boost they need to start lessons."

Doug Campbell interacts musically with young people by using his composing skills to bring to life poems and other lyrics written by Tennessee high school students. One of his music friends is a high school teacher who would assign students to write a poem about something they love. Mr. Campbell and friends would set the poems to music. Then he, the teacher, and other friends would record the songs and give the recordings to the students at the end of the school year. "Some students continued to submit poems to us unsolicited and we set them to music, recorded them, and

Cover art for the CD of the musical *The Aroostook War*. The musical's text was written by students of Roane County High School in Kingston, Tennessee. The music was written by Doug Campbell and his friends.

returned them to the students, too," notes Mr. Campbell. They did this for about eight years until the teacher moved on to teaching AP US history and his students decided to write a humorous musical about a little known nineteenth century boundary dispute between the United States and Canada called the Aroostook War, which, despite the name, was settled diplomatically. The students wrote the script, Mr. Campbell and his friends wrote the music, and he and his music friends made an audio recording for the school. "We had a great time," he says. "After ten years, the project has grown in scope to include an army of composers. One year we had 72 submissions and writing had to be farmed out to additional songwriters."

Boards and Fundraising

Quite a few members of our advice panel serve on the boards of the community ensembles in which they perform, often helping with fundraising to keep the groups going. Several team members are on the boards of other music organizations, as Dr. Mann was with Music Haven. Violinist Joan Herbers is on the board of the ProMusica Chamber Orchestra, a professional orchestra in Columbus, Ohio, and has commissioned a piano concerto for the orchestra to perform. Cellist Ken Williams is a board member of Chamber Music Madness, a Seattle nonprofit that promotes chamber music playing for young people. Mr. van Eeghen serves on the board of several music organizations, including the Marlboro Music Festival in Vermont, and Music for Food, a concert series that raises money for hunger-relief organizations.

Clarinetist Dr. Alvin Crawford serves on the board of the Cincinnati Symphony Orchestra and is also on the Dean's Advisory Board for the University of Cincinnati's conservatory, helping the school "promote inclusivity and diversity," he says. For many years he was in a jazz combo with other non-pro musicians who called themselves the Wannabes. "We played gigs for nonprofits, performing for free, which allowed them to make more on their affairs. Everybody loved us." Many of our team members' small ensembles perform gratis to help nonprofits raise funds, including the band of child psychiatrists that Dr. Eugene Beresin started. It performs each year at the annual meeting of the American Academy of Child and Adolescent Psychiatry. They sell T-shirts and hats with the band's name— Pink Freud and the Transitional Object—donating the proceeds to a fund for children's health care. Pink Freud members, including Dr. Brad Reddick, work at different medical centers around the country. They tried rehearsing via Skype or other online venues, but without much success due to online transmission lag times. So the band members practice their set list tunes on their own and then show up early for the conference. "They get a space for us to rehearse. We rehearse non-stop for three days, and then play for an hour and a half at a Wednesday night opening reception for the conference. It's the same every year," explains Dr. Reddick.

CLOSE UP: DR. WEN DOMBROWSKI, PERCUSSIONIST, CORPORATE INNOVATION CONSULTANT

"When I was 14, out of curiosity I bought a three-CD set on world drumming. I was fascinated by the intricacies of the rhythms and sounds from distant lands. It didn't dawn on me until later that I don't have to be Indian to play Indian drums," says Dr. Wen Dombrowski. She got her first taste of world percussion in college by learning Irish step dancing and Spanish flamenco castanets. After medical school, she began playing flamenco's cajon box drum and also explored the Middle Eastern doumbek, African djembe, Latin conga, Indian tabla, and others. To share the joy of music-making with colleagues, she organized impromptu drum circles at health-care conferences by bringing a doumbek (portable enough to carry on a plane) and asking others to bring drums. These drum circles have been a big hit. "At some conferences, we had over a hundred senior executives playing drums and dancing in conga lines," she says. She now includes drum and movement activities in her consulting work to encourage out-of-the-box thinking and collaboration. "The shared experience of music-making can break down hierarchical barriers, get people to let down their guard, and empower people from different walks of life to connect on a musical, cultural, and personal level."

Ensembles with a Mission

Faith-based ensembles at churches and synagogues are the original ensembles with a mission. Their performances enhance the spirituality of the services in which they perform. "I love how music adds to the meaning of the service," says Dr. Rena Johnson, who sings in a church choir.

Other ensembles also make serving others an important part of their mission. "Our chorus is designed to make great music, make people feel welcome, and support the community at the same time," remarks Christine Anderson-Morehouse about the Midcoast Community Chorus of Rockport, Maine (described in chapters 5 and 8). Its mission statement says it all: "Singing as a community for the community." The chorus began as an outgrowth of a small church choir whose director, Mimi Bornstein, wanted to give her singers more challenging music. She put together a community-wide chorus to perform the Paul Winter Consort's "Earth Mass." To encourage people to join the chorus, she made it a concert in honor of Earth Day to benefit the local 4-H program, "to give back to the community," she says. "It took off and became this magical thing." More than a hundred singers took part in two sold-out performances that raised $10,000 for the 4-H group. Ms. Bornstein organized another benefit concert that drew just as many people. That led to her creating the Midcoast Community Chorus. It is a 501(c)(3) nonprofit and gives two concerts a year—one to raise money to support the chorus and the other to benefit a local charitable organization. During rehearsals, chorus members learn about the nonprofit that their concert will benefit. "We also build community with our audiences. At least twice in each concert there's a community song when everybody joins in," says Ms. Bornstein.

The Harmony Project chorus of Columbus, Ohio, engages in community service not by raising money for nonprofits, but by requiring the 250 members of this non-auditioned chorus to take part in community service projects. "You can't sing and not serve. I love it," notes chorus member Janae Miller. The group's diverse membership adds to its sense of community. "I've met people in the chorus I would not otherwise have met," says Tom Krouse. He was glad that David Brown, Harmony Project's director, let him bring his 14-year-old son to rehearsals one year. "We live in a predominantly white, upper class neighborhood and I wanted him to have more exposure to the idea of harmony, with people from different backgrounds coming together."

"What's beautiful about the choir is it promotes inclusiveness," adds Ms. Miller. "We live in a world that is so divided, we don't realize that if you sit down with people of different backgrounds, religions, and orientations, we find we have more in common than not in common." Even the ensemble's rehearsal strategy promotes inclusiveness, with Mr. Brown teaching all the songs by ear (as described in chapter 5).

Neela Wickremesinghe with her baritone saxophone.

The Harmony Project's public service activities range from serving at food pantries or homeless shelters to taking part in neighborhood spruce-ups, during which a group of chorus members adopts a neighborhood for a week. They do whatever is needed to help the neighborhood, such as fix up things, plant trees, or build a playground. "We assign people by zip codes so we have people who live in different parts of our city meeting and working together," says Mr. Brown. Another project involves several chorus members who join him each Thursday to sing with a chorus he leads inside the Ohio Reformatory for Women. "Music is our tool that we use to bring like-minded people together."

The Windy City Gay Chorus that Mark Sherkow sings with sees itself as both a chorus and a social justice organization. "We do a lot of outreach with other LGBT organizations in the city," says Justin Fyala, the general manager of this auditioned chorus. "When anyone is not quite ready to be in the chorus, we give them the option to be part of our volunteer corps." Neela Wickremsinghe, who plays baritone saxophone with the New York Lesbian and Gay Big Apple Corps, notes that this band "is about so much more than making music. We are also making a statement. It becomes hard to hate a group of people that can sound so great!"

Spreading the Fun

All of the public performances that non-pro musicians give—whether in ensembles or in solo recitals—fulfill another mission: to help close the information gap about avocational music-making that has kept many musically inclined adults from becoming involved because they didn't know that such opportunities existed. These performances demonstrate that this kind of music-making is alive and well, that lifelong learning is possible, and that busy adults with non-musical jobs can fit music-making into their lives and have a great time. Simply performing in public can encourage others to make music more a part of their lives, too.

Knowing that their performing plays this important role can add to the enjoyment that non-pros feel when they pull off a successful performance, despite being a bit under-rehearsed or over-extended. Dr. Reddick feels that this is one of the best parts of his music-making. "Watching the joy in others in reaction to the music one is creating feels similar to watching family members open up their holiday presents, or gifts on their birthdays," he says. "Witnessing others listening, interacting, and enjoying the music is by far the biggest treat."

The Sanctified Symphony Orchestra of Alfred Street Baptist Church, Alexandria, Virginia, with two advice-team members on the front row: Alecia Watson and Joshua Dadeboe (fourth and seventh from left). Music director Jamal Lee is front row center.

Stop thinking about it and do it already! Life is too short to be afraid of increasing your happiness.
> —Kathy Dockins, flutist, pre-employment background investigator

About the Advice Panel

A big round of applause goes to the 441 musicians, music educators, research scientists, health-care professionals, professional musicians, and others who shared their music-making experiences for this book by filling out questionnaires, being interviewed by telephone or in person, or by contributing comments via email. There isn't room in the text of this book to mention everyone by name, but the observations and suggestions from each one played a role in shaping the framework and contents of this book.

AMATEUR MUSICIANS ON THE ADVICE PANEL

A total of 363 amateur musicians are part of the advice panel for this book: 274 completed an online questionnaire on their music-making experiences; 41 others answered nearly all the questions on the questionnaire; another 48 amateur musicians did not complete the questionnaire but described their musical experiences while being interviewed by the author by phone, in person, or via email. The questionnaire (created and distributed using the Survey Monkey online questionnaire-creation service) consists of fifty-one questions. A few questions on the survey are multiple choice, but most are open-ended, permitting respondents to write as much as they wish. Most of the amateur musicians on the advice panel worked on the questionnaire or were interviewed from late 2015 through 2016. A few were interviewed in early

2017. Thirty-two questionnaire respondents provided additional information via follow-up telephone interviews. Others updated their responses by email.

The author solicited amateur musicians to join the advice panel from the music schools, organizations, ensembles, and summer programs in the list that follows, as well as from these individuals: Dr. Serap Bastepe-Gray, Dr. Eugene Beresin, Mark Dalrymple, Brenda Dillon, Juli Elliot, Norma Foege, Judy Gutmann, Rebecca Henry, Jonathan Herman, Jean Hess, Glenn Kramer, Polly van der Linde, Dr. Yeou-Cheng Ma, Sarah Muffly, Eric Nathan, Dr. Jonathan Newmark, Ann Hess Smith, Dominique van de Stadt, Rebecca Vaudreuil, and Dr. Marc Wager.

MUSIC SCHOOLS AND ENSEMBLES THAT HELPED WITH THE ADVICE PANEL

Alfred Street Baptist Church, Alexandria, VA: http://www.alfredstreet.org

Camerata Notturna, New York, NY: http://camerata-notturna.org

Chhandayan Center for Indian Music, New York, NY: http://tabla.org

Chicago Bar Association Symphony Orchestra, Chicago, IL: http://cbasymphonyandchorus.blogspot.com, cbaso.cochairs@gmail.com

DC Youth Orchestra Program, Washington, DC: http://www.dcyop.org

Eastman New Horizons Chorus, Rochester, NY: https://www.esm.rochester.edu

Energy City New Horizons Music, Houston, TX: https://www.ecnhm.org

Glass City Swing Band, Jeannette, PA: http://glasscityswingband.com

Handel Choir of Baltimore, Baltimore, MD: https://www.handelchoir.org

Harmony Project, Columbus, OH: http://www.harmonyproject.com

Heritage Signature Chorale, Washington, DC: http://www.heritagesignaturechorale.org

Larchmont Music Academy, Larchmont, NY: http://larchmontmusicacademy.com

Levine Music, Washington, DC: http://www.levinemusic.org

Longwood Symphony Orchestra, Boston, MA: http://longwoodsymphony.org

Midcoast Community Chorus, Rockport, ME: http://www.mccsings.org

Michigan State University Community Music School, Detroit, MI: http://www.cms.msu.edu

Montréal New Horizons Band, Montréal, Canada: http://nhmontreal-en.weebly.com

Music Center of the Northwest, Seattle, WA: http://www.mcnw.org

Music and Medicine, New York, NY: http://weill.cornell.edu/music

New Horizons Jazz Band, Detroit, MI: http://www.cms.msu.edu/el/adults/horizonsBand.php

Old Town School of Folk Music, Chicago, IL: http://www.oldtownschool.org

Peabody Preparatory, Baltimore, MD: http://www.peabody.jhu.edu/preparatory

Piano Pathways, Baton Rouge, LA: http://thepianopathway.com

Really Terrible Orchestra-Pennsylvania, Bethlehem, PA: http://rto-pa.com

San Francisco Community Music Center, San Francisco, CA: http://sfcmc.org

Seattle Pro Musica, Seattle, WA: http://www.seattlepromusica.org

Third Street Music School, New York, NY: http://www.thirdstreetmusicschool.org

University of Cincinnati College-Conservatory of Music, Cincinnati, OH: http://ccm.uc.edu

Will Baily Piano Tunes, Scottsbluff, NE: http://www.willbailypianotunes.com

Village Singers, Rye Brook, NY: http://www.thevillagesingers.com

Windy City Gay Chorus, Chicago, IL: http://windycitysings.org

Young New Yorkers' Chorus, New York, NY: http://ynyc.org

MUSIC ORGANIZATIONS THAT HELPED WITH THE ADVICE PANEL

The following organizations also helped with assembling the advice panel. Their websites are listed in the resources section: Adult Music Student Forum (AMSF); Associated Chamber Music Players (ACMP); Amateur Classical Musicians Association (ACMA); Amateur Pianist; Baltimore Symphony Orchestra and its Academy Week, Rusty Musicians, and OrchKids programs; Chaparral Music Fest; Chorus America; National Guild for Community Arts Education; Sonata Piano Camp; Bennington Chamber Music Conference.

MUSIC EDUCATORS, RESEARCHERS, AND OTHERS ON THE ADVICE PANEL

The author conducted interviews by telephone, email, or in person with more than seventy other individuals: music educators or officials with music organizations, scientists or health-care professionals, professional musicians, and a few others.

Educators or officials of music organizations: Michael Alstad, Will Baily, Audrey-Kristel Barbeau, Ysaye Barnwell, Rebecca Bellelo, Mimi Bornstein, David Brown, Lauren Campbell, Meghan Carye, Jeremy Castillo, Samir Chatterjee, Bai-Chi Chen, Chris Corsale, Paul Dab, Amy Dennison, Brenda Dillon, Mark Dvorak, Juli Elliot,

Marcus Elliot, Gavin Farrell, Liz Fleischer, Sean Fleming, Justin Fyala, Joyce Garrett, BettyAnne Gottlieb, Bau Graves, Matthew Harre, Louise Hildreth-Grasso, Jeanne Kelly, Danielle La Senna, Brian Leatherwood, Carmelia Lee, Reggio McLaughlin, Lois Narvey, Patrick O'Donnell, David Peretz-Larochelle, Richard Rejino, Nelson Rodríguez-Parada, Martha Rodríguez-Salazar, Jesse Rosen, Cindy Runkel, Glenn Sewell, Katherine Shields, Carl Stone, Brandon Tesh, Jimmy Tomasello, Terry Tullos, Charles Williams, Larry Williams, Anne Wilson, and Nozomi Yamaguchi.

Scientists and health-care professionals: Jill Abernethy, Nancy Amigron, Dr. Serap Bastepe-Gray, Debbie Bates, Jennifer Bugos, Dr. Michael Charness, Dr. Jayme Dowdall, Joel Ginn, Dr. Michael Haben, Brenda Hanna-Pladdy, Julene Johnson, Aline Moussard, Dr. Alexander Pantelyat, Karen Popkin, Marlene Riley, Dr. Robert T. Sataloff, Rebecca A. Sayles, Dr. David Shapiro, Rebecca Vaudreuil, Wen Chang-Lit, and Robert Zatorre.

Professional musicians: Adam Kent, Jane Marvine, Ursula Oppens, Stanley J. Thurston, and Vivian Weilerstein. *Others interviewed:* Jen Laury and Irwin Niedober.

Resources

These organizations often have helpful information on their websites including listings of summer programs, workshops, competitions, and general advice for amateur musicians.

Adult Music Student Forum, AMSF (Washington, DC)
http://www.amsfperform.org

Amateur Classical Musicians Association, ACMA (New York, NY)
http://www.nycclassical.com

Amateur Pianist (San Diego, CA)
https://www.meetup.com/Amateur-Pianists-San-Diego/

Associated Chamber Music Players, ACMP (New York, NY)
http://www.acmp.net

Boston Piano Amateurs Association (Boston, MA)
http://www.bostonpianoamateurs.org

CAMMAC: Canadian Amateur Musicians/Musiciens Amateurs du Canada
https://cammac.ca

Chamber Music Society of Santa Barbara (Santa Barbara, CA)
http://www.sbchambermusic.org

Chamber Musicians of Northern California
http://www.cmnc.org

Choirs in the Puget Sound
http://www.openharmony.org/casa/choral.html

Choruses of Northern California
http://www.choralarchive.org/Directory/choruses.html

Cliburn International Amateur Piano Competition
https://www.cliburn.org/cliburn-international-amateur-piano-competition/

CoMA: Contemporary Music for All (in the UK)
http://www.coma.org

Encore Creativity for Older Adults
http://www.encorecreativity.org

The Friday Morning Music Club (Washington, DC)
http://www.fmmc.org

Greater Summerville Music Forum (Summerville, SC)
https://www.facebook.com/
Greater-Summerville-Music-Forum-170640926330710/

Massachusetts Choruses and Choral Societies
http://www.masshome.com/choruses.html

Music for People
http://www.musicforpeople.org

New Horizons International Music Association
http://newhorizonsmusic.org

Singing in Harmony
http://www.singinharmony.org/eastbay/

The Vocal Area Network Choir Directory (New York City metro area)
http://www.van.org/choirdirectory.htm

GENERAL MUSIC ORGANIZATIONS

These organizations have information on their websites on music education and the value of music.

American Composers Forum
http://www.composersforum.org

American Guild of Organists
https://www.agohq.org

American Music Therapy Association
http://www.musictherapy.org

American Society of Composers, Authors and Publishers (ASCAP)
http://www.ascap.com

American String Teachers Association
http://www.astaweb.com

Association of Adult Musicians with Hearing Loss
https://www.musicianswithhearingloss.org/wp/

Association of Concert Bands
http://www.acbands.org

Association for Popular Music Education
http://www.popularmusiceducation.org/

Chamber Music America
http://www.chamber-music.org

Choral Canada
http://www.choralcanada.org

Chorus America
http://www.chorusamerica.org

Classical Revolution
http://classicalrevolution.org

Dalcroze Society of America
http://www.dalcrozeusa.org

Gospel Music Workshop of America, Inc.
http://www.gmwanational.net

International Alliance for Women in Music
http://www.iawm.org

International Council for Traditional Music
http://www.ictmusic.org/

Jazz at Lincoln Center
http://www.jazz.org

Johns Hopkins Center for Music and Medicine
https://www.facebook.com/hopkinscmm/

League of American Orchestras
http://www.americanorchestras.org

Muascor: Musicians as a Community Resource
http://www.Musacor.com

Music and Medicine, Weill Cornell Medical College
http://weill.cornell.edu/music/

Music-in-Education National Consortium
http://music-in-education.org

Music Teachers National Association
http://www.mtna.org

Musical America
https://www.musicalamerica.com

Musicians' Clinics of Canada
http://www.musiciansclinics.com

The NAMM Foundation (National Association of Music Merchants)
http://www.nammfoundation.org

National Association for Music Education
http://www.nafme.org

National Association of Schools of Music
http://nasm.arts-accredit.org

National Association of Teachers of Singing
http://www.nats.org

National Guild for Community Arts Education
http://www.nationalguild.org

Orchestras Canada
http://orchestrascanada.org

Organization of American Kodály Educators
http://www.oake.org

Performing Arts Clinic, Brigham and Women's Hospital, Boston, MA
http://www.brighamandwomens.org/Departments_and_Services/neurology/
services/PerformingArtsClinic.aspx

Performing Arts Medicine Association
http://www.artsmed.org

Playing for Change
https://playingforchange.com

Resounding Joy
http://resoundingjoyinc.org

Seattle Recorder Society
http://www.seattle-recorder.org

Sing for Hope
http://www.singforhope.org

Suzuki Association of the Americas
http://suzukiassociation.org

VH1 Save the Music Foundation
http://www.vh1savethemusic.com

INSTRUMENT ORGANIZATIONS

American Harp Society
http://www.harpsociety.org

American Pianists Association
http://www.americanpianists.org

Chhandayan Center for Indian Music
http://tabla.org

Chinese Arts and Music Association in the United States
http://www.uschinamusic.org

Guitar Foundation of America
http://www.guitarfoundation.org

International Clarinet Association
http://www.clarinet.org

International Double Reed Society
http://www.idrs.org

International Horn Society
http://www.hornsociety.org

International Society of Bassists
http://www.isbworldoffice.com

International Trombone Association
http://www.trombone.net

International Trumpet Guild
http://www.trumpetguild.org

International Tuba Euphonium Association
http://www.iteaonline.org

International Women's Brass Conference
http://myiwbc.org/

Internet Cello Society
http://www.cello.org

National Flute Association
http://www.nfaonline.org

National Piano Foundation
http://pianonet.com

North American Saxophone Alliance
http://www.saxalliance.org

Percussive Arts Society
http://www.pas.org

Viola da Gamba Society of America (VdGSA)
https://vdgsa.org

Violin Society of America
http://www.vsaweb.org

AARP: An organization geared to the interests of older people.
http://www.aarp.org

Aroha Philanthropies: A funder of arts programs.
https://www.arohaphilanthropies.org

The Art of Freedom: Website of Alexander Technique instructor Jennifer Roig-Francolí has information on practice, performance, and links to her e-newsletter/blog.
http://www.artoffreedom.me

The Bulletproof Musician: Website of Noa Kageyama, PhD, with articles on practice and performance, and information about his blog and his course.
http://www.bulletproofmusician.com

Classical Connect: Offers an archive of free classical music recordings online.
http://www.classicalconnect.com

CyberBass: Free digital recordings of major choral works.
http://www.cyberbass.com/

Dystonia Medical Research Foundation: A nonprofit focused on focal dystonia.
https://www.dystonia-foundation.org

Fractured Atlas: Offers services for arts organizations, including use of the Fractured Atlas nonprofit status.
https://www.fracturedatlas.org

Freecycle Network: A nonprofit that offers free items donated by others.
https://www.freecycle.org

Foundation Center: Has information on filing for nonprofit status.
http://foundationcenter.org

Grand Piano Passion: Features articles on practice, performance, and hearing loss, and information on its e-newsletter.
http://www.grandpianopassion.com

IMSLP—Internet Music Score Library Project, Petrucci Library: Free public-domain sheet music.
http://imslp.org

J. W. Pepper: A music retailer with recordings of sheet music to listen to for free.
http://www.jwpepper.com

Keys44Kids: A nonprofit that offers used pianos for sale.
http://www.keys44kids.org

Lifetime Arts: A nonprofit that encourages the creation of creative aging arts programs; its website has a resources list and toolkit.
http://www.lifetimearts.org

Making Music (UK): A British organization that provides "advice, support and resources for leisure-time musicians."
https://www.makingmusic.org.uk/

Meetup: Clearing house for online Meetup groups for people with shared interests.
https://www.meetup.com

The Musician's Way: The companion website for the book *The Musician's Way* has information on practice, performance, wellness, and other topics.
http://musiciansway.com

Music and Wellness: A section on the Pittsburgh Symphony's website with a guide for musicians performing in health-care facilities.
http://wellness.pittsburghsymphony.org

Musopen: Offers free recordings and sheet music, without copyright restrictions.
https://musopen.org

National Center for Creative Aging: Has a database on arts programs nationwide.
http://creativeaging.org

National Public Radio: Archive of NPR music stories and interviews.
http://www.npr.org/series/100920965/music-articles/

Next Avenue: A website and e-newsletter geared to older people.
http://www.nextavenue.org

Osher Lifelong Learning Institutes: Offer programs for older people.
https://www.osherfoundation.org

Piano Society: Offers classical keyboard recordings to listen to for free online.
http://www.pianosociety.com

St. James Music Press: A subscription service for choral music.
https://www.sjmp.com

The following orchestras offer online "extras" on their websites—blogs, podcasts of performances, master classes, texts of program notes, videos, and other educational materials: Berlin Philharmonic (https://www.berliner-philharmoniker.de/en/), Boston Symphony Orchestra (http://www.bso.org), Los Angeles Philharmonic (http://www.laphil.org), National Symphony Orchestra (http://www.kennedy-center.org/nso), New York Philharmonic (http://www.nyphil.org), Pittsburgh Symphony (http://wellness.pittsburghsymphony.org), and San Francisco Symphony Orchestra (http://www.sfsymphony.org). Several orchestras offer summer programs and workshops for avocational musicians, as noted in the following section and also in chapter 9.

SUMMER PROGRAMS AND YEAR-ROUND WORKSHOPS

Two organizations noted earlier in the resources section list summer programs and workshops on their websites: Adult Music Student Forum (AMSF) and Associated Chamber Music Players (ACMP). Three others list their own programs and workshops: CAMMAC, Encore Creativity for Older Adults, and New Horizons International Music Association. Local music schools may also have summer programs and workshops. Those that follow are ones that members of our advice panel have participated in and enjoyed. The programs on the list have not been vetted for quality or effectiveness but are presented here as a starting point for further research by prospective participants. See chapters 7 and 9 for more on these types of programs.

IN THE UNITED STATES AND CANADA

Alaria Chamber Ensemble Class, New York, NY
http://www.alaria.org/classes.shtml

Alessi (Trombone) Seminar, Eugene, OR
http://www.alessiseminar.com

Amy Porter Anatomy of Sound Flute Workshop, Ann Arbor, MI
http://porterflute.com/anatomy-of-sound/

Apple Hill Summer Chamber Music Workshop, Nelson, NH
http://applehill.org

Augusta Heritage Center, Elkins, WV
https://augustaheritagecenter.org

Baltimore Symphony Orchestra: Rusty Musicians and BSO Academy Week,
Baltimore, MD
https://www.bsomusic.org

Bennington Chamber Music Conference, Bennington, VT
http://cmceast.org

Berkshire Choral International, Sheffield, MA
http://www.berkshirechoral.org

Blue Lake Adult Arts Program, Twin Lake, MI
https://bluelake.org/adultcamp/

British Columbia Swing Camp, Sorrento, BC, Canada
http://www.bcswingcamp.ca

Buffalo Philharmonic Orchestra BPO Fantasy Camp, Buffalo, NY
https://bpo.org/

California Concerto Weekend, Saratoga, CA
http://www.californiaconcerto.org

Chamber Music Workshop, Chapel Hill, NC
http://music.unc.edu/unc-cms/workshops/

Chamberre in The Rockies, Boulder and Estes Park, CO
https://www.rockyridge.org/program/chamberre-in-the-rockies/

Chaparral Music Fest, Prescott, AZ
http://www.chaparralmusicfest.org

Colorado Suzuki Institute, Beavercreek, CO
https://www.coloradosuzuki.org/chamber-music/curriculum/adult-amateurs/

Composers Conference Chamber Music Workshop, Wellesley, MA
https://www.composersconference.org

Detroit Symphony Orchestra's Community Ensembles
http://www.dso.org/page.aspx?page_id=11

Edmonton Symphony Orchestra Rusty Musicians, Edmonton, AB, Canada
https://www.winspearcentre.com/learning/rusty-musicians/

Fall Foliage Chamber Workshop, Rockport, ME
http://fallfoliagechambermusic.com

Gamba Conclave, various locations in United States
https://vdgsa.org

Garth Newel Workshop, Warm Springs, VA
http://www.garthnewel.org/amateur-chamber-music-workshop/

Gettysburg Chamber Music Workshop, Fairfield, PA
http://www.gettysburgchambermusic.org

Golandsky Institute Summer Symposium, Princeton, NJ
https://www.golandskyinstitute.org/symposium/

Interlochen Music Programs for Adults, Interlochen, MI
http://college.interlochen.org

Jamey Aebersold's Summer Jazz Workshops, Louisville, KY
http://workshops.jazzbooks.com/about-us/summer-jazz-workshops/

International Keyboard Institute & Festival, New York, NY
http://www.ikif.org

John Mack Oboe Camp, Little Switzerland, NC
http://www.johnmackoboecamp.org

Kent/Blossom Music Festival, Kent, OH
https://www.kent.edu/blossom

Kinhaven Adult Piano Workshop, Weston, VT
http://www.kinhaven.org

Manhattan String Quartet Workshops, in United States and Europe
http://www.manhattanstringquartet.com/conferences.html

MasterWorks, Indianapolis, IN
https://masterworksfestival.org

Midsummer Musical Retreat, Walla Walla, WA
http://www.musicalretreat.org

Midwest Banjo Camp, Olivet, MI
http://midwestbanjocamp.com

Music Camps North, Charlton, MA
http://musiccampsnorth.com

Music Etc., Ocean Grove, NJ
https://www.facebook.com/chambermusicetc/

Music for People
http://musicforpeople.org

New England Adult Music Camp, Sidney, Maine
https://adultmusiccamp.com

Next Level Recorder Retreat, Carmel Valley, CA
https://www.hiddenvalleymusic.org/event-next-level-recorder-retreat_110.htm

Pacific Symphony Orchestra, OC Can You Play with Us, Irvine, CA
https://www.pacificsymphony.org/education/community_participation/
oc_can_you_play_with_us

Piano Texas Institute and Festival Amateurs Program, Fort Worth, TX
http://www.pianotexas.org

Playweek Virginia, Lexington, VA
http://www.playweek.net/virginia.html

Puget Sound Chamber Music Workshop, Seattle WA
http://www.mcnw.org/programs/workshops/workshops.htm

Puget Sound Guitar Workshop, Bremerton, WA
http://www.psgw.org

Raphael Trio Chamber Music Workshop, Wilton, NH
http://www.raphaeltrioworkshop.com

Richmond Symphony Orchestra Come & Play, Richmond, VA
https://www.richmondsymphony.com

SCOR! String Camps for Adults, various US locations.
http://www.stringcamp.com

Seattle Recorder Society Workshop, Tacoma, WA
http://www.seattle-recorder.org/workshop

Somerset Harp Folk Festival, New Jersey
http://www.somersetharpfest.com

Sonata Piano Camps for Adults, Bennington, VT
http://www.sonatina.com/sonatas.html

St. Lawrence String Quartet Seminar, Palo Alto, CA
https://music.stanford.edu/ensembles-lessons/ensemble-in-residence-slsq

Strathmore Uke and Guitar Summit, North Bethesda, MD
https://www.strathmore.org

Summer Acoustic Music in the Pines, Bremerton, WA
http://www.summeracousticmusic.org

Summerkeys, Lubec, ME
http://summerkeys.com

SummerTrios, Lancaster, PA
http://www.summertrios.org

Uke Fest—Ashokan Music and Dance Camps, Olivebridge, NY
https://ashokan.org/uke-fest/

Walden Creative Musicians Retreat, Dublin, NH
http://waldenschool.org/creative-musicians-retreat

Western Wind Vocal Workshops, Northampton, MA
http://www.westernwind.org

IN THE UK AND EUROPE

AlpenKammerMusik, Austria
http://alpenkammermusik.com

Benslow Music Festival, Hertfordshire, UK
http://www.benslowmusic.org

Bournemouth Symphony Orchestra Rusty Musicians, Bournemouth, UK
https://www.bsolive.com/rustymusicians/

East London Late Starters Orchestra, London, UK
http://www.ellso.org/summer-school

Grittleton Chamber Music Course, Grittleton, UK
http://www.grittletonmusiccourse.co.uk

Trevor Wye Flute Workshops, Kent, UK
http://flutesenvacances.co.uk/wp

MEDICAL SCHOOL AND MEDICAL CENTER ENSEMBLES

Medical schools and medical centers of the following universities sponsor musical ensembles for students, faculty, and staff: Albert Einstein, Cornell University's Weill Cornell Medical College, Duke, Johns Hopkins, University of California San Francisco, University of Michigan, and Yale. Texas Medical Center in Houston sponsors the Texas Medical Center Orchestra. There are also regional orchestras with a link to the medical profession that are not tied to one specific medical school, including Longwood Symphony (Boston), Los Angeles Doctors Symphony Orchestra, World Doctors Orchestra, Philadelphia Doctors Chamber Orchestra, and the European Doctors Orchestra.

COMPETITIONS FOR AMATEUR MUSICIANS

Several organizations listed earlier in the resources section post information about competitions for amateur musicians on their websites: Adult Music Student Forum (AMSF), Amateur Pianist, Associated Chamber Music Players (ACMP), Boston Piano Amateurs Association, and Cliburn International Amateur Piano Competition. Music schools may sponsor competitions, such as the Misbin Family Memorial Chamber Music Competition sponsored by Levine Music and Washington Performing Arts in Washington, DC (http://www.levinemusic.org). Community ensembles may also have competitions, such as the one described in chapter 10 offered by Kenwood Symphony Orchestra, Minneapolis, MN (http://kenwoodsymphonyorchestra.org/mcac).

ONLINE COURSES

There are too many instructional videos available on YouTube to list here, but following are a few sources for more in-depth online courses.

Coursera: Courses with university instructors that charge tuition, with financial aid available. Courses that advice-team members took include: "Developing Your Musicianship," "Write Like Mozart: An Introduction to Classical Music Composition," "Songwriting: Writing the Lyrics," and "Fundamentals of Music Theory."
https://www.coursera.org/

Earmaster: Courses in ear training, sight-singing, music theory, with a free trial period.
https://www.earmaster.com

EdX: Free courses from universities, including an introductory version of "Developing Your Musicianship" offered on Coursera.
https://www.edx.org

Juilliard Open Classroom: Live-streamed master classes and other educational options.
http://open.juilliard.edu/courses?gclid=CPOF79Kqn9MCFdyCswod91INnQ

MusicTheory.net: Free music theory lessons, with some helpful tools in the Tenuto section of the website (a pop-up piano and staff paper generator) that can be used for free or purchased as apps for Apple products.
https://www.musictheory.net

The Practice Room: Online sight-singing course available for purchase.
http://www.thepracticeroom.net

teoría : Music theory lessons and sight-singing exercises, available for free online, with optional membership fee for fuller use of the exercises.
https://www.teoria.com

Violinlab: Tuition charged for its online violin instruction, but there is an archive of excerpts from its lessons to sample for free.
http://violinlab.com

MUSIC NOTATION SOFTWARE

Finale
http://www.finalemusic.com

NoteWorthy Composer: For Windows computers.
https://noteworthycomposer.com/

Pro Tools
http://www.avid.com/pro-tools

Sibelius
http://www.avid.com/sibelius

OTHER ONLINE EDUCATIONAL OPTIONS

Hal Leonard play-alongs: Sheet music books with play-along CDs or online audio files.
https://www.halleonard.com

iReal Pro: Play-along app with a band that accompanies you as you practice.
https://itunes.apple.com/us/app/ireal-pro/id298206806?mt=8

Jamey Aebersold series: Play-along jazz sheet music books with CDs.
http://www.jazzbooks.com

Music Minus One: Play-along sheet music books with CDs on a wide range of musical styles, including some for vocal music; some books include links to online audio tracks.
https://www.musicdispatch.com/index.jsp?subsiteid=325

SmartMusic: Software program that keeps track of your accuracy as you practice.
https://www.smartmusic.com

TECHNOLOGICAL AIDS FOR PRACTICING

There are many versions of online metronomes and tuners available, but the following are other kinds of technological aids that advice-team members used. Technology changes quickly. An online search may uncover other products.

Amazing Slow Downer: Slows down music without changing the pitch.
https://itunes.apple.com/us/app/amazing-slow-downer/id308998718?mt=8

Anytune: Slows down music without changing the pitch.
https://itunes.apple.com/us/app/anytune-slow-down-music-without/
id415365180?mt=8

Audacity: Free multitrack audio editor and recorder.
https://sourceforge.net/projects/audacity/

Cadenza: Play-along program that lets the accompaniment match your tempo.
http://www.sonacadenza.com/the-app/

Capo: App to slow down music.
https://capo.en.softonic.com/mac

Doodle: Online scheduler.
http://doodle.com

forScore: App for storing scores on an iPad.
https://forscore.co

Henle Library: App for downloading scores for an iPad or Android tablet.
http://www.henle-library.de/en/

Meludia: Computer program for enhancing listening skills.
https://www.meludia.com/en/

MusicReader: Turns an iPad, laptop, or desktop computer into a digital music stand.
http://www.musicreader.net

PiaScore: App that turns an iPad into a digital music stand.
http://piascore.com

Tempo SlowMo: App for iPhones and iPads to slow down music.
https://itunes.apple.com/us/app/tempo-slowmo-bpm-music-practice-slow-downer/
id460008289?mt=8

Bibliography

Listed below are memoirs of amateur musicians, as well as general books on music, music-making, practicing, adult education, and aging that were either recommended by members of the advice team or were used for research. There are too many methods books and biographies of professional musicians and composers to list here, but an online search can turn up good examples of those kinds of books.

MEMOIRS OF AMATEUR MUSICIANS

Adams, Noah. *Piano Lessons*. New York: Delacorte, 1996.
Booth, Wayne. *For the Love of It: Amateuring and Its Rivals.* Chicago: University of Chicago Press, 1999.
Carhart, Thad. *The Piano Shop on the Left Bank: Discovering a Forgotten Passion in a Paris Atelier.* New York: Random House, 2002.
Cooke, Charles. *Playing the Piano for Pleasure*. Westport, CT: Greenwood, 1941.
Goldman, Ari L. *The Late Starters Orchestra*. New York: Algonquin Books of Chapel Hill, 2014.
Holt, John. *Never Too Late*. New York: Da Capo Press, 1991.
Horn, Stacy. *Imperfect Harmony: Finding Happiness Singing with Others*. New York: Algonquin Books of Chapel Hill, 2013.
Rees, Jasper. *I Found My Horn: One Man's Struggle with the Orchestra's Most Difficult Instrument.* London: Phoenix, 2009.
Robinson, Bernard. *An Amateur in Music*. Newbury, UK: Countryside Books, 1985.

Rusbridger, Alan. *Play It Again: An Amateur against the Impossible*. New York: Farrar, Straus and Giroux, 2013.

Solovitch, Sara. *Playing Scared: A History and Memoir of Stage Fright*. New York: Bloomsbury, 2015.

BOOKS ON MUSIC, PRACTICING, ADULT EDUCATION, AND AGING

*Books with asterisks include practice suggestions.

* Bernstein, Seymour. *With Your Own Two Hands: Self-Discovery Through Music*. New York: G. Schirmer, 1981.

Boyer, Johanna Misey. *Creativity Matters: The Arts and Aging Toolkit*. New York: National Guild for Community Arts Education, 2007.

* Bruser, Madeline. *The Art of Practicing: A Guide to Making Music from the Heart*. New York: Bell Tower, 1997.

Bugos, Jennifer. *Contemporary Research in Music Learning Across the Lifespan: Music Education and Human Development*. London: Routledge, 2016.

* Cheng, Wendy, and Willa Horwitz. *Making Music with a Hearing Loss: Strategies and Stories*. Gaithersburg, MD: AAMHL Publications, 2016.

* Chung, Brian, and Brenda Dillon. *Recreational Music Making Handbook for Piano Teachers*. Los Angeles: Alfred Music Publishing Company, 2009.

Cohen, Gene D. *The Creative Age: Awakening Human Potential in the Second Half of Life*. New York: Harper Collins, 2000.

Colvin, Geoff. *Talent Is Overrated: What Really Separates World-Class Performers from Everybody Else*. New York: Penguin Group, 2010.

Csikszentmihalyi, Mihaly. *Flow: The Psychology of Optimal Experience*. New York: Harper Perennial Modern Classics, 2008.

* Dillon, Brenda. *Piano Fun for Adult Beginners—Recreational Music Making for Private or Group Instruction*. New York: Hal Leonard, 2010.

Giddan, Jane, and Ellen Cole. *70 Candles: Women Thriving in Their 8th Decade*. Chagrin Falls, OH: Taos Institute Publications, 2015.

* Green, Barry, with W. Timothy Gallwey. *The Inner Game of Music*. New York: Doubleday, 1986.

* Green, Barry. *The Mastery of Music: Ten Pathways to True Artistry*. New York: Broadway Books, 2003.

Gwande, Atul. *Being Moral: Medicine and What Matters in the End*. New York: Henry Holt, 2014.

* Heman-Ackah, Yolanda, Robert T. Sataloff, and Mary J. Hawkshaw. *The Voice: A Medical Guide for Achieving and Maintaining a Healthy Voice*. Narberth, PA: Science & Medicine, 2013.

* Horvath, Janet. *Playing Less Hurt: An Injury Prevention Guide for Musicians*. New York: Hal Leonard, 2010.

* Kaplan, Burton. *Practicing for Artistic Success: The Musician's Guide to Self-Empowerment*. New York: Perception Development Techniques, 2004.

Katz, Mark. *Capturing Sound: How Technology Has Changed Music*. Berkeley: University of California Press, 2010.

* Klickstein, Gerald. *The Musician's Way: A Guide to Practice, Performance, and Wellness*. New York: Oxford University Press, 2009.

Koufman, Jamie, Jordan Stern, and Marc Bauer. *Dropping Acid: The Reflux Diet Cookbook & Cure*. Elmwood Park, NJ: G & H Soho, 2015.

Lawrence-Lightfoot, Sara. *The Third Chapter: Passion, Risk, and Adventure in the 25 Years after 50.* New York: Sarah Crichton Books, 2009.

Levitin, Daniel J. *This Is Your Brain on Music: The Science of a Human Obsession.* New York: Penguin Group, 2006.

* Maris, Barbara English. *Making Music at the Piano: Learning Strategies for Adult Students.* New York: Oxford University Press, 2000.

* Marsalis, Wynton. *Marsalis on Music.* New York: Norton, 1995.

* Mathieu, W. A. *The Listening Book: Discovering Your Own Music.* Boston: Shambhala, 2011.

* Mathieu, W. A. *The Musical Life: Reflections on What It Is and How to Live It.* Boston: Shambhala, 1994.

* Meredith, Victoria. *Sing Better as You Age: A Comprehensive Guide for Adult Choral Singers.* Santa Barbara, CA: Santa Barbara Music Publishing, 2007.

Merriam, Sharan B., and Laura L. Bierma. *Adult Learning: Linking Theory and Practice.* San Francisco: Jossey Bass, 2014.

Merriam, Sharan B., Rosemary S. Caffarella, and Lisa M. Baumgartner. *Learning in Adulthood: A Comprehensive Guide.* San Francisco: Jossey Bass, 2007.

* Miller, Richard. *Solutions for Singers: Tools for Performers and Teachers.* New York: Oxford University Press, 2004.

* Nathan, Amy. *Meet the Musicians: From Prodigy (or Not) to Pro.* New York: Henry Holt, 2006.

* Nathan, Amy. *The Music Parents' Survival Guide.* New York: Oxford University Press, 2014.

* Nathan, Amy. *The Young Musician's Survival Guide.* New York: Oxford University Press, 2000, 2008.

Philip, Robert. *Performing Music in the Age of Recording.* New Haven, CT: Yale University Press, 2004.

* Ristad, Eloise. *A Soprano on Her Head: Right-Side-Up Reflections on Life and Other Performances.* Moab, UT: Real People Press, 1982.

* Roseman, Ed. *Edly's Music Theory for Practical People.* Hadley, MA: Musical EdVentures, 2009.

Sacks, Oliver. *Musicophilia: Tales of Music and the Brain.* New York: Random House, 2008.

* Sataloff, Robert T., Mary J. Hawkshaw, Jaime Eaglin Moore, and Amy L. Russ. *50 Ways to Abuse Your Voice: A Singer's Guide to a Short Career.* Oxford, UK: Compton Publishing, 2014.

* Sudo, Philip Toshio. *Zen Guitar.* New York: Simon and Schuster, 1997.

* Tunstall, Tricia. *Note By Note: A Celebration of the Piano Lesson.* New York: Simon and Schuster, 2008.

* Westney, William. *The Perfect Wrong Note: Learning to Trust Your Musical Self.* Pompton Plains, NJ: Amadeus Press, 2006.

* Williams, Bernie, Dave Gluck, and Bob Thompson. *Rhythms of the Game: The Link Between Musical and Athletic Performance.* Milwaukee, WI: Hal Leonard, 2011.

RESEARCH ARTICLES ABOUT MUSIC AND MUSIC-MAKING

Archie, Patrick. "Music-Based Interventions in Palliative Cancer Care: A Review of Quantitative Studies and Neurobiological Literature." *Support Care Cancer* 21, no. 9 (2013): 2609–2624.

Balbag, M. Alison, Nancy L. Pedersen, and Margaret Gatz. "Playing a Musical Instrument as a Protective Factor against Dementia and Cognitive Impairment: A Population-Based Twin Study." *International Journal of Alzheimer's Disease* 2014 (2014), ID 836748.

Beck, R. J., T. C. Cesario, A. Yousefi, and H. Enamoto. "Choral Singing, Performance Perception, and Immune System Changes in Salivary Immunoglobulin A and Cortisol." *Music Perception: An Interdisciplinary Journal* 18, no. 1 (Fall 2000): 87–106.

Bensimon, Moshe, Dorit Amir, and Yuval Wolf. "Drumming through Trauma: Music Therapy with Post-Traumatic Soldiers." *The Arts in Psychotherapy* 35 (2008): 34–48.

Blood, Anne J., and Robert J. Zatorre. "Intensely Pleasurable Responses to Music Correlate with Activity in Brain Regions Implicated in Reward and Emotion." *Proceedings of the National Academy of Sciences* 98, no. 20 (2001): 11818–11823

Brown, Raschel M., Joyce L. Chen, Avrum Hollinger, Virginia B. Penhune, Caroline Palmer, and Robert J. Zatorre. "Repetition Suppression in Auditory-Motor Regions to Pitch and Temporal Structure in Music." *Journal of Cognitive Neuroscience* 25, no. 2 (2013): 313–328.

Bugos, Jennifer A. "Adult Learner Perceptions: Perspectives from Beginning Musicians (Ages 60–86 years)." *Applications of Research in Music Education* 32, no. 2 (2014): 26.

Bugos, Jennifer. "Community Music as a Cognitive Training Programme for Successful Ageing." *International Journal of Community Music* 7, no. 3 (2014): 319–331.

Bugos, Jennifer. "Intense Piano Training on Self-Efficacy and Physiological Stress in Aging." *Psychology of Music* 44, no. 4 (2015): 611–624.

Bugos, J. A. "The Benefits of Music Instruction on Processing Speed, Verbal Fluency, and Cognitive Control in Aging." *Music Education Research International* 4 (2010): 1–9.

Bugos, J. A., and W. M. Perlstein, C. S. McCrae, T. S. Brophy, and P. H. Bedenbaugh. "Individualized Piano Instruction Enhances Executive Functioning and Working Memory in Older Adults." *Aging & Mental Health* 11, no. 4 (2007), 464–471.

Canga, Bernardo, Ronit Azoulay, Jonathan Raskin, and Joanne Loewy. "AIR: Advances in Respiration—Music Therapy in the Treatment of Chronic Pulmonary Disease." *Respiratory Medicine* 109 (2015): 1532–1539

Canga, Bernardo, Cho Long Hahm, David Lucido, Michael L. Grossbard, and Joanne Loewy. "Environmental Music Therapy: A Pilot Study of the Effects of Music Therapy in a Chemotherapy Infusion Suite." *Music and Medicine* 4, no. 4 (2012): 221–230.

Chanda, Mona Lisa, and Daniel J. Levitin. "The Neurochemistry of Music." *Trends in Cognitive Sciences* 17, no.4 (2013): 179–193.

Cooper, T. "Adults' Perceptions of Piano Study: Achievements and Experiences." *Journal of Research in Music Education* 49 (2001) 156–168.

Creech, A., S. Hallam, M. Varvarigou, H. McQueen, and H. Gaunt. "Active Music Making: A Route to Enhanced Subjective Well-Being among Older People." *Perspectives in Public Health* 133, no. 1 (2013): 36–43.

Creech, Andrea, Susan Hallam, Hilary McQueen, and Maria Varvarigou. "The Power of Music in the Lives of Older Adults." *Research Studies in Music Education* 35, no. 1 (2013): 87–102.

Demorest, Steven M., and Peter Q. Pfordresher. "Singing Accuracy Development from K-Adult: A Comparative Study." *Music Perception: An Interdisciplinary Journal* 32, no. 3 (2015): 293–302.

Drummond, John. "An International Perspective on Music Education for Adults." In *The Oxford Handbook of Music Education* Vol. 2 (2nd ed., pp. 303–315), edited by Gary E. McPherson and Graham F. Welch. Oxford University Press, 2012.

Dunbar, R. I., K. Kaskatis, I. MacDonald, and V. Barra. "Performance of Music Elevates Pain Threshold and Positive Affect: Implications for the Evolutionary Function of Music." *Evolutionary Psychology* 10, no. 4 (2012): 688–702.

Eiluned Pearce, Jacques Launay, and Robin I. M. Dunbar. "The Ice-Breaker Effect: Singing Mediates Fast Social Bonding." *Royal Society Open Science* 28 (2015).

Ertel, Karen A., M. Maria Glymour, and Lisa F. Berkman. "Effects of Social Integration on Preserving Memory Function in a Nationally Representative US Elderly Population." *American Journal of Public Health* 98, no. 7 (2008): 1215–1220.

Fancourt, Daisy, Rosie Perkins, Sara Ascenso, Livia A. Carvalho, Andrew Steptoe, and Aaron Williamon. "Effects of Group Drumming Interventions on Anxiety, Depression, Social Resilience, and Inflammatory Immune Response among Mental Health Service Users." *PLOS,* March 14, 2016. Available: https://doi.org/10.1371/journal.pone.0151136

Fancourt, Daisy, Aaron Williamon, Livia A Carvalho, Andrew Steptoe, Rosie Dow, and Ian Lewis. "Singing Modulates Mood, Stress, Cortisol, Cytokine, and Neuropeptide Activity in Cancer Patients and Carers." *eCancer* 10, 631 (2016). Available: http://ecancer.org/journal/10/full/631-singing-modulates-mood-stress-cortisol-cytokine-and-neuropeptide-activity-in-cancer-patients-and-carers.php

Gooding, Lori F., Erin L Abner, Gregory A Jicha, Richard J Kryscio, and Fredrick A Schmitt. "Musical Training and Late-Life Cognition." *American Journal of Alzheimer's Disease and other Dementias* 29, no 4 (2014): 333–343.

Guzmán-Vélez, Edmarie, and Daniel Tranel. "Does Bilingualism Contribute to Cognitive Reserve? Cognitive and Neural Perspectives." *Neuropsychology* 29, no.1 (2015): 139–150.

Hanna-Pladdy, Brenda, and Byron Gajewski. "Recent and Past Musical Activity Predicts Cognitive Aging Variability: Direct Comparison with General Lifestyle Activities." *Frontiers in Human Neuroscience* 6, no. 198 (2012): 1–11.

Hanna-Pladdy, Brenda, and Alicia MacKay. "The Relation between Instrumental Musical Activity and Cognitive Aging." *Neuropsychology* 25, no. 3 (2011): 378–386.

Hartshorne, Joshua K., & Laura T. Germine. "When Does Cognitive Functioning Peak? The Asynchronous Rise and Fall of Different Cognitive Abilities across the Lifespan." *Psychological Science* 26, no. 4 (2015).

Hollinger, Avrum. "Optical Sensing, Embedded Systems, and Musical Interfaces for Functional Neuroimaging." McGill Library and Collections eScholarship@McGill (2014). Available: http://digitool.library.mcgill.ca/R?func=dbin-jump-full&object_id=123054

Hyde, Krista L., Jason Lerch, Andrea Norton, Marie Forgeard, Ellen Winner, Alan C. Evans, and Gottfried Schlaug. "The Effects of Musical Training on Structural Brain Development: A Longitudinal Study." *Annals of the New York Academy of Sciences* 1169 (2009): 182–186.

Jäncke, Lutz. "Music Drives Brain plasticity." *Molecular Biology Reports* 1 (2009): 78.

Jäncke, Lutz. "The Plastic Human Brain." *Restorative Neurology and Neuroscience* 27 (2009) 521–538.

Jentzsch, Ines, Anahit Mkrtchian, and Nayantara Kansal. "Improved Effectiveness of Performance Monitoring in Amateur Instrumental Musicians." *Neuropsychologia* 52, no. 100 (2014):117–124.

Johnson, Julene, Jukka Louhivuori, Anita L. Stewart, Asko Tolvanen, Leslie Ross, and Pertti Era. "Quality of Life (QOL) of Older Adult Community Choral Singers in Finland." *International Psychogeriatrics* 25, no. 7 (2013): 1055–1064.

Jutras, P. "The Benefits of New Horizons Band Participation as Self-reported by Selected New Horizons Band Members." *Bulletin for the Council of Research on Music Education* 187 (2011): 65–84.

Kraus, Nina, and Bharath Chandrasekaran. "Music Training for the Development of Auditory Skills." *Nature Reviews Neuroscience* 11 (2010): 599–605.

Kreutz, Gunter, Stephan Bongard, Sonja Rohrmann, Volker Hodapp, and Dorothee Grebe. "Effects of Choir Singing or Listening on Secretory Immunoglobulin A, Cortisol, and Emotional State." *Journal of Behavioral Medicine* 27, no. 6 (2004): 623–635.

Levitin, Daniel J. "Neural Correlates of Music Behaviors: A Brief Overview." *Music Therapy Perspectives* 31, no. 1 (2013): 15–24.

Loewy, Joanne V., Jamée Ard, and Naoko Mizutani. "Music Therapy in Neurologic Dysfunction to Address Self-Expression, Language, and Communication: The Impact of Group Singing on Stroke Survivors and Caregivers." In *Communication and Aging* (2nd ed., pp. 269–300), edited by Jon F. Nussbaum, Loretta L. Pecchioni, James D. Robinson, and Teresa L. Thompson. New York: Routledge, 2000.

Meister, I. G., T. Krings, H. Foltys, B. Boroojerdi, M. Müller, R. Töpper, and A. Thron. "Playing Piano in the Mind—An fMRI Study on Music Imagery and Performance in Pianists." *Brain Research Cognitive Brain Research* 19, no. 3 (2004): 219–228.

Moussard, A., P. Bermudez, C. Alain, W. Tays, and S. Moreno. "Life-long Music Practice and Executive Control in Older Adults: An Event-Related Potential Study." *Brain Research* 1642 (2016): 146–53.

Myers, David E. "Including Adulthood in Music Education Perspectives and Policy: A Lifespan View." *National Society for the Study of Education* 111, no. 1 (2012): 74–92.

Parbery-Clark, Alexandra, Dana L. Strait, Samira Anderson, Emily Hittner, and Nina Kraus. "Musical Experience and the Aging Auditory System: Implications for Cognitive Abilities and Hearing Speech in Noise." *PLoS One* 6, no. 5, (2011): 1–8.

Rohwer, D. "Going to the Source: Pedagogical Ideas from Adult Band Members." *Journal of Band Research* 48, no. 1 (2012): 45–57.

Rohwer, D., M. Raiber, and D. Coffman. "Random or Non-random Thoughts: What Senior Adults Think about within their Ensemble Settings." *International Journal of Community Music* 5, no. 3 (2013): 289–302

Schlaug, G., L. Jäncke, Y. Huang, J. F. Staiger, and H. Steinmetz. "Increased Corpus Callosum Size in Musicians." *Neuropsychologia* 33, no. 8 (1995):1047–1055.

Seinfeld, Sofia, Heidi Figueroa, Jordi Ortiz-Gil, and Maria V. Sanchez-Vives. "Effects of Music Learning and Piano Practice on Cognitive Function, Mood, and Quality of Life in Older Adults." *Frontiers in Psychology* 4 (2013): 810.

Skoe, Erika, and Nina Kraus. "A Little Goes a Long Way: How the Adult Brain Is Shaped by Musical Training in Childhood." *Journal of Neuroscience* 32, no. 34 (2012): 11507–11510.

Tsugawa, S. "Motivation and Meaning among Members of Two Senior Adult Music Ensembles." In *Situating Inquiry: Expanded Venues for Music Education Research* (pp. 179–203), edited by L. K. Thompson and M. R. Campbell. Charlotte, NC: Information Age Publishing, 2012.

Verghese, Joe, Richard B. Lipton, Mindy J. Katz, Charles B. Hall, Carol A. Derby, Gail Kuslansky, Anne F. Ambrose, Martin Sliwinski, and Herman Buschke. "Leisure Activities and the Risk of Dementia in the Elderly." *New England Journal of Medicine* 348 (2003): 2508–2516.

Wan, Catherine Y., and Gottfried Schlaug. "Music Making as a Tool for Promoting Brain Plasticity across the Life Span." *Neuroscientist*, 16, no. 5 (2010): 566–577.

Weinstein, D., J. Launay, E. Pearce, R. Dunbar, and L. Stewart. "Group Music Performance Causes Elevated Pain Thresholds and Social Bonding in Small and Large Groups of Singers." *Evolution and Human Behavior* 37, no. 2 (2016):152–158

White-Schwoch, Travis, Kali Woodruff Carr, Samira Anderson, Dana L. Strait, and Nina Kraus. "Older Adults Benefit from Music Training Early in Life: Biological Evidence for Long-Term Training-Driven Plasticity." *Journal of Neuroscience* 33, no. 45 (2013): 17667–17674.

Zatorre, Robert J. "Music the Food of Neuroscience?" *Nature* 434 (2005): 312–315.

Zelazny, Colleen M. "Therapeutic Instrumental Music Playing in Hand Rehabilitation for Older Adults with Osteoarthritis: Four Case Studies." *Journal of Music Therapy* 38, no. 2 (2001)): 97–113.

Zuk, Jennifer, Christopher Benjamin, Arnold Kenyon, and Nadine Gaab. "Behavioral and Neural Correlates of Executive Functioning in Musicians and Non-Musicians." *PLOS One* 9, no. 6 (2014).

OTHER ARTICLES OF INTEREST

Charness, Michael F. "Suggestions for Preventing Injury in Musicians." Performing Arts Clinic. Boston: Brigham and Women's Hospital. Available: http://www.brighamandwomens.org/Departments_and_Services/neurology/Images/Injury%20prevention%20for%20musicians.pdf

Cole, Diane. "Your Aging Brain Will Be in Better Shape If You've Taken Music Lessons." *National Geographic,* January 2014.

"How to Rock an Open Mic Night." Guitar Tricks, April 9, 2014. Available: https://www.guitartricks.com/blog/How-to-Rock-an-Open-Mic-Night

Jamieson, Sophie. "'Tuneless Choir' for People Who Can't Sing Plans to Hold First Concert." *The Telegraph*, April 4, 2017.

Lee, Anna. "Amateur." *Theories of Media, Keywords Glossary* (Winter 2007). Chicago School of Media Theory, University of Chicago. Available: http://csmt.uchicago.edu/glossary2004/amateur.htm

Marshall, Amy Milgrub. "Probing Questions: Can Anyone Be Taught How to Sing?" *Penn State News*, April 5, 2017. Available: http://news.psu.edu/story/141974/2012/07/20/research/probing-question-can-anyone-be-taught-how-sing

McLennan, Douglas. "Hail the Amateur, Loved by the Crowd." *New York Times*, June 10, 2011.

Midgette, Anne. "Amateur Musicians Savor Performance Opportunities." *Washington Post*, September 16, 2011.

Povoledo, Elisabetta. "In the Land of Opera, a Choir for the Tone Deaf." *New York Times,* February 19, 2017.

Quilter, Deborah. "The Surprising Health Benefits of Drumming." Next Avenue e-newsletter, October 19, 2016. Available: http://www.nextavenue.org/health-benefits-drumming/

Raschke, Heidi. "Chorus Lets Those Dealing with Dementia Make New Memories." Next Avenue e-newsletter, June 30, 2016. Available: http://www.nextavenue.org/giving-voice-chorus/

Rienzi, Greg. "Musicians Get Hurt a Lot: Paging Dr. Serap Bastepe-Gray." *Johns Hopkins Magazine* (Fall 2016). Available: https://hub.jhu.edu/magazine/2016/fall/peabody-doctor-for-musicians-injuries/

Tagawa, Beth. "Lifelong Learners Thrive at OLLI Program." *San Francisco State University News*, February 2015. Available: http://news.sfsu.edu/lifelong-learners-thrive-olli-program

"Taking Care of Your Voice." National Institutes of Health. Available: https://www.nidcd.nih. gov/health/taking-care-your-voice#4

"Task Specific Focal Dystonia." US National Library of Medicine. Available: https://ghr.nlm. nih.gov/condition/task-specific-focal-dystonia#diagnosis

"Tips to Keep You Talkin.'" National Center for Voice and Speech. Available: http://www.ncvs. org/products_tips.html

"This is Your Brain on Jazz: Researchers Use MRI to Study Spontaneity, Creativity." *Johns Hopkins Medicine News and Publications*, February 26, 2008). Available: http://www. hopkinsmedicine.org/news/media/releases/this_is_your_brain_on_jazz_researchers_use_ mri_to_study_spontaneity_creativity

Tommasini, Anthony. "Playing by Heart, With or Without a Score." *New York Times*, December 31, 2012.

Umberson, Debra, and Jennifer Karas Montez. "Social Relationships and Health: A Flashpoint for Health Policy." *Journal of Health and Social Behavior* 51, Suppl. (2010): S54–S66.

Wakin, Daniel J. "For Music's Sake." *New York Times*, October 21, 2006.

Wakin, Daniel J. "Reviving Music Dreams in Middle Age." *New York Times*, February 29, 2012.

"What Do I Need to Know to Survive at a Jazz Jam Session." Ask MetaFilter, August 26, 2010. Available: http://ask.metafilter.com/163309/What-do-I-need-to-know-to-survive-at-a-jazz-jam-session

Zatorre, Robert J., and Valorie N. Salimpoor. "Why Music Makes Our Brain Sing." *New York Times*, June 7, 2013.

ONLINE BOOKLETS AND REPORTS

"Artful Aging Resource Guide." Aroha Philanthropies. Available: https://www. arohaphilanthropies.org/wp-content/uploads/2016/07/070716ResourceGuide_Linked.pdf

"The Chorus Impact Study." Chorus America, 2009. Available: https://www.chorusamerica.org/ publications/research-reports/chorus-impact-study

"Creative Aging Toolkit For Public Libraries." Lifetime Arts. Available: http:// creativeagingtoolkit.org

"A Decade of Arts Engagement: Findings from the Survey of Public Participation in the Arts, 2002–2012." National Endowment for the Arts. Available: https://www.arts.gov/publications/ decade-arts-engagement-findings-survey-public-participation-arts-2002-2012

"The Demographics of Aging." Transgenerational Design Matters. Available: http:// transgenerational.org/aging/demographics.htm

"Directory of Creative Aging Programs in America." National Center for Creative Aging. Available: http://creativeaging.org/programs-people/cad

"Music and the Brain." Auditory Neuroscience Laboratory. Available: http://www.brainvolts. northwestern.edu/projects/music/index.php

"New Gallup Survey by NAMM Reflects Majority of Americans Agree with Many Benefits of Playing Musical Instruments." National Association of Music Merchants, April 29, 2009. Available: https:// www.namm.org/news/press-releases/new-gallup-survey-namm-reflects-majority-americans%20

"A Profile of Older Americans: 2015." US Department of Health and Human Services. Available: https://www.acl.gov/sites/default/files/Aging%20and%20Disability%20in%20America/ 2015-Profile.pdf

Raschke, Heidi, ed. *Artful Aging: How Creativity Sparks Vitality and Transforms Lives.* E-book. St. Paul, MN: Next Avenue, Twin Cities PBS (TPT), 2016.

"Staying Engaged: Health Patterns of Older Americans Who Participate in the Arts." National Endowment for the Arts, September 2017. Available: https://www.arts.gov/sites/default/files/StayingEngaged_0917_0.pdf

BLOGS AND E-NEWSLETTERS

The Art of Freedom e-newsletter. http://www.artoffreedom.me

Borkopolis—Mark Dalrymple's blog (advice-team member): https://borkopolis.wordpress.com/2011/04/07/the-social-contact-network/

Bulletproof Musician e-newsletter: http://www.bulletproofmusician.com

Grand Piano Passion e-newsletter: http://www.grandpianopassion.com/

Grant Space, a blog of the Foundation Center: http://grantspace.org

Making Music e-newsletter: http://makingmusicmag.com

Musical America blogs: http://www.musicalamerica.com/mablogs/

Next Avenue e-newsletter: http://www.nextavenue.org/newsletter/

The Rest Is Noise blog by *New Yorker* music critic Alex Ross. Lists many music blogs: http://www.therestisnoise.com/2004/11/music_blogs.html

Mary Schons' blog (advice-team member): http://www.hammondlovesmusic.blogspot.com

Violinist blog: http://www.violinist.com

EDUCATIONAL VIDEOS AND DVDS

Alive Inside, a documentary "to demonstrate music's ability to combat memory loss and restore a deep sense of self to those suffering from it." Michael Rossato-Bennett, director/producer. Available: http://www.aliveinside.us/#about

Bastepe-Gray, Serap. *Putting It All Together: A Musician's Guide to Day-to-Day Healthy Play.* Health and Wellness Seminar Series, Peabody Institute of the Johns Hopkins University, September 2014 (YouTube, January 2015). Exercise video starts at minute 17:00. Available: https://www.youtube.com/watch?v=YK_NxxD5bbM

Collins, Anita. *How Playing an Instrument Benefits Your Brain.* TEDEd Lessons Worth Sharing. Available: http://ed.ted.com/lessons/how-playing-an-instrument-benefits-your-brain-anita-collins

Music and the Brain. Slide show produced by Northwestern University's Auditory Neuroscience Laboratory. Available: http://www.brainvolts.northwestern.edu/projects/music/index.php

Music for Life: The Story of New Horizons. WXXI Public Broadcasting, Rochester, NY. Available for purchase: http://interactive.wxxi.org/musicforlife

Pantelyat, Alexander Y. *Motor Control in Musicians.* Health and Wellness Seminar Series, Peabody Institute of the Johns Hopkins University, September 2014 (YouTube, January 2015). Available: https://www.youtube.com/watch?v=RSfiOZqOYr8

Playing Musical Instruments in the MRI—The Brain on Music. YouTube, November 6, 2014. Available: https://www.youtube.com/watch?v=DrlAYaJw8Qk

Seymour: An Introduction. A movie by Ethan Hawke about Seymour Bernstein, whose book *With Your Own Two Hands* was recommended by several team members. MPI Home Video (2015). http://www.imdb.com/title/tt2219650/

Author's Note

Doing research for all three books on music that I've written for Oxford University Press has helped me navigate various aspects of my own musical life. Interviewing professional musicians, music educators, and parents for *The Young Musician's Survival Guide* and *The Music Parents' Survival Guide* helped my husband and me find ways to be supportive as we tried to guide our two sons on their musical journeys. Research for the current book has helped me in a more personal way, by giving me a sense of confidence in being a "sometime musician" who sings in a choir and plays piano at home. As was true of a few members of this book's advice team, I used to feel embarrassed if people who found out that I wrote books on music—or who knew about my musical sons—would ask whether I too was a musician. My standard answer was to mumble, "I play piano very badly."

The enthusiastic self-confidence of the vast majority of the avocational musicians featured in this book—at all levels of skill and experience—proved contagious. They let me realize that we're all part of the musical family, from struggling beginner to confident pro. We all participate each in our own way in the calming beauty and invigorating wonder of making music. Absorbing a bit of their musical confidence has helped me sing better at choir practice. My piano playing has also benefited from the advice that professional pianist Ursula Oppens gives in chapter 8, to keep learning new, challenging pieces, instead of just playing the few old chestnuts learned in the past.

In addition, the comments by the amateurs and educators on the advice panel taught me the wisdom of resuming lessons. I've done so with singing. The voice lessons and a sight-singing class that I have taken since starting work on this book have refreshed the skills learned from voice lessons taken years ago.

Another benefit of working on this book has been re-establishing personal connections from earlier in my own musical journey and in the musical journeys of our sons. When word about this project reached friends from the Baltimore neighborhood where I grew up, several volunteered to fill out the questionnaire for this book and to suggest friends of their own who agreed to join the advice team. The same happened with friends and colleagues of my sons. Another plus has been the opportunity to see many terrific performances by amateur music ensembles, widening the scope of our concert-going possibilities.

Acknowledgments

Warm thanks go to all the musicians, educators, researchers, health-care professionals, and others who took time from their busy lives to be interviewed for this book, to fill out questionnaires, or to suggest others to include in the research, and who, in some cases, also searched through their files to find photos to share in the book. Although more than two hundred people are quoted in this book, there are so many others who participated—too many to quote directly or list here—but all their comments and suggestions helped define the issues covered in this book and the nature of the discussion.

Thanks also go to the following organizations and schools that made available photographs to use in this book: Alfred Street Baptist Church, Amateur Classical Musicians Association, Annapolis Summer Garden Theatre, Around the Sound Community Band, Baltimore Symphony Orchestra, Chicago Bar Association Symphony Orchestra, Harmony Project, Heritage Signature Chorale, Levine Music, Midcoast Community Chorus, Montréal New Horizons Band, Piano Pathways, Queen City Concert Band, San Francisco Community Music Center, Seattle Pro Musica, Strings Collaborative at UCSF, Third Street Music School, University of Cincinnati's College-Conservatory of Music, and Young New Yorkers' Chorus.

I'm also grateful to the photographers who graciously allowed their photos to appear in the book: Kenneth Adam, Annemarie Bain, Steve Behrens, Kathleen

Cei, Alberto De Salas, Carlos Gomez, Alison Harbaugh, Nancy Harris, Lois Kebe, Nancy P. Mack, Terry Medert, Rabbi Jack Moline, Eric Nathan, Erin Oswalt, Steven Schnur, Claire Stefani, Katharine Whisler, Tony Willis, Benjamin Zibit, and Nick Zorzi. Thanks also to Nicole Sharlow and to Douglas Kostner, Larchmont Avenue Church music director, for letting me observe a rehearsal of the Larchmont Symphonia at the church. In addition, I appreciate the kind invitation I received from Marilyn Bell and the Bennington Chamber Music Conference to be a fly on the wall at some of the program's rehearsals for two days during July 2016.

Special thanks go to Liz Fleischer for her many helpful suggestions and her wonderful sight-singing class at the Lucy Moses School, which I took during the summer of 2015; it helped revive my vocal music skills and reminded me again of the value of sight-singing. Others who helped move this project along that I am very grateful to include Nancy Amigron, Michael Barnett, Ysaye Barnwell, Dr. Serap Bastepe-Gray, Kitty Benton, Mimi Bornstein, Liza W. Beth, Katie Brill, Barbara Butterworth, Sonia Caltvedt, Lauren Campbell, Katherine Carleton, Alberto De Salas, Amy Dennison, Brenda Dillon, Andre Dowell, Mark Dvorak, Juli Elliot, Roy Ernst, Gavin Farrell, Norma Foege, Kristy Fox, Shelbi Franklin, Joyce Garrett, Bau Graves, Judy Gutmann, Rebecca Henry, Jonathan Herman, Jean Hess, Sarah Hoover, Claudia Huter, Victoria Hutter, Sunil Iyengar, Mandi Jackson, Terry Joshi, David Katz, Adam Kent, Glenn Kramer, Jamal Lee, Dr. Yeou-Cheng Ma, Joan Magagna, Amber Marek, Hana Morford, Sarah Muffly, Lois Narvey, Eric Nathan, Noah Nathan, Alexandra Newman, Dr. Jonathan Newmark, Shebbie Robinson Rice, Afa Sadykhly Dworkin, Rebecca A. Sayles, Rachelle Schlosser, Elizabeth Schurgin, Glenn Sewell, Dr. David Shapiro, Sylvia Sherman, Katherine Shields, Katie Skovholt, Ann Hess Smith, Dominique van de Stadt, Johnnia Stigall, Carl Stone, Jennifer Alexander Thorpe, Rebecca Vaudreuil, Dr. Marc Wager, Anne C. A. Wilson, Lauren Winther-Hansen, Jill Woodward, and Carole Wysocki.

In addition, special thanks go to my editor Suzanne Ryan, who believed in this project right from the start and has been encouraging throughout, as have the terrific editorial and production teams at Oxford University Press. My sons and daughters-in-law have been encouraging and helpful in so many ways. Also believing in the value of this project, offering support, enthusiasm, love (and gentle editing) has been my concert-going partner to whom I am grateful beyond words, my husband Carl.

Credits

QUOTED MATERIAL

Other than the quotation references listed here, all of the direct quotes from individuals in this book come from questionnaires they filled out for this book, from personal telephone or in-person interviews conducted by the author, or through email communications with the author.

The quote from Heidi Raschke on page 13 comes from Raschke, Heidi, ed. *Artful Aging: How Creativity Sparks Vitality and Transforms Lives.* E-book. St. Paul, MN: Next Avenue. Twin Cities PBS (TPT), 2016.

The quote from Wayne Booth on page 14 comes from his book *For the Love of It: Amateuring and Its Rivals.* Chicago: University of Chicago Press, 1999.

The quote from Robert J. Zatorre on page 22 comes from Zatorre, Robert J., Joyce L. Chen, and Virginia B. Penhune. "When the Brain Plays Music: Auditory–Motor Interactions in Music Perception and Production." *Nature Reviews Neuroscience* 8 (2007): 547–558. Other quotes from Robert Zatorre come from a telephone interview with him on April 10, 2017.

The quote on page 25 about the twins study that begins "twins who played a musical instrument . . . . " comes from Balbag, M. Alison, Nancy L. Pedersen, and Margaret Gatz. "Playing a Musical Instrument as a Protective Factor against Dementia and Cognitive Impairment: A Population-Based Twin Study." *International Journal of Alzheimer's Disease* 2014 (2014): ID 836748.

The quote from Daniel Levitin on page 27 comes from his book *This Is Your Brain on Music: The Science of a Human Obsession.* New York: Penguin Group, 2006.

The quote from John Holt on page 58 comes from his book *Never Too Late*. New York: Da Capo Press, 1991.

Quotes from Steven Demorest on page 86 come from Demorest, Steven M., and Peter Q. Pfordresher. "Singing Accuracy Development from K-Adult: A Comparative Study." *Music Perception: An Interdisciplinary Journal* 32, no. 3 (2015): 293–302.

The quote from Wynton Marsalis on page 146 comes from his book *Marsalis on Music*. New York: Norton, 1995.

The quotes from Dr. Alexander Pantelyat on page 148 ("You are athletes ... keep in mind, too") and on page 150 ("Prevention is possible . . . . Treatment is available") come from Pantelyat, Alexander Y. *Motor Control in Musicians*. Health and Wellness Seminar Series, Peabody Institute of the Johns Hopkins University, January 20, 2015. Available: https://www.youtube.com/watch?v=RSfiOZqOYr8. Other quotes from Dr. Pantelyat come from a personal telephone interview with the author.

The quotes from Dr. Serap Bastepe-Gray on page 149 come from Bastepe-Gray, Serap. *Putting It All Together: A Musician's Guide to Day-to-Day Healthy Play*. Health and Wellness Seminar Series, Peabody Institute of the Johns Hopkins University, January 20, 2015. Her exercise video starts at minute 17:00. Available: https://www.youtube.com/watch?v=YK_NxxD5bbM

The quote from Joshua Bell on page 204 comes from Nathan, Amy, *The Young Musician's Survival Guide*. New York: Oxford University Press, 2000 (2nd Ed., 2008).

PHOTO CREDITS

Cover (top left)—Courtesy Colleen Schoneveld; cover (top right)—Courtesy Nancy Harris, photographer; cover (bottom)—© Seattle Pro Musica, photo by Chris Bennion; Pages x, 43, 47, 131, 162—© Amy Nathan; 4—Courtesy Colleen Schoneveld; 7, 104—Courtesy Amanda and Brandon Ray; 9, 45—© Eric Nathan; 16—Courtesy Chicago Bar Association's Barristers Big Band and Judge Blanche M. Manning; 18—© Seattle Pro Musica, photo David Rither; 20—© (2016) Carlos Gomez, Courtesy Young New Yorkers' Chorus; 26—Courtesy Rufus Browning; 27—Courtesy Wen Dombrowski, M.D.; 30—Courtesy Fritz Lustig; 31, 187—Courtesy Nancy Harris, photographer; 36—© Seattle Pro Musica, photo by Chris Bennion; 40 (top)—Photo Claire Stefani; 40 (bottom)—Courtesy Mark Dalrymple; 48—Courtesy Angela Bowman, Photo Nick Zorzi; 53—Courtesy Joshua Dadeboe; 54—© Strings Collaborative at UCSF, photo by Kwiri Yang; 56 (top)—© Steven Schnur, courtesy Hoff Barthelson Music School; 56 (bottom)—Courtesy Darlene Ifill-Taylor, M.D.; 65—Courtesy Montréal New Horizons Band; 69—Courtesy Rebecca Berg; 70—Courtesy Amateur Classical Musicians Association (ACMA); 72—© Katharine Whisler; 77—Courtesy Third Street Music School New Horizons Band; 78—Photo Nancy P. Mack; 79—Courtesy Janet Blume; 85—Courtesy Barbara J. Try; 88—Courtesy of Jessica Levant for SF Community Music Center (www.sfcmc.org); 92—Photo by Laurel Lisez; 95—© 2017 Alison Harbaugh for Sugar Farm Productions; 106—Courtesy Alfred Street Baptist Church, photo taken by Aaron Watson, Jemarion Jones; 107—Courtesy Sarah Wright; 110—Photo by Rabbi Jack Moline; 112—Courtesy Levine Music; 115—Photo by Terry Medert; 125—Courtesy Piano Pathways, Baton Rouge, LA, photo taken by Erin Oswalt; 129—University of Cincinnati College-Conservatory of Music New Horizons program, © BettyAnne Gottlieb; 134—Photo by Winnie Barouch; 142 (top)—© Benjamin Zibit, photographer; 142 (bottom)—Courtesy Around the Sound Community Band; 145—Courtesy Ellen Shepard; 147—Courtesy Stephen R. DeMont, photo by Debi Quirk; 154— Courtesy Midcoast Community

Chorus; 160—Courtesy Harmony Project; 164—Courtesy Fritz Hessemer; 170—© Baltimore Symphony Orchestra, photographer Kenneth Adam; 175—Courtesy Chicago Bar Association Symphony Orchestra (Mark Bergeron, photographer); 178—Courtesy Chicago Bar Association Symphony Orchestra; 182—Courtesy Elizabeth Sogge; 191—Courtesy Carol Katz; 200— Courtesy The Heritage Signature Chorale; 202— Courtesy Kenneth P. Williams; 206—Photo by Tony Willis; 209— Courtesy Michelle Billingsley; 211—© 2015, Steve Behrens; 214—Courtesy Energy City New Horizons Music; 218—Courtesy Dale Backus; 220—© Music Haven, photo by Kathleen Cei; 224—Courtesy Sofia Axelrod; 227—Courtesy Deborah Edge, MD; 228— Courtesy Doug Campbell; 231—Photo by Annemarie Bain- image AMB; 232-233— Courtesy Alfred Street Baptist Church, photo by Lois Kebe.

Index